NATURALLY HUMAN,
SUPERNATURALLY GOD

NATURALLY HUMAN, SUPERNATURALLY GOD

DEIFICATION IN PRE-CONCILIAR CATHOLICISM

ADAM G. COOPER

Fortress Press
Minneapolis

NATURALLY HUMAN, SUPERNATURALLY GOD

Deification in Pre-Conciliar Catholicism

Cover image: Scala / Art Resource, NY

Cover design: Laurie Ingram

Library of Congress Cataloging-in-Publication Data

Print ISBN: 978-1-4514-7202-8

eBook ISBN: 978-1-4514-8426-7

The paper used in this publication meets the minimum requirements of American National Standard for Information Sciences — Permanence of Paper for Printed Library Materials, ANSI Z329.48-1984.

Manufactured in the U.S.A.

This book was produced using PressBooks.com, and PDF rendering was done by PrinceXML.

CONTENTS

Acknowledgments

Many kind and generous people have assisted me in the writing of this book. My thanks go first of all to the John Paul II Institute in Melbourne and the Archdiocese of Melbourne for granting me time for research and for underwriting it with generous funding. Alexandra Diriart, José Granados, Kevin O'Shea, and Matthew Levering all read through part or the whole of the manuscript in its earlier stages and offered helpful criticism and feedback. The staff of the Mannix Library also deserve mention for their professional and ready help in acquiring sources. Michael Gibson, Lisa Gruenisen, Amy Sleper, and David Cottingham from Augsburg Fortress have proved a stirling editorial support team, and colleagues from the John Paul II Institute in Melbourne merit praise for their collegial support. Above all I would like to thank my wife Elizabeth and son Benjamin for their always affectionate and faithful love.

O wisest love! that flesh and blood
Which did in Adam fail,
Should strive afresh against their foe,
Should strive and should prevail.

And that a higher gift than grace
Should flesh and blood refine,
God's presence and His very Self,
And Essence all-divine.

J. H. Newman

Abbreviations

CCSG   *Corpus Christianorum Series Graeca*, Turnhout, Brepols 1977–

CCSL   *Corpus Christianorum Series Latina*, Turnhout, Brepols 1953–

DS   H. Denzinger and A. Schönmetzer A., eds., *Enchiridion Symbolorum: Definitionum et Declarationum de Rebus Fidei et Morum*, Freiburg in Breisgau 1965

DV   Thomas Aquinas, *De Veritate*, ET: *Truth* 3 vols., trans. R. W. Mulligan et al., Chicago, Regnery 1952–54

LXX   *Septuaginta*, ed. A. Rahlfs, Stuttgart, Deutsche Bibelgesellschaft 1979

NPNF   *A Select Library of Nicene and Post-Nicene Fathers of the Christian Church* 14 vols., ed. P. Schaff and H. Wace, Grand Rapids, Eerdmans Second Series 1978

PG   *Patrologiae cursus completus. Series Graeca* 161 vols. ed. J.-P. Migne, Paris 1857–66

PL   *Patrologiae cursus completus. Series Latina* 221 vols. ed. J.-P. Migne, Paris 1844–64

SC   *Sources chrétiennes*, Paris, Cerf 1941–

SCG   Thomas Aquinas, *Summa contra gentiles* 5 vols., trans. A. C. Pegis et al., Notre Dame, University of Notre Dame 1955–57

ST   Thomas Aquinas, *Summa theologiae: Latin text and English translation* 60 vols., trans. English Province Dominicans, Oxford and New York, Blackfriars 1964–

TI   Karl Rahner, *Theological Investigations* vols. 1–20, trans. C. Ernst, London, Darton, Longman & Todd 1961–81 (= *Schriften zur Theologie* vols. 1–16, Einsiedeln, Benziger 1954–84)

ET   English translation

Introduction

This book had its beginnings in a personal quest to understand better the key doctrinal trends characterizing the Catholic theological landscape in the decades leading up to the Second Vatican Council. It is published here as the culmination of a lengthy and satisfying, even if occasionally arduous, investigation. Rather than offering a comprehensive or systematic survey, of which there are many, it limits its scope in two unique ways, thereby presenting its readers with an analysis of the period that is at once accessible and atypical.

First, it settles upon the work of three theologians who are widely regarded as representative of three main currents or traditions in the pre–conciliar period. The three theologians concerned are Réginald Garrigou-Lagrange O.P., Karl Rahner S.J., and Henri de Lubac S.J. It is widely acknowledged that the differences between these three figures, and the traditions subsequently associated with them, sometimes run so deep as to defy resolution. All have been designated "Thomists," but qualifying descriptors are often added that suggest alternative and even competing loyalties, with Garrigou-Lagrange being called a "strict observance Thomist," Rahner a "transcendental Thomist," and de Lubac an "Augustinian Thomist." All belong to that rich period of *ressourcement* in the Catholic Church from which the Second Vatican Council arose as a kind of culminating watershed, but it is especially de Lubac who may be said finally to represent this *ressourcement*, for Garrigou-Lagrange, sometimes despite himself, expressly opposed it, while Rahner sought to craft an alternative to it.[1]

The second way this study limits its scope is through focusing not just on these three theologians in general, but, as the title indicates, in particular on the presence in their theology of the motif of deification or divinization, a theological subject matter whose provenance spans the whole history of Christianity, but which comes to special light in their respective works. In doing so, this book opens a small window upon an oddly surprising case of theological convergence. For as I shall argue, despite sometimes quite far-reaching differences, Garrigou-Lagrange, Rahner, and de Lubac were strangely united in a shared conviction: today's church urgently needs to renew its acquaintance with an ancient Christian theme, namely, the doctrine of

---

1. See Gabriel Flynn and Paul D. Murray, eds., *Ressourcement: A Movement for Renewal in Twentieth-Century Catholic Theology* (Oxford: Oxford University Press, 2012).

deification. Only in a self-transcending, supernaturally wrought participation in the life of God do human beings reach their proper fulfillment.

In this way, this book functions as an introduction to the doctrine of deification in modern Catholic theology, as it is expounded by three of its most able and influential protagonists in the twentieth century. It is true that the doctrine of deification has undergone a veritable explosion of renewed interest in recent decades.[2] Far from being a subject of merely peripheral concern, or the quirky whim of a few oriental mystics, deification has been recognized as figuring throughout Christian history as mainstream orthodox catholic teaching, held in common by such epochal and diverse thinkers as Irenaeus, Athanasius, Augustine, Aquinas, Luther, and Newman. Yet it is also true that the doctrine has sometimes suffered a certain eclipse, even disparagement, particularly in the west. Anxieties about it have partly arisen from the fact that in the Scriptures the primal sin consists in consent to the temptation to be "like God" (Gen. 3:5). The proposal that human beings can and should "become God" or "divine" or "gods" may to some sound disturbingly like the old temptation in new guise. But deification really only started coming under systematic criticism following the anti-hellenistic sentiments of nineteenth-century scholars who interpreted it as an alien Greek or Platonic philosophical incursion into the pure Semitic "essence" of primitive Christianity. According to Adolf von Harnack, writing around 1900, once the Christian religion "was represented as the belief in the incarnation of God and as the sure hope of the deification of man, a speculation that had never got beyond the fringe of religious knowledge was made the central point of the system and the simple content of the Gospel was obscured."[3] This criticism was fueled by suspicion that the doctrine, thought anyway to be unbiblical and more associated with the eastern Christian tradition, lent itself to pantheism and involved a failure to distinguish adequately between the human

---

2. More recent studies include David Meconi and Carl E. Olson, eds., *Called to Be Children of God: Deification in the Catholic Tradition* (San Francisco: Ignatius, forthcoming); Paul L. Gavrilyuk, "The Retrieval of Deification: How a Once-Despised Archaism Became an Ecumenical Desideratum," *Modern Theology* 25, no. 4 (2009): 647–59; Paul. M. Collins, *Partaking in Divine Nature: Deification and Communion* (New York: Continuum, 2008); M. J. Christensen and J. A. Wittung, eds., *Partakers of the Divine Nature: The History and Development of Deification in the Christian Traditions* (Grand Rapids: Baker, 2007); Roger E. Olson, "Deification in Contemporary Theology," *Theology Today* 64 (2007): 186–200; David Meconi, "The Consummation of the Christian Promise: Recent Studies in Deification," *New Blackfriars* 87, no. 1007 (2006): 3–12; Stephen Finlan and Vladimir Kharlamov, eds., *Theosis: Deification in Christian Theology* (Eugene, OR: Pickwick, 2006); Jean Borella, *The Sense of the Supernatural* (New York: Continuum, 2002).

3. Adolf von Harnack, *History of Dogma*, vol. II, trans. Neil Buchanan (New York: Dover, 1961), 318.

and divine natures, between nature and grace.[4] Misunderstandings have been further compounded by various misrepresentations of the doctrine, making of what the ancients taught about the human person's vocation to become God by grace an affirmation of his becoming God by nature.

With such critical sentiments boiling around near the turn of the twentieth century, it was all the more remarkable that the winds of fortune ended up taking the Catholic Church toward the recovery and reinstatement of this biblical and patristic insight to its rightful prominence. For all its inner contradictions, the twentieth can go down in history as the century in which deification almost universally rose to the top of the theological and ecumenical agenda. The full scope of this recovery is still be to realized, and new publications on the topic continue to spring up in every circle, but certain definitive outlines have been adumbrated in the christocentric and Trinitarian anthropological vision outlined in Vatican II's Pastoral Constitution, *Gaudium et Spes*, and then developed by Pope John Paul II, according to which the mystery of the incarnation, itself the key to human self-understanding, leads the individual human being beyond herself toward the goal of a deifying communion of persons.[5] Without explicitly using the language of deification, the Council Fathers proposed an "ultimate goal" for human beings that lies exclusively in the mystery of God, adopting the famous *cor inquietum* metaphor of St. Augustine: "[O]nly God . . . meets the deepest longings of the human heart, which is never fully satisfied by what this world has to offer."[6] These same words were echoed by John Paul II on the occasion of his Bull of Indiction welcoming the Third Millennium. There he proclaimed to the world that supernatural life alone "can bring fulfilment to the deepest aspirations of the heart. . . . Proclaiming Jesus of Nazareth, true God and perfect Man, the Church opens to all people the prospect of being 'divinized' and thus of becoming more human."[7]

The three theologians selected for special focus in this book have each played an important role in that recovery. They of course were not alone

---

4. See e.g., Ben Drewery, "Deification," in *Christian Spirituality: Essays in Honour of Gordon Rupp*, ed. Peter Brooks (London: SCM, 1975), 33–62.

5. See David Meconi, "Deification in the Thought of John Paul II," *Irish Theological Quarterly* 71 (2006): 127–41; Tracey Rowland, "Deification after Vatican II," in Meconi and Olson, *Called to Be Children of God* (San Francisco: Ignatius, forthcoming).

6. *Gaudium et Spes* 41.

7. *Incarnationis Mysterium: Bull of Indiction of the Great Jubilee of the Year 2000* §2, quoted in David V. Meconi, "Deification in the Thought of John Paul II," *Irish Theological Quarterly* 71 (2006): 127–41, at 133.

in this endeavor, and there are a number of other worthy theologians whose works I could have selected for focus. Mention may be made of Jules Gross's important historical study, *The Divinization of the Christian According to the Greek Fathers* (1938), along with key articles by G. W. Butterworth (1916), Otto Faller (1925), Yves Congar (1935), Henri Rondet (1949), and the long multi-authored study on "Divinisation" published in the *Dictionnaire de Spiritualité* under the oversight of Édouard des Places (1957).[8] Yet for all these profound studies, there are good reasons to zero in especially on the seminal contribution of our three figures in particular. Let me give four.

First, deification arguably features as systematically central to their respective theological visions, not just as one theme among many, nor only by way of analysis and commentary on doctrinal history. Each of them explicitly expounded their soteriology using the traditional conceptual instruments and technical vocabulary of *theosis* or graced participation in the intra-Trinitarian intimacy of the divine nature, giving the lie to unfounded claims that deification is an exclusively eastern Christian concept. While studies have brought these features out for each individually, it has recently come to the surface as an implicitly global claim for all three in an article by Peter Ryan, in which he compares the responses of Garrigou-Lagrange, Rahner, and de Lubac to the question how a natural being can find its fulfillment in a gratuitously given supernatural finality.[9]

8. Gross's work, written in French, has been translated into English by Paul A. Onica (Anaheim, CA: A and C Press, 2002); G. W. Butterworth, "The Deification of Man in Clement of Alexandria," *Journal of Theological Studies* 17 (1916): 157–69; O. Faller, "Griechische Vergottung und christliche Vergöttlichung," *Gregorianum* 6 (1925): 405–35; M.-J. Congar (=Yves), "La Déification dans la tradition spirituelle de l'Orient," *Vie spirituelle* 43 (1935): 91–107; H. Rondet, "La divinisation du chrétien," *Nouvelle Révue Théologique* 71 (1949): 449–76, 561–88; Édouard des Places, "Divinisation," in *Dictionnaire de Spiritualité*, vol. 3 (Paris, 1957), columns 1370–1459. Another important contribution came from the Russian Orthodox scholar Myrrha Lot-Borodine. Her articles, first published between 1932 and 1933 in *Revue d'histoire des religions*, were reprinted in the single volume *La Déification de l'homme selon la doctrine des Pères grecs* (Paris: Cerf, 1970), with a Preface by Jean Daniélou.

9. Peter F. Ryan, "How Can the Beatific Vision both Fulfill Human Nature and Be Utterly Gratuitous?" *Gregorianum* 83, no. 4 (2002): 717–54. I analyze elements of Ryan's critique in the conclusion. For individual studies see Denis Edwards, *How God Acts: Creation, Redemption and Special Divine Action* (Minneapolis: Fortress Press, 2010); Francis J. Caponi, "Karl Rahner: Divinization in Roman Catholicism," in *Partakers of the Divine Nature: The History and Development of Deification in the Christian Traditions*, ed. M. J. Christensen and J. A. Wittung (Grand Rapids: Baker, 2007), 259–80; John Milbank, *The Suspended Middle: Henri de Lubac and the Debate Concerning the Supernatural* (Grand Rapids: Eerdmans, 2005); Aidan Nichols, *Reason with Piety: Garrigou-Lagrange in the Service of Catholic Thought* (Ave Maria, FL: Sapientia, 2008).

Second, as already suggested, each has proven to be an especially influential theologian in the twentieth century, not only in the period between the so-called *nouvelle théologie* controversy and the Second Vatican Council, but also in the postconciliar period right up to the present day.[10] Garrigou-Lagrange continues to be heralded by a vanguard of mainly North American Neothomists as the faithful champion of a rigorous scholastic method and commonsense philosophy in a world that has lost its reason. Rahner, having held sway in seminary curricula around the world for decades, is increasingly becoming passé, but continues to hold attraction for all kinds of revisionist trends in theology, education, and ethics, and is still especially beloved among promoters of popular liturgies, egalitarian ecclesiologies, and women's ordination. De Lubac appears most influential in circles of the younger orthodox generation who, hungry for theological and liturgical substance, want to drink from the sources of the church's deepest and most longstanding spiritual wellsprings. His famous insistence on the primacy of paradox echoes true for a generation simultaneously skeptical of totalitarianizing claims to truth and convinced by the absolute trustworthiness of the gospel of the crucified and risen God-man, Jesus Christ.

Third, each may be taken as foundationally representative of three distinct "streams" of Catholic theology in the twentieth century, whose respective emphases continue to shape and inspire their witting or unwitting heirs in the postconciliar Church, and whose commitments and sensibilities have come to be recognized as standing in a certain tension with and even antithesis to one another.[11] One way to characterize them would be to identify their respective emphases: Garrigou-Lagrange represents an emphasis upon reason, Rahner upon relevance, and de Lubac on revelation. Another way would be to identify the way they deal with theological difficulties. Garrigou-Lagrange relies on systematization, Rahner on resolution, and de Lubac on paradox.

---

10. On the emergence and meaning of the term *nouvelle théologie*, see Jürgen Mettepenningen, *Nouvelle Théologie: Inheritor of Modernism, Precursor of Vatican II* (London: T. & T. Clark, 2010); Hans Boersma, *Nouvelle Théologie and Sacramental Ontology: A Return to Mystery* (Oxford: Oxford University Press, 2009); Brian Daley, "The *Nouvelle Théologie* and the Patristic Revival: Sources, Symbols and the Science of Theology," *International Journal of Systematic Theology* 7, no. 4 (2005): 362–82; Aidan Nichols, "Thomism and the *Nouvelle Théologie*," *The Thomist* 64 (2000): 1–19; A. Darlapp, "Nouvelle Théologie," *Lexikon für Theologie und Kirche*, vol. 7 (Freiburg: Herder, 1963): 1060.

11. See Tracey Rowland, *Culture and the Thomist Tradition: After Vatican II* (London: Routledge, 2003); Fergus Kerr, *After Aquinas: Versions of Thomism* (Oxford: Blackwell, 2002); Joseph A. Komonchak, "Theology and Culture at Mid-Century: The Example of Henri de Lubac," *Theological Studies* 51 (1990): 579–602.

These are generalizations to be sure, but they help to classify certain features that characterize still-pertinent convictions and commitments among their respective devotees.

Fourth, and this is a very practical reason, the major theological writings of all three figures have been translated into English and therefore have exercised greater impact on the English-speaking theological world than the lesser-known works of their contemporaries.

What we find as we study their works is that, despite striking disparities in circumstance, formation, vocation, method, and theological output, despite also their more or less direct criticisms of one another, their lives strangely intersected and aspects of their thought converged in their common invocation of deification as the fundamental and ultimate goal of fulfilled human existence. While showing how each expressed this central Christian doctrine in his own particular way, it will be intimated in various comparative comments that the approach of Henri de Lubac, with its roots more deeply in biblical and patristic theology, and with its more explicit and determinative christocentrism, ecclesiocentrism, and theology of the *imago Dei*, best coheres with the theological anthropology that subsequently has been formally corroborated in the Catholic Church's magisterial teaching.

Before launching into the first chapter, some readers may find it useful to know what rationale I have followed in my adoption of certain terminology. In the main I have relied on translated works of the authors studied. However, to gain a more critical understanding of certain terms or ideas I have also consulted many of their works in their original languages. The question therefore arises as to what terminology they themselves used to designate deification. The English word "deification," the term used in the title of this book and in the main preferred throughout, has its origins in the Latin noun *deificatio*, whose verb *deifico* was not infrequently used by Thomas Aquinas.[12] It is not, strictly speaking, a biblical term, although this is not to say the idea has no biblical foundation.[13] The *locus classicus* for the doctrine of deification in the New Testament speaks of human beings becoming θείας κοινωνοὶ φύσεως,

12. See R. J. Deferrari, *A Lexicon of Saint Thomas Aquinas* (Dover, NH: Loreto Publications, 2004), 278.

13. See the excellent syntheses of the biblical foundations of the theology of deification in Gregory Glazov, "Theosis, Judaism, and Old Testament Anthropology," in Finlan and Kharlamov, *Theosis: Deification in Christian Theology*, 16–31; Stephen Finlan, "Second Peter's Notion of Divine Participation," in Finlan and Kharlamov, *Theosis: Deification in Christian Theology*, 32–50; Al Wolters, "Partners of the Deity: A Covenantal Reading of 2 Peter 1:4," *Calvin Theological Journal* 25 (1990): 28–40; Jules Gross, *The Divinization of the Christian according to the Greek Fathers*, 80–92.

participants or sharers in the divine nature (2 Pet. 1:4). This idea fits hand-in-glove with two other central New Testament soteriological motifs: divine adoption and mutual indwelling. These mysteries were explored by the earliest Church Fathers using a number of Greek terms, including θεοποίησις, θεοποιεῖν, ὁμοίωσις τῷ Θεῷ, μετουσία, or μέθεξις τοῦ Θεοῦ, with a formal definition of the term θεώσις as "assimilation to God as far as possible" finally appearing in the late fifth or early sixth century in the pseudonymous writings of Dionysius the Areopagite.[14] In the Latin tradition, Augustine expounded a clear doctrine of deification, providing an orthodox foundation for the further development of the term *deificare*. Ultimately, for Augustine, God is the *deificator* who through adoptive grace enables those who worship him to become gods themselves: *Deus facitque suos cultores deos.*[15]

When we come to the native language of the three theologians under consideration in this book, the terminology they use for deification does not appear to depart from these basic terms in Christian tradition. The preference for Garrigou-Lagrange and de Lubac seems to be for the French noun *divinisation* and the verb *diviniser*, and although one sometimes gets the impression that the term *deification* raises for Francophones connotations of impious human hubris, de Lubac uses it interchangeably with *divinisation* with no indication of any change in meaning, explaining them variously as "l'union divine," "la participation de la vie trinitaire," "la vision de Dieu," and "l'élévation surnaturelle de la creature." In Rahner's German, the primary term is the noun *die Vergöttlichung*, which has been in existence at least since Luther.[16] Rahner often uses it adjectivally in such formulae as "die vergöttlichenden Gnade"

14. See Norman Russell, *The Doctrine of Deification in the Greek Patristic Tradition* (Oxford: Oxford University Press, 2004), 1–15, 248–61.

15. See David V. Meconi, "Becoming Gods by Becoming God's: Augustine's Mystagogy of Identification," *Augustinian Studies* 39, no. 1 (2006): 61–74; Robert Puchniak, "Augustine's Conception of Deification, Revisited," in Finlan and Kharlamov, *Theosis: Deification in Christian* Theology, 122–33; Gerald Bonner, "Augustine's Conception of Deification," *Journal of Theological Studies* 37 (1986): 369–86; "Deification, Divinization," in *Augustine Through the Ages: An Encyclopedia*, ed. A. D. Fitzgerald (Grand Rapids: Eerdmans, 1999), 265–56; "Deificare," in *Augustinus-Lexicon*, vol. 2, ed. C. Mayer (Basel: Schwabe, 1996), 265–67.

16. See Tuomo Mannermaa, *Christ Present in Faith: Luther's View of Justification*, trans. Kirsi Irmeli Stjerna (Minneapolis: Fortress Press, 2005); B. D. Marshall, "Justification as Declaration and Deification," *International Journal of Systematic Theology* 4 (2002): 3–28; Paul D. Lehninger, "Luther and Theosis: Deification in the Theology of Martin Luther," Ph.D. Dissertation (Milwaukee: Marquette University Press, 1999); Carl E. Braaten and Robert W. Jensen, eds., *Union with Christ: The New Finnish Interpretation of Luther* (Grand Rapids: Eerdmans, 1998); S. Peura and A. Raunio, eds., *Luther und Theosis: Vergöttlichung als Thema der abendländischen Theologie* (Erlangen: Martin-Luther, 1990).

and "die vergöttlichenden Teilnahme an der gottliche Natur," phrases that are almost always accompanied by discussion of "die Selbstmitteilung Gottes" (the self-communication of God). Along with "the supernatural elevation of the creature," this last formula represents an interpretative move beyond the traditional terms. The significance of such shifts will become apparent in due course.

1

Setting the Scene
Deification, a Fruit of Ressourcement

Before studying our three theologians and the way deification features in their works, a brief outline of the immediate history of deification in modern Catholic thought will be helpful. This chapter serves as a kind of summary index, rather than an in-depth history. It offers snapshots that indicate the presence of deification as a programmatic theological theme in various centers around Europe. It also illustrates how in the period just prior to and contemporary with our authors, deification was regarded as a central Christian doctrine that had somehow been neglected and needed urgent recovery. As a new historical consciousness led theologians to inquire about doctrinal development, and as research with an ever wider range of newly available texts increasingly revealed the centrality of deification in earlier periods of Christian history, a way was opened for the richer articulation of the Christian mystery beyond the confines of comparatively recent scholastic and polemical categories.

The First Vatican Council (1869–1870) is most widely remembered for promulgating the decree on papal primacy and infallibility, not for contributing in any way to the doctrine of deification. Yet in its other decree, the Dogmatic Constitution on the Catholic Faith of April 24, 1870 (*Dei filius*), Vatican I touched upon a theme that in the ensuing decades was to become a key focal point in attempts to revitalize the longstanding catholic teaching that human beings are gratuitously ordained to deifying union with God. To the question why, beyond the knowledge of divine things attainable by reason, special revelation and faith are necessary, the Council Fathers answered that "God has directed human beings to a supernatural end, that is, to share in the good things of God that utterly surpass the understanding of the human mind."[1] True enough, the Constitution tends to present revelation as a process of supernatural instruction, with a corresponding understanding of faith as docile intellectual assent to divine authority. Nowhere does it seem to appreciate the way the Scriptures depict revelation unfolding also in events, progressively, within the pedagogical drama of interpersonal action. But against the complicated historical backdrop of theology's struggle with an increasingly ubiquitous rationalism, the clear assertion of humanity's God-given transcendent end could be read as fruit of a lengthy and still-blossoming movement of renewal whose aim was to restore to the church and its mission a properly supernatural vision of the human vocation, according to which "sanctifying grace" is not simply a therapeutic salve for sin but theology's name for the human person's actual and substantial communication in the inner life of the holy Trinity.

Two Nineteenth-Century Streams

Reading the modern history of the doctrine of deification in this way requires us to go back into the decades before Vatican I to uncover two main streams in the tradition whose long-term influence along the lines of such a renewal deserve attention. The first is the renewal represented by the Tübingen school of theology, pioneered by Johann Sebastian Drey (1777–1853) and Johann Adam Möhler (1796–1838). Avoiding the subjectivism of Schleiermacher, their influential Protestant counterpart, the Catholic Tübingen theologians sought nonetheless to reinsert the subject back into the theological enterprise and so to reunite theology and culture, doctrine and life. In Möhler's theology especially we glimpse the revitalization of the ancient sense of the church as an organic extension of the incarnation and therefore as the living, historical community in which human beings are granted a vital share in the life of God.[2]

The second main stream to which Vatican I's affirmation of the human being's supernatural end bears witness is the work of Cologne patristic and dogmatic theologian Matthias Scheeben (1835–1888). Hans Urs von Balthasar hailed Scheeben as "the greatest German theologian to date...."[3] Aidan Nichols characterized his theology as "lyrical Scholasticism."[4] Ultramontane populist and defender of Vatican I's Constitution on the Petrine office, Scheeben

---

1. *Dei filius* §5.

2. See Donald J. Dietrich and Michael J. Himes, *The Legacy of the Tübingen School: The Relevance of Nineteenth Century Theology for the Twenty-first Century* (New York: Crossroad, 1997); Michael J. Himes, *Ongoing Incarnation: Johann Adam Möhler and the Beginnings of Modern Ecclesiology* (New York: Crossroad, 1997).

3. Hans Urs von Balthasar, *Glory of the Lord*, vol. 1 (San Francisco: Ignatius, 1982), 104.

nonetheless emerges as an early protagonist of what would later become known as *ressourcement*: a return to the primary wellsprings of theological reflection, combined with the affective and speculative appropriation of the fruits of that reflection in the light of contemporary thought and life. Scheeben's dogmatic expositions on traditional scholastic categories was integrated with a lively pneumatology, a profound pastoral bent, and an unshakable conviction that grace brings about not just a new situation but a "new being."[5] As a result, the theology that emerged was at once both more Trinitarian, more pastoral, and more anthropological than what was found in many of the manuals of the day.

Typically, Scheeben did not dedicate a separate *locus* to deification, but expressed the ancient teaching primarily under the *loci* of christology and the doctrines of grace, resurrection, and beatitude. In *The Glories of Divine Grace* (1863),[6] the first and second parts exhibit a rich synthesis of patristic thought with scholastic categories. Grace makes us partakers in the divine nature, establishes union with God, and ushers the Holy Spirit, "the personal expression of divine love," into the soul.[7] By grace "the soul is made deiform, godlike . . . ; it is made like God's holiness and thereby becomes partaker of God's own beauty."[8] Indeed, it is not enough to reduce deification to the bestowal of grace, for in giving the Holy Spirit God gives not just an extrinsic gift but "the very Giver of the gifts and the very principle of supernatural power."[9] Scheeben's way of expressing this truth is both beautiful and striking:

> The Spirit who binds God the Father with the Son and the Son with the Father in the unity of inexpressible love, the same Spirit has been sent into our heart through sanctifying grace. He comes to teach us to stammer the name of the Father, to impart to us a childlike trust of Him, and to give testimony of His love, to console us in our needs and sufferings and to bind us now already with our heavenly Father in most intimate love.[10]

---

4. "Homage to Scheeben," in Aidan Nichols, *Scribe of the Kingdom: Essays on Theology and Culture* (London: Sheed & Ward, 1994): 205–13 at 213.

5. Yves Congar, *A History of Theology*, trans. H. Guthrie (New York: Doubleday, 1968), 193.

6. 2 vols., trans. P. Shaugnessy (St. Meinrad, IN: Grail, 1947, orig. 1863).

7. Scheeben, *Glories of Divine Grace*, vol. 2., 1.

8. Ibid., 101.

9. Ibid., 3–4.

10. Ibid., 58–59.

By grace then we human beings possess God not just as an object known and loved, but "immediately" and "intimately."[11] Grace makes us "capable of the divine being and of the divine persons."[12] This doctrine of divine indwelling is paramount. Our deification "presupposes union with the divine Persons and is caused by this union."[13] And while Scheeben affirms that the entire indivisible Trinity indwells the Christian, it is the Holy Spirit "especially" whose intimate presence in the soul effects a real ontological transformation. Not only so, but the Holy Spirit dwells also in our bodies, making them worthy of great reverence and admiration.[14] Through the Spirit we are reborn and adopted as "sons of God," not in name and right only, but in such a way that we share the same relation the Son has with the Father.[15] Indeed, through grace and the sanctifying Spirit we are made not just sons but spouses of God, an analogy that indicates an even more intimate kinship inasmuch as "the spouse obtains through marriage a greater right to participate in the dignity and honor of the husband than the son to that of the father."[16]

Yet even the relation between spouses, along with that between father and son, presents an inadequate analogy, because "they are not a real, permanent union of the body." In contrast, God—being infinite—is able to unite himself to us "as the soul is united to the body which it vivifies."[17] Our bodies thereby become integral members of Christ's own body. His body "unites to itself the bodies of those who receive it" and "fills them with divine life."[18] Clearly Scheeben is thinking here of the eucharist along the same lines as such Fathers as Ignatius of Antioch and Cyril of Alexandria. "The divine being is spiritual food to us. . . . It is a food that possesses in itself the marrow of divine life."[19] Citing Francis de Sales, he writes, "[T]he divine essence is as intimately united to our soul through grace as corporal food and the body of Christ is united with our body in the holy Sacrament of the altar."[20]

In *Nature and Grace* (1861),[21] Scheeben presents a full-scale patristic theological anthropology, going beyond the categories supplied by the anti-

11. Ibid., 5.
12. Ibid., 6.
13. Ibid., 143.
14. Ibid., 12–13.
15. Ibid., 48–60.
16. Ibid., 128.
17. Ibid., 137.
18. Ibid., 140.
19. Ibid., 71.
20. Ibid., 71.
21. Trans. C. Vollert (St. Louis: Herder, 1954).

Pelagian theology of the west and adopting the Greek patristic notion of grace "in its supernatural and divine excellence" and in its "relations with the mysteries of the Trinity, the Incarnation, and the Eucharist."[22] Nowhere does Scheeben allege that the great scholastics like Albert, Bonaventure, and Thomas were not inspired by the same notion. Nor does he seek to abandon the established scholastic terms. For example, using traditional language, he distinguishes between two kinds of deification, one "accidental," peculiar to us, and the other "substantial," peculiar to Christ. "[W]e are born of God and become like Him through an accidental form and nature, as the only-begotten Son is born of the Father and is like Him through the substantial and essential communication of the Father's nature to Him."[23] This contrast, which presages later debates over formal causality and created versus uncreated actuation, was taken over into manuals of theology in terms of a distinction between the union of sanctifying grace, defined as "an accidental assimilation and union with the Godhead" and the grace of union, exclusive to Christ, defined as "substantial deification."[24]

Another distinction Scheeben draws, and one for which he was criticized, is between the image of the divine essence in the soul, common to all people by nature, and the image of the Trinity, granted by grace alone and exclusive to the regenerate.[25] For him it is akin to the patristic distinction between the image and likeness of God. The difference between the two lies in the immediacy with which the Trinitarian processions are established and represented in the graced recipient. To speak of an *imago Trinitatis* in the created soul is to presume that the divine processions are there faithfully mirrored and reproduced, something impossible without divine illumination and a holy love. He cites an old analogy from Bonaventure: by grace the soul becomes son of the Father, bride of the Son, and temple of the Holy Spirit.[26] Only by a very imperfect and remote analogy is the unregenerate person, as Augustine taught, an image of the Trinity.[27]

22. "Author's Preface," *Nature and Grace*, xviii–xix.

23. *Nature and Grace*, 107.

24. Joseph Wilhelm and Thomas B. Scannell, *A Manual of Catholic Theology*, vol. 2 (London: Kegan Paul, Trench, Kübner & Co., 1908), 141–42.

25. *Nature and Grace*, 176–81. On the controversy over this teaching, see C. M. Aherne, "Grace, Controversies On," in *The New Catholic Encyclopedia*, vol. 6 (Detroit: Gale, 2003, 2nd ed.), 401–5 at 404.

26. *Nature and Grace*, 175.

27. Ibid., 181.

Scheeben's masterpiece was *The Mysteries of Christianity* (1865).[28] Here, besides offering a similarly rich exposition of the deifying effects of grace and the divine indwelling, Scheeben treats another important theme in the elaboration of the doctrine of deification, namely, the motive for the incarnation. By it God intends far more than simply to restore the human race to the same status it occupied before sin.[29] Christ is "not merely a supplement, a substitute for the first Adam," with the purpose of "supplying for the deficiency" caused by him.[30] Rather he is "a complement to the first Adam, preordained by God,"[31] so that we are to think of the incarnation not as a factor required by a preexisting and determinative order, whether that of creation or sin, but

> as the basis of its own proper order, of a special and altogether sublime order of things, in which the orders of nature and of grace are absorbed. We must soar up to the heights of the immeasurable power, wisdom, and love of God, which in an extraordinary, extravagant manner, such as no creature can surmise and apprehend, are revealed in this work and lay open the uttermost depths of the divinity, in order to submerge creatures in it and to flood the world with its illimitable riches.[32]

Once again we discern a deeply Trinitarian logic at work. The incarnation appears "as the flower springing from the root buried in the Trinitarian process."[33] Christ does not simply reveal God in general, but effectively incorporates creation into the ineffably blessed communion of the three divine Persons.

THE HOLY SPIRIT AND UNCREATED LOVE

The effects of Scheeben's revitalization of the doctrine of deification were far-reaching, but formal ecclesial substantiation for developing theology in this direction would only come after his death during the pontificate of Leo XIII (d. 1903). Pope Leo was the author of the famous encyclical *Aeterni patris* (1879) whose aim was to restore Thomism as the authentic systematization of Christian

---

28. Trans. C. Vollert (St. Louis: Herder, 1964).

29. Ibid., 354.

30. Ibid.

31. Ibid.

32. Ibid., 356.

33. Ibid., 359.

philosophy. Yet numerous figures, including the influential Salamancan Dominican Juan Gonzalez Arintero (1860–1928), would invoke this Pope's promotion of renewed devotion to the Holy Spirit and surrender to "uncreated Love" enshrined in such encyclicals as *Divinum illud munus* (1897), as authorization for an all-out recovery of deification as the lost but crucial plot of the Christian gospel and the key to human fulfillment.

Arintero joined the Dominican novitiate in 1875, and after studying at the University of Salamanca, lectured all over Europe in the natural sciences until a dramatic turn to spiritual theology in 1903.[34] In Arintero's definitive *magnum opus, The Mystical Evolution in the Development and Vitality of the Church* (1908),[35] all the themes that we have encountered in Scheeben are developed with explicit and vigorous urgency. Arintero set out by highlighting the cruciality of the doctrine of deification for spiritual existence, repeatedly lamenting the loss of its central profile in Christian consciousness. "This deification, so well known to the Fathers but unfortunately forgotten today, is the primary purpose of the Christian life."[36] "So common were these ideas concerning deification that not even the heretics of the first centuries dared to deny them."[37] And again: "Unfortunately these sublime and consoling doctrines are utterly forgotten, as Cornelius a Lapide asserts: 'few there are who know the privilege of such a dignity; fewer still who ponder it with the gravity it deserves.'"[38] Yet despite "the universal forgetfulness" and "the shameful deviations" from this traditional teaching, it can still be heard from numerous "dominant and authoritative voices." It is here that Arintero refers especially to Pope Leo XIII and his advocacy of devotion to the paraclete. "This augurs a happy rebirth of these fundamental doctrines which are the very soul and substance of the Christian life."[39]

What are the features of Arintero's exposition of the doctrine? Like Scheeben, and echoing Athanasius' famous line, Arintero identifies deification as the very goal and purpose of the incarnation. "For this was God made man: to make men gods and to take His delight in them."[40] His definitions likewise follow traditional lines. Quoting Dionysius the Areopagite, he defines

34. See "Biographical Note," in John G. Arintero, *The Mystical Evolution in the Development and Vitality of the Church*, vol. 1, trans. J. Aumann (St. Louis: Herder, 1950), xi–xiii.

35. 2 vols., trans. J. Aumann (St. Louis: Herder, 1950–51).

36. *Mystical Evolution*, vol. 1, 23.

37. Ibid., 29.

38. Ibid., 38.

39. Ibid., 38.

40. Ibid., 350. Cf. Athanasius, *De Incarnatione* 54 (PG 25, 192B).

deification as "the most perfect possible assimilation, union, and transformation in God. . . ."[41] He denies any association between this teaching and any "absurd Gnostic emanation" or "repugnant pantheistic fusion." "God remains ever the same—God is immutable—but man, without ceasing to be man, is deified."[42]

Two problems confront the proponent of deification, which Arintero tackles head on. To be deified, "we need the animation of a new vital principle that far transcends our own." In other words, we need a new life from outside of us. On other hand, "[w]e need a principle that will give us a new sort of being, a second nature with its own proper faculties or potencies, so that we shall be able to live and work divinely and produce fruits of eternal life."[43] In other words, this new life needs to be within us; it needs to be intrinsically our own, fitted to our creaturely and psycho-physical nature, and not merely imposed from above. Sanctifying grace, the seed and sap of divine life as communicated and adapted to the created order, fulfills both these conditions:

> God respects us and does not destroy the nature formed by Him to be a subject of grace. . . . When [God's own life] is reproduced in us to the greatest possible extent and in harmony with our own life, it does not make us cease to be men; rather it makes us perfect men at the same time that it deifies us.[44]
>
> Sanctifying grace truly gives us a participation in the divine life so far as it deifies us. It transforms us to our very depths and makes us like unto God as His sons in truth, and not in name only or merely in appearance. It is the true divine life . . .[45]

Constantly we find Arintero emphasizing this intrinsic character of our deifying transformation, the fact that it consists not simply in an extrinsic relation with God or his grace, or only in a moral or affective inclination, but in an organic and ontological transformation of the human person. Sanctifying grace is not received, like the virtues, only into the faculties. "It is received into the very substance of the soul and makes us a new creature and so transforms and divinizes us. It gives a manner of life which is truly divine; whence flow certain powers and energies likewise divine. . . ."[46] In order to be truly deified, "the

---

41. *Mystical Evolution,* vol. 1, 355 and 65. Cf. Dionysius the Areopagite, *Ecclesiastical Hierarchy* I, 3.
42. *Mystical Evolution,* vol. 1, 57.
43. Ibid., 71.
44. Ibid., 60.
45. Ibid., 67.
46. Ibid., 24.

conformity of wills is not enough; there must be a conformity of nature. . . ."[47] God must become the very life of our souls, as the soul is the life of our bodies. "To dwell in the soul, to vivify and refashion it, God must penetrate it substantially, and this is proper and exclusive to God."[48] This explains why, like Scheeben, Arintero finds human adoption a poor analogy for divine adoption. "Earthly adoption is nothing more than a moral union. It confers new rights, but it does not change the nature of the adopted. . . . Divine adoption, on the other hand, not only implies the name, but also the reality of filiation. . . ."[49] In fact in finding all earthly analogies falling far short, Arintero anticipates the rejection of the two-tiered theology of nature and grace that we will find by theologians of the so-called *nouvelle théologie*:

> The supernatural order is not . . . anything that our reason can trace out by analogy with the natural order. Nor is it a superior order which has been "naturalized" so as to fit our mode of being. It is not simply "an order which exceeds all the natural exigencies of creatures, whether existing or purely possible," as others have defined it. Such an order is still in some way a projection of the natural; it could easily be a superadded perfection or gratuitous complement to the natural order, without transubstantiating it or deifying it.[50]

The intrinsic transformation of the human person by grace brings about a range of new and divine acts. Human beings become capable of knowing and loving God as God knows and loves himself. But it is Arintero's description of the Trinitarian "shape" of this knowing and loving that is most interesting.

> The functions and essential or characteristic operations of this [deified] life are a divine love and knowledge caused in us by the Spirit. . . . As directed to the Father, this love should be a filial love; as directed to the Son, it should be fraternal, marital, and even organic, vital, for He is the first-born, the Spouse of our souls, and the Head of the mystical body of the Church. Finally, as directed to the Holy Ghost, that love must be a love of affectionate friendship and, so to speak, an experimental and vital love, full of sentiment and life and intimate affections. . . .[51]

47. Ibid., 33.
48. Ibid., 30.
49. Ibid., 348.
50. Ibid., 349–50.
51. Ibid., 353–54.

Two comments are pertinent here. First, Arintero, like Scheeben, believes that the deified soul properly bears the marks of the Trinitarian processions. He argues that current opinion on the "appropriation" of sanctification to the Holy Spirit is erroneous. He invokes not only the ancient Fathers but also such authors as Petau, Scheeben, Thomassin, and Ramière[52] in support of his affirmation that the indwelling by grace is an action "proper" to the Holy Spirit, and not simply an *ad extra* work of God in general and only nominally "appropriated" to the Spirit. Of course, all the Persons together, and each in his own way, "contribute to the work of our deification."[53] But it is the Spirit in particular "who directly unites Himself with souls in order to vivify and sanctify them"[54] and who inserts them into the relations constitutive of the Trinitarian processions. That is why, at one point, Arintero can call deification a "trinification" inasmuch as it is "a resemblance of and participation in the inner life of God, one and three."[55]

Second, by the word "experimental" Arintero is tapping back into an old tradition according to which deification is as much experienced or "suffered" as it is actively achieved. "Experimental" knowledge is not the fruit of discursive reason, but a "knowing" that arises from the intimate experience of another through love. As Arintero puts it, "The knowledge which accompanies this love must not be an abstract knowledge but one that is concrete and ever more experimental, because it treats of an admirable and incomprehensible fact that can be realized only by living and experiencing it."[56] We shall see how these two characteristics come to feature significantly, though in different ways, in the works of our three theologians.

GERMAN THEOLOGY AND FRENCH NEOPLATONISM

While Arintero was championing deification among Neothomists in Rome and Spain, who included, as I shall soon reveal in more detail, the philosophically inclined Réginald Garrigou-Lagrange, Karl Adam (1876–1966) was doing so in

---

52. Denis Petau S.J. (1583–1652) was a renowned patristics scholar; Louis Thomassin (1619–1695) was an Oratorian from the age of thirteen; Henri Ramière S.J. (1821–1884) was a theological consultant at Vatican I but is better known for editing the writings of J.-P. de Caussade and publishing them in the form of the spiritual classic *Abandonment to Divine Providence*. Other favorite authors Arintero drew on heavily included Guy de Broglie S.J. and Jean Vincent Bainvel S.J.

53. *Mystical Evolution*, vol. 1, 350.

54. Ibid., 36.

55. Ibid., 44.

56. Ibid., 354.

Germany in the spirit and eventually also the surrounds of the great Tübingen school. Trained in Regensburg and Munich with doctoral theses on Tertullian and Augustine, Adam became one of the most widely read theologians in the twentieth century.[57] Given that his life and work "spanned the period from the First Vatican Council to the Second Vatican Council," to recollect them is virtually "to review one hundred years of drastic changes in governments, culture, church polity, and theology."[58] In his justly famous book *The Spirit of Catholicism* (1924), which manifests deep affinity with the mystical ecclesiology that eventually flowered at Vatican II,[59] we discover a strongly ecclesiocentric and sacramental exposition of deification that Adam expounds in terms of participation in the church which, as the body of Christ, has been established by Christ as the living and dynamic *locus deificandi* in history. Like Arintero and Scheeben, Adam argued that the church's message of salvation does not simply concern the redemption of humanity from a state of sin and its restitution to a pristine natural condition. "The Church's doctrine of justification is based upon the presupposition that man is not only called to a natural end, . . . but also beyond that, to a supernatural elevation of his being which entirely surpasses all created aptitudes and powers, to sonship with God, to participation in the divine life itself."[60] This glorious end constitutes "the central fact" of the gospel. The likeness to which we are being conformed "consists, according to the Second Epistle of St. Peter, in an enrichment by grace, in a fulfilling and permeation of our being by divine and holy forces. . . . Therefore man's end lies, not in mere humanity, but in a new sort of superhumanity, in an elevation and enhancement of his being, which essentially surpasses all created powers and raises him into an absolutely new sphere of existence and life, into the fullness of the life of God."[61]

For Adam, deification and incarnation are almost reversible terms. He speaks of "this incarnation, this raising of man to the fullness of the divine life. . . ."[62] Grace is "a vital force" that "does not come from outside like some alien charm," but rather presupposes our humanity and calls for accompanying human activities and psychological points of contact.[63] Yet it is thoroughly

57. See Robert Anthony Krieg, *Karl Adam: Catholicism in German Culture* (Notre Dame: University of Notre Dame Press, 1992).

58. Ibid., 177–78.

59. Trans. J. McCann (London: Sheed & Ward, 1929, from the 4th German ed.). Cf. Krieg, *Karl Adam*, 51–56.

60. *Spirit of Catholicism*, 177.

61. Ibid., 177–78.

62. Ibid., 178.

divine, "a sort of overflow of the eternal and infinite life within the soul." "It is not of me, yet it is wholly mine." The expression "infusion of charity" means "that the new love flows into me out of a primal source which is not my own self. But this primal source is not far from me, but within me, for it is the basis of my being. . . ." It is on this transcendent, intrinsically communicated divine power that the entire Christian life depends. "If man denies it theological substance, then his theology is an unsatisfactory subjectivism."[64] Adam's modes of expression were not as precise as those of Arintero or Scheeben, but he has certainly become the better-known theologian outside his own circle, and remains even today one of the key inspirations behind many Protestant conversions to the Catholic Church.

This chapter would not be complete without a brief final word about the philosopher Maurice Blondel, who through his lasting friendships with Etienne Gilson and Henri de Lubac provided a formidable philosophical backbone for the *ressourcement* movement in theology. The revolutionary character of de Lubac's project in particular is better appreciated when it is read in the light of its formative background in the wider intellectual movement of French Augustinian Neoplatonism, of which Blondel was an early representative. In this movement, philosophy—and indeed, any truly human pursuit—was regarded as an intrinsically religious and mystical enterprise. In his 1893 *L'Action*, Blondel described the way God stands behind all human knowing as a kind of presupposition. "God is the immediate certitude without which there is no other, the first clarity, the language known without having learned it." No one can act "without co-operating with Him and without having Him collaborate with us by a sort of necessary *theergy*." If human action is to be authentic, if it is not to be short-circuited by blind self-containment, then it must eventually lead toward "a synthesis of man with God."[65] Yet it is important to note that for Blondel this synthesis did not imply any kind of effacement of the ontological heterogeneity between God and human beings. Writing to de Lubac in 1932 on the subject of the latter's nascent work in progress, he wrote:

> One of the errors in perspective that must be avoided, it seems to me, has to do with the bad habit of considering that the state in which the supernatural vocation places us eliminates the "state of nature." No, the latter remains immanent to the divine adoption itself. And it

---

63. Ibid., 179–81.

64. Ibid., 181.

65. Maurice Blondel, *Action (1893): Essay on a Critique of Life and a Science of Practice*, trans. Oliva Blanchette (Notre Dame: University of Notre Dame Press, 2003), 325.

is in this sense that one can, as a philosopher and a theologian, speak of the essential and indestructible incommensurability of created beings and God, in order better to understand the creations of the divine Charity, the paradoxical ways of transforming union, the metaphysical and properly hyperphysical wonder of our *consortium divinae naturae*. . . . Like you, I believe that God created only with a view to a deifying elevation; but that does not prevent the radical heterogeneity of the first gift of rational life and the second (and *antecedent* in the order of finality) gift of supernatural life, which, in order to be both received and acquired demands of us a *denuo nasci*. . . .[66]

This pregnant paragraph encapsulates some of the most fundamental themes of what would become de Lubac's panoramic theological vision. It also demonstrates, as Wayne Hankey has argued, that the kind of Platonism adopted by Blondel and de Lubac was "intellectualist and ontological, as opposed to henological, and Augustinian as opposed to Iamblichan."[67] This observation may be illustrated by the way Blondel responded to the claim that there is fundamentally no difference between creation and incarnation, between "the gifts of the creator" and "the gifts of the incarnation and redemption," in short, to the claim that the natural order *is* supernatural. In reply, Blondel asserted: "Well, for my part I believe that there is an abyss to cross, and in order not to see it one must not *realize in concreto what God is*."[68] In other words, Blondel's account of the human person's deifying *itinerarium* toward mystical union with God remained firmly embedded in the metaphysical realism supplied by the patristic, and indeed soundly catholic doctrines of God, creation, and incarnation.

---

66. Quoted by Henri de Lubac, *At the Service of the Church: Henri de Lubac Reflects on the Circumstances That Occasioned His Writings*, trans. A. E. Englund (San Francisco: Ignatius, 1993), 186–87.

67. Wayne J. Hankey, "One Hundred Years of Neoplatonism in France: A Brief Philosophical History," in J.-M. Narbonne and W. J. Hankey, *Levinas and the Greek Heritage Followed by One Hundred Years of Neoplatonism in France: A Brief Philosophical History* (Leuven: Peeters, 2006), 99–162 at 112.

68. Quoted by Alexander Dru in the introduction to Maurice Blondel, *Letter on Apologetics and History and Dogma*, trans. A. Dru and I. Trethowan (Grand Rapids: Eerdmans, 1994), 75–76.

2

Entering the Fray
Three Theologians, Three Schools

With the broad historical and theological background of chapter 1 in place, it is now time to introduce one by one the three figures whose theology of deification constitutes the subject of this book, and whose respective theological approaches have become representative of three quite distinct schools or traditions in Catholic theology in the twentieth century, lasting right down until the present day. Biographical details about them abound, though only a few monographs in English are dedicated solely to an account of their life, and many details have to be gleaned from articles. Garrigou-Lagrange's life is briefly but handily outlined in a single chapter in Richard Peddicord's *Sacred Monster of Thomism* (2004).[1] A still authoritative account of Rahner's life is given by Herbert Vorgrimmler, *Understanding Karl Rahner* (1986), while de Lubac's life and work are the combined subject of Rudolph Voderholzer's *Meet Henri de Lubac* (2008).[2] From these and a range of other sources it is possible to construct the following summary resumé.

---

1. Richard Peddicord, *The Sacred Monster of Thomism: An Introduction to the Life and Legacy of Reginald Garrigou-Lagrange* (South Bend, IN: St. Augustine's Press, 2004). I was fortunate enough to enjoy a number of informal conversations with one of his students from the 1950s and '60s, Fr. Kevin F. O'Shea, who both personally confirmed and candidly filled out the portrait given in Peddicord's account.

2. Herbert Vorgrimmler, *Understanding Karl Rahner: An Introduction to His Life and Thought* (New York: Crossroad, 1986); Rudolph Voderholzer, *Meet Henri de Lubac: His Life and Work* (San Francisco: Ignatius, 2008).

RÉGINALD GARRIGOU-LAGRANGE

Réginald Garrigou-Lagrange (1877–1964) is best known in accounts of the first half of the twentieth century for two very different things. The first is his role in the offensive against the so-called *nouvelle théologie* movement culminating in the suspension in June 1950 of Henri de Lubac from teaching and publishing, and in the publication of Pius XII's encyclical *Humani Generis* (August 1950). The second is his role in supervising the doctoral research of the young Karol Wojtyla—the future pope John Paul II—on St. John of the Cross's understanding of faith, successfully defended at the Angelicum in 1948.[3]

In relation to the first, any probing into Garrigou-Lagrange's confrontation with the theologians of the *nouvelle théologie* tends to uncover an unhappy tale. His dislike of the driving historical thrust in the works of the likes of Maurice Blondel, Jean Daniélou, and Marie-Dominique Chenu and his suspicion that their philosophy and theology was merely a front for modernist subjectivism, have been well documented.[4] So bitter and *ad hominem* did the polemics become, however, that in a personal letter to his superior in 1947 de Lubac was led to refer to a "dictatorship" and "systematic offensive on the part of Father G.-L., who seeks to provoke scandal everywhere and who is succeeding to a certain degree."[5]

On the question of Garrigou-Lagrange's contact with Wojtyla, a brief comment is worthwhile insofar as it bears upon our topic of deification and the theological anthropology of Vatican II and of subsequent magisterial teaching. Wojtyla had been reading and studying the writings of John of the Cross well before he came under Garrigou-Lagrange's academic oversight in Rome. Weigel suggests that what followed was a "creative tension," evident in the dissertation, between two approaches to reading the Carmelite: a Thomistic, speculative reading, fostered by Garrigou-Lagrange, and a more mystical,

---

3. See Karol Wojtyla, *Faith according to St. John of the Cross*, trans. J. Aumann (San Francisco: Ignatius, 1981).

4. See John Sullivan, "Fifty Years Under the Cosh: Blondel and Garrigou-Lagrange," *New Blackfriars* 93, no. 1043 (2012): 58–70; Fergus Kerr, "A Different World: Neoscholasticism and Its Discontents," *International Journal of Systematic Theology* 8, no. 2 (2006): 128–48; Aidan Nichols, "Thomism and the *Nouvelle Théologie*," 1–19. Blondel (1861–1949), a philosopher, spearheaded a renaissance in Catholic thought in opposition to the prevailing extrinsicism. He came under fire from Garrigou-Lagrange for "pragmatism" and "meddling" with the traditional definition of truth. Fr. Chenu (1895–1990), a Dominican, did his doctoral studies under Garrigou-Lagrange's supervision. His manifesto, *Une école de théologie: Le Salchoir* (1937), had him hauled before a tribunal in Rome headed by Garrigou-Lagrange.

5. Henri de Lubac, *At the Service of the Church: Henri de Lubac Reflects on the Circumstances That Occasioned His Writings*, trans. A. E. Englund (San Francisco: Ignatius, 1993), 275–76.

experiential one, fostered by Wojtyla.[6] Weigel further reports that Garrigou-Lagrange, in reviewing the thesis, "criticized Wojtyla for not using the phrase 'divine object' [*objectum*] of God."[7] Bulzacchelli poses an even sharper opposition between Garrigou-Lagrange and Wojtyla, especially in the way the latter developed his mystical theological vision in his office as pope, under the fraternal influence of Joseph Ratzinger.[8] According to Bulzacchelli, the Cajetanian doctrine of pure nature defended by Garrigou-Lagrange against those who, like de Lubac, hold to the human being's natural desire for supernatural finality, is essentially irreconcilable with the theological anthropology of *Gaudium et Spes* 22, whose composition has been shown to owe much to de Lubac and whose content was so cherished by John Paul II.[9] Be that as it may, it is notable that Wojtyla ended up defending an interpretation of St. John in which the goal of the Christian life is to become *Dios par participación*: God by participation.[10] As we shall see, and perhaps ironically, this was a theme more than agreeable to Garrigou-Lagrange, for whom John of the Cross ranked among his most well-loved theologians.

In studying Garrigou-Lagrange's spiritual theology, especially his understanding of human deification, we shall be hard-pressed to discover anything like a full recovery of the deeply felt mysticism of earlier centuries. Despite his love for such monumental mystics as St. Thomas Aquinas, St. Catherine of Siena, and St. John of the Cross, he has not been called a Thomist of the "strict observance" for nothing. His thought seems too formal, too

6. George Weigel, *Witness to Hope: The Biography of Pope John Paul II 1920-2005* (London: HarperCollins, 2005), 85.

7. Ibid., 86. See also Kerr, "A Different World," 138.

8. R. H. Bulzacchelli, "Dives in Misericordia: The Pivotal Significance of a Forgotten Encyclical," in *Karol Wojtyla's Philosophical Legacy*, ed. N. M. Billias et al. (Washington, DC: The Council for Research in Values and Philosophy, 2008), 125–62 at 136. Bulzacchelli's characterization of Garrigou-Lagrange's Augustinian and Thomistic predestinarianism over against a biblical and evangelical doctrine of election of all humanity by grace in Christ leads him to argue that Garrigou-Lagrange's opposition to John Paul II pales in comparison to his opposition to Ratzinger. "One can only believe that he [Ratzinger] escaped Garrigou-Lagrange's inquisition on account of his age; he was too young and green to show up in the spotlight. But, by Garrigou-Lagrange's criteria, he is every bit as threatening to orthodoxy as de Lubac, and would do more, concretely, in his academic and ecclesiastical career to undermine Garrigou-Lagrange's theology than de Lubac ever did on his own." Ibid., 136.

9. For a detailed study of *Gaudium et Spes* 22, see the dissertation by T. Gertler, *Jesus Christus: Die Antwort der Kirche auf die Frage nach dem Menschsein*, Erfurt Theologischen Studien 52 (Leipzig: St. Benno, 1986). On de Lubac's involvement, see Jared Wicks, "Further Light on Vatican Council II," *Catholic Historical Review* 95 (2009): 546–69.

10. Weigel, *Witness to Hope*, 86.

systematic, too schematized, too heavily wedded to the seemingly endless categories and distinctions of Baroque scholasticism to warrant the name spiritual or mystical theology. Indeed, not a few assessments of the Dominican's character paint a picture of a staunch heresy hunter distinctly lacking in what we might call spiritual or mystical sensitivity. Chenu famously criticized Garrigou-Lagrange's style of theology as a Thomism that had lost its Augustinian sap and Dionysian mysticism and become a virtual positivism.[11] In the April 1947 issue of the *Bulletin de littérature ecclésiastique*, Bruno de Solanges published a damning critique of Garrigou-Lagrange's famous "Nouvelle théologie: Ou va-t-elle?" essay, in which the latter had railed against leading figures in the *ressourcement* movement. Garrigou-Lagrange, de Solanges says, "constantly uses Thomism as a club to crush its adversaries."[12] In the judgment of another critic, Benedictine Guy Mansini, the Dominican

> read little and wrote the same thing often. One gathers that his theology was produced with the *Tabula Aurea* in one hand and Cajetan in the other. . . . He lived ascetically, but at the expense of rendering himself impervious to modern (at least modern popular) culture.

All the evidence leads Mansini to this sorry conclusion: all in all, Garrigou-Lagrange is "an unattractive figure. . . ."[13]

But alongside this bleak and negative portrait, a number of factors may be mentioned that allow us to mitigate the picture somewhat. By virtue of his professorial appointment at the Angelicum in Rome, Garrigou-Lagrange played a pivotal role in the inauguration of a unique position devoted to the study and teaching of spiritual and mystical theology, a chair he held for some forty years (1917–1959). Through his studies and teaching he sought to achieve a coherent and plausible synthesis marrying the more abstract philosophical theology of St. Thomas Aquinas to the experiential mysticism of St. John of the

11. M.-D. Chenu, *Une école de théologie: Le Salchoir* (1937), as summarized by Fergus Kerr, "Chenu's Little Book," *New Blackfriars* 66, no. 777 (1985): 108–12.

12. Quoted by Mettepenningen, *Nouvelle Théologie*, 108. Garrigou-Lagrange's article "La Nouvelle théologie: Ou va-t-elle?" *Le Bulletin de l'Angelicum* 23 (1946): 126–45 was originally submitted to *Revue Thomiste*, the prestigious Dominican journal, but rejected.

13. Guy Mansini, *"What Is a Dogma?" The Meaning and Truth of Dogma in Eduoard le Roy and His Scholastic Opponents* (Rome: Editrice Pontificia Università Gregoriana, 1985), 281. The *Tabula Aurea* was a compendious and definitive guide to the writings of Aquinas penned by Peter de Bergamo in the fifteenth century. For a (satirical?) summary of its contents and uses, see George Tyrrell, "The 'Tabula Aurea' of Peter de Bergamo," *The Heythrop Journal* 10, no. 3 (1969): 275–79.

Cross. Students of his lectures (which were well attended), far from finding him "unattractive," discovered him to be an engaging and passionate teacher. "He communicated the delight and the love of the truth that he lived."[14] Nor was he without a sense of humor. Emonet remembers Garrigou-Lagrange's "gift for comedy." Apparently it was rare for a class to go by "without at least a moment or two of hilarity." Yet it was the synthesis of metaphysics, theology, and mysticism that animated him most of all, being as it was not simply an abstract aspiration but an affective inspiration: "This synthesis made him live."[15]

The belief that there is needed a living and human experience of the divine realities that Christians profess was dear to Garrigou-Lagrange. Even before he had even begun teaching philosophy at Le Saulchoir in 1905 or theology at the Angelicum in 1909, Garrigou-Lagrange spoke of himself having had a kind of personal "conversion" experience while a medical student. It came about through his reading of Ernest Hello's *L'Homme: La vie, la science, l'art* in 1897. Hello was the avowed enemy of all forms of mediocrity, with a prophetic-like ability to diagnose the spiritual languor of his age. As one reads in the introduction to one of his major works,

> Hello was absolutely fearless in his deductions from first principles, and with spirit and confidence his voice rang out, reminding men that God is THAT WHICH IS, and that outside God is nothing but darkness, disorder, negation, and the most utter boredom.[16]

Hello stressed the ordinariness of mystical experience and extraordinary Christianity: saintliness is not the preserve of a chosen few too heavenly minded to be of any earthly use, but a universal and dire human need. He criticized those who over the centuries "have believed Christianity to be, as it were, a speciality—the speciality of those who fix their thoughts on another life, the speciality of mystics," and who regarded mysticism merely "as one of the forms assumed by dreams—worthy of a certain respect, perhaps, but assuredly useless."[17] In contrast to these parodies, Christianity presents not a religious option or a more refined lifestyle choice, but the truth of the total human reality

14. M.-B. Lavaud, "Le Père Garrigou-Lagrange: *In Memoriam,*" *Revue Thomiste* 64 (1964): 181–99 at 188, quoted by Peddicord, *The Sacred Monster of Thomism,* 18.

15. P.-M. Emonet, "Un maître prestigieux," *Angelicum* 42 (1965): 195–99 at 197, quoted by Peddicord, *The Sacred Monster of Thomism,* 19.

16. E. M. Walker, "Introduction," in E. Hello, *Life, Science, Art: Being Leaves from Ernest Hello,* trans. E. M. Walker (London: R. and T. Washbourne, 1912), 14–15.

17. Hello, *Life, Science, Art,* 24.

and the urgent summons and gratuitous power to embrace it. "[Jesus Christ] remains the one universal necessity. Men do not want Him—they say that he is a dream; but He is the Reality, and nothing can ever get on without Him."[18]

The experience of reading Hello's work precipitated a veritable vocational turnaround on Garrigou-Lagrange's part. He promptly left his medical studies, embarked on a course of discernment in first a Trappist and then a Carthusian monastery, and finally entered the Dominican novitiate in 1897. His later recollection of the experience bears the marks of dogmatic stylization, yet it is still possible to sense the way in which he must have been captivated at the time by the conviction that the truth of all things is somehow bound up with the person of Jesus Christ and with his Church:

> I was able to glimpse how the doctrine of the Catholic Church is the absolute truth concerning God, his intimate life, and concerning man, his origin and his supernatural destiny. I saw in the blink of an eye that it was not a truth relative to the actual state of our understanding, but an absolute truth that will not change but will become more and more apparent up to the time when we see God face to face. A ray of light shone before my eyes and made clear the words of the Lord: "Heaven and the earth will pass away, but my words will not pass away."[19]

Another important factor in Garrigou-Lagrange's life that deeply affected his spiritual doctrine was his encounter at the Angelicum with Arintero (d. 1928). Peddicord refers to Arintero as the figure who, next to Thomas Aquinas and Garrigou-Lagrange's teacher at Le Saulchoir, Ambrose Gardeil, made "the most impact" on Garrigou-Lagrange's theological project, while Lavaud says that their discussions together were "decisive for the definitive orientation of Garrigou's thought. . . ."[20] As we have seen in the previous chapter, Arintero was a bold champion of the patristic doctrine of deification—understood not simply as a conformity of wills but as the human being's ontological and substantial fellowship with God—and argued for the necessity of its recovery in the contemporary church. Arintero lamented the "universal forgetfulness" of and "shameful deviations" from the traditional spiritual doctrine that deification is the primary purpose of the Christian life. Arintero was of the view that every Christian must embrace the way of holiness, that mystical union with God is

---

18. Ibid., 28.
19. Quoted in Peddicord, *The Sacred Monster of Thomism*, 9, slightly amended.
20. Ibid., 14.

not an exceptional vocation for clergy, religious, or the uniquely gifted, but the common calling of all the baptized. Garrigou-Lagrange met Arintero in Rome in 1909, the year the former moved from Le Saulchoir to the Angelicum to teach dogmatic theology. Although they were only together a year before Arintero left Rome, Arintero confirmed Garrigou-Lagrange's love for John of the Cross, which he had gained through reading Ernest Hello. In 1920 Garrigou-Lagrange reviewed the second edition of Arintero's *Cuestiones místicas* in a new journal that Garrigou-Lagrange had just founded with Vincent Bernadot called *La vie spirituelle*. "[I]f there are few contemplatives," he wrote, "it is not that contemplation is properly an extraordinary gift, in a miraculous sense; it is because of our lack of perseverance, abnegation, and love for the Cross. . . ."[21]

Both of these intensely personal encounters—with Hello first, then with Arintero—played a part in Garrigou-Lagrange's rejection of the commonly fostered two-tiered version of Christian spirituality: one for the clergy and religious, the other for the common layperson. In this sense Garrigou-Lagrange's spiritual theology may be interpreted as an early example of a more widespread contemporary revival of mystical theology in Catholic circles that emphasizes the unity of all spheres of life. It is true that his spiritual writings betray a certain over-systematization, a failure to allow adequately for variations in each individual's psychological temperament. Yet in this systematization one may detect an underlying pedagogical concern. For example, the carefully demarcated three-tiered ascent delineated in *The Three Conversions in the Spiritual Life* (1933), which draws upon ancient analogies that relate the passage to holiness through various levels of purgation to human development through childhood and youth to adulthood, provides spiritual directors with a practical pedagogical instrument by which to cultivate growth and measure progress in those under their pastoral care.[22] In adopting this schema, Garrigou-Lagrange wanted to emphasize that spiritual progress and advancement in holiness is no less normal—or vital—in a Christian than organic development in a living body. He believed that any division between spiritual and intellectual life was invalid, and his writing and lecture activity confirm it. His involvement in the famous "*cercles de St. Thomas*," initiated by Jacques and Raissa Maritain in 1919, saw him give the opening lecture at the first retreat in Versailles in 1922 on the topic, "The union of the intellectual life and the spiritual life." It was followed the next

21. Quoted in ibid., 187.

22. "The distinction between the three periods or stages of the spiritual life is clearly of great importance, as those who are charged with the direction of souls well know." Réginald Garrigou-Lagrange, *The Three Conversions in the Spiritual Life* (Rockford, IL: Tan Books, 2002), 29–30.

day by a second lecture, "The ultimate end of human life," devoted, as Jacques Maritain recalled, to "the natural desire to see God."[23] The following year (1923) saw the publication of his *Christian Perfection and Contemplation according to St. Thomas Aquinas and St. John of the Cross*, then *The Love of God and the Cross of Jesus* in 1929, and the already-mentioned *The Three Conversions in the Spiritual Life* in 1933. Finally he published what has been acclaimed as his "*summa*" of Catholic spirituality, *The Three Ages of the Spiritual Life* (two volumes, 1938), designated by the late Benedict Ashley as "[t]he fullest theological analysis of spiritual life from a Dominican perspective."[24]

As for the later period of Garrigou-Lagrange's life, his influence waned as his own health declined and as the church increasingly took up the challenge of engaging the modern world. However, in researching for this book I was privileged to have extensive correspondence with Fr. Kevin O'Shea, an Australian philosopher, theologian, and author of many scholarly articles on deification in the 1950s and '60s, and who spent several years at the Angelicum in Rome during the last years of Garrigou-Lagrange's teaching career. He writes:

> As far as Garrigou-Lagrange goes, I knew him rather personally (he had his 80th birthday while I was there). He had a reputation of being a really difficult man, and had been so re: the "nouvelle théologie," but I never found him like that. He used to lift his skull cap to me on arrival early every morning, when he would walk the courtyard saying a rosary. He went out every Thursday and came home without any of the money he took in his pocket. . . . As long as you weren't bullshitting, he was a friend of every real search for truth.[25]

As is so often the case, the weariness of age and ill-health seemed to have had the effect of softening the temperament and ushering into clearer perspective the things that really matter.

---

23. See Jacques Maritain's *Notebooks*, chapter 5: "Thomist Study Circles and Their Annual Retreats," published online at the Jacques Maritain Center, http://martian.nd.edu/jmc/etext/nb05.htm, accessed November 9, 2011.

24. Benedict Ashley, *Spiritual Direction in the Dominican Tradition* (New York: Paulist, 1995), 159.

25. Kevin O'Shea, private email correspondence (August 16, 2010).

KARL RAHNER

With Karl Rahner (1904–1984) we have an altogether different personality. Like many others of his generation, Rahner stood out from such strict-observance Thomists as Garrigou-Lagrange in that he was "nourished on the Fathers of the Church."[26] His doctorate in theology, examining the typological interpretation of the nuptial nativity of the church from the side of Christ as expounded by Scripture and the Fathers, stands as lasting testimony to the soundness of his formation.[27] His love for the spirituality of St. Ignatius of Loyola and its devotion to the Sacred Heart leave their profound mark in many of his writings, especially sermons, prayers, and retreats. His entry into the Jesuit order may have been precipitated by his early contact in 1920 with Romano Guardini at a Quickborn youth retreat at Castle Rothenfels in Bavaria. He was counted among the close colleagues of the circle of theological renewal that included Henri de Lubac and Hans Urs von Balthasar, and with them he was moved painfully by de Lubac's disciplinary exile in 1950. An illuminating remark arises from that time in a letter written by von Balthasar to de Lubac: "I fear that Karl Rahner is very discouraged now—he, who is almost our only hope. We must support him; you and he must help one another."[28]

Unlike Garrigou-Lagrange, and like de Lubac, Rahner never attempted a systematic theology or philosophy. His writings seek instead to respond to different questions in different circumstances, and are thus classified in German as *Anlasstheologie*. He was nevertheless a remarkably gifted and bold speculative and philosophical theologian, especially gripped by the challenges presented to theological discourse by the transcendental philosophy of Maréchal and Heidegger, the latter of whom was his teacher and, later, mutually respected intellectual colleague. Although Rahner was no systematician, that is not to say his writings possess no unifying theme, which surely lies in the nexus of divine self-communication and human self-transcendence. Yet here and there they betray a sense of ambivalence about his true convictions. There is a feeling of incoherence and inconsistency about their theological content, which Rahner himself admitted,[29] and which is perhaps not so surprising for a life that had its own inner inconsistencies.[30] Von Balthasar has justly spoken of Rahner's

---

26. De Lubac, *At the Service of the Church*, 318.

27. Karl Rahner, "E Latere Christi: Der Ursprung der Kirche als zweiter Eva aus der Seite Christi des zweiten Adam (1936)," in Rahner, *Sämtliche Werke*, vol. 3: *Spiritualität und Theologie der Kirchenväter*, ed. A. R. Batlogg et al. (Benziger: Herder, 1999), 4–83.

28. Quoted by Voderholzer, *Meet Henri de Lubac*, 74.

29. "Karl Rahner, himself, often pointed out how easily you can come up with inconsistencies in his work. . . . There are ruptures in his work and you do not have to harmonize everything. . . ." A. R.

"bold but often one-sided proposals, which are not always coordinated among themselves (there are many Karl Rahners!). . . ." In his role as *peritus* at Vatican II, Rahner was remembered among other things for monopolizing discussion. As Yves Congar reported in his diary at the time, "Il est magnifique, il est courageux, il est perspicace et profond, mais finalement indiscret."[31] While Rahner's orthodoxy never formally came under suspicion, he "often had to suffer the fate of the sorcerer's apprentice who was no longer able to exorcise from his disciples the spirits he had conjured up."[32]

Moved by the new historical and evolutionary consciousness called for by modern advances in the physical and cosmological sciences, Rahner belonged to an emerging movement in twentieth-century theology that increasingly gave considered reflection to the intimate relation between God's acts of creation and incarnation in an effort to make better sense of the mysterious fact that in Jesus God himself has entered into the world of signs and become "flesh" in such a way as to constitute the radical and centripetally definitive epicenter of all matter and time. It has become increasingly common for theologians from across a broad range of Christian traditions to acknowledge the truly cosmic character and profoundly universal scope of the new creation established in Jesus Christ the eternal Son of God made man. One need not go too far to find this very contemporary perception extending deep into the history of Christian thought. From Teilhard de Chardin's *Hymn of the Universe* to Gerard Manley Hopkins's "dearest freshness deep down things," from Justin Martyr's *logos spermatikos* to the great Christ hymns in the opening chapters of Ephesians and Colossians: each in its own way speaks of a Christ whose identity and meaning and mission are not limited to the sphere of soteriology.

This more "global" and historical way of reading the incarnation within the context of creation has many worthy advocates. We need only to mention, for example, the deeply incarnational theology of Emil Mersch, which in its own way prepared the ground for the "logic of the gift" so prominent in the conciliar and postconciliar theology of creation and especially in John Paul

---

Batlogg and M. E. Michalski, ed., *Encounters with Karl Rahner: Remembrances of Rahner by Those Who Knew Him* (Milwaukee: Marquette University Press, 2009), 300.

30. I am thinking of his somewhat secretive long-term relationship by correspondence with Luise Rinser. See Luise Rinser's share of the exchange in her *Gratwanderung: Briefe der Freundschaft an Karl Rahner 1962-1984* (Munich: Kösel, 1994). Also Pamela Kirk, "Reflections on Luise Rinser's Gratwanderung," *Philosophy and Theology* 10 (1997): 293–300.

31. Quoted by Jared Wicks, "Yves Congar's Doctrinal Service of the People of God," *Gregorianum* 84, no. 3 (2003): 499–550 at 529.

32. Hans Urs von Balthasar, *The Moment of Christian Witness* (San Francisco: Ignatius, 1994), 148.

II's nuptial and communional anthropology. In a manner not dissimilar to the way the Holy Spirit in St. Paul's theology of the new creation is understood as the ἀρραβών or "pledge" of a more complete inheritance (2 Cor. 1:22; Eph. 1:14), Mersch asserts that "creation is the first token of a total donation." In giving to human beings their whole being in creation, says Mersch, God foreshadows his intention to endow them with *his* whole being in Christ.[33] While the incarnation is an utterly novel and unexpected event, there is a sense in which the ground for it had already begun to be prepared not only in Israel's prophetic history, nor even in the creation of the first man and woman, but right back in the primordial beginnings of the world's aboriginal formation. "When the original chaos rose up, all the elements that in the fullness of time would go to form the body of the Savior were there, scattered throughout the universal mass. God was even then fashioning a body for Himself." In this way it is possible to perceive in the God-man Jesus Christ "the supreme achievement of all creation."[34] These and similar words by Mersch express thoughts with which Rahner felt deep affinity.

Although Rahner served as a *peritus* for the Council, as did de Lubac, his theology increasingly came to bear the problematic mark of his concern to "demythologize" the theological language and concepts of the Bible and the Fathers in order to translate the riches of the Christian faith into contemporary modes of thought. In this approach, however laudable in intent, something becomes lost. Nowhere is this clearer than in Rahner's curious proposal, in the epilogue to his mature work *Foundations of Christian Faith*, of three prospective "creeds" intended—alongside any number of alternatives suited to the plurality of theologies and cultural settings of today—to replace the Apostles' Creed.[35] Quite apart from their intolerably abstract philosophical style and story-less, ahistorical content, they exhibit no sense of the nature of creed as narrative *confessio* (a speaking with) and ecclesial *homologia* (saying the same thing), as answer to the question: "Who do you say that I am?" (Matt. 16:13-20). This is a question that is finally not interested in this or that opinion drawn from the plurality of theological speculation ("Some say . . . , others say . . ."), but demands a faithful accounting in response to divinely revealed realities ("Flesh

---

33. Emil Mersch, *The Theology of the Mystical Body*, trans. C. Vollert (St. Louis: Herder, 1952), 133.

34. Ibid., 134–35.

35. Karl Rahner, *Foundations of Christian Faith: An Introduction to the Idea of Christianity*, trans. W. V. Dych, (New York: Crossroad, 1978), 448–59. See the critique of Rahner's proposal, first broached in 1967, by Joseph Ratzinger, *Principles of Catholic Theology: Building Stones for a Fundamental Theology*, trans. Mary Frances McCarthy (San Francisco: Ignatius, 1987), 122–30.

and blood did not reveal this to you . . ."), and for whose rendering the church, in her head, receives her Lord's approval ("Blessed are you . . .").

But rather than end with this rather critical observation, it may be better to close with an amusing anecdote. It has sometimes been said that Rahner was a rather boring character, overly preoccupied with his theological work, with little interest in music and the arts. However, in an interview late in his life, when it was reported to him that he apparently lacked a hobby, Rahner retorted: "Well, I don't know about no hobbies at all. For many years I smoked, beginning with my bee-keeping days in Valkenburg. But other than that, I don't know what particular hobbies I've had."[36] It seems even the greatest theologians have their mundane pursuits!

HENRI DE LUBAC

Although Henri de Lubac S.J. (1896–1991) was born before Rahner, I have placed him third in our overall schema not only because he outlived his Jesuit confrere but in order to emphasize my sense that his theology of deification brings together what is best in both Garrigou-Lagrange and Rahner, at the same time supplementing and correcting them along lines that are more expressly in keeping with the *fontes* of Christian tradition and that better cohere with the ecclesiological and christological emphases of Vatican II. He is also distinguished among the other two by having been appointed a cardinal (in 1983), an honor that can be taken as vindication of his fundamental theology.

How is it possible to classify his theological output? "Whoever stands before the forty or so volumes of Henri de Lubac's writings . . . feels as though he is at the entrance to a primeval forest."[37] Here is a mind immersed and completely conversant with and at home in the entire tradition of Christian thought, who complained about his lack of facility in Greek and German, but who benefited in his patristic studies and publications by the collaboration of expert colleagues such as Daniélou and von Balthasar. De Lubac's earliest reading in the Greek Fathers, often snatched in free time during his formative years of seminary exile in Britain—especially in Canterbury and Jersey in the second period after the war between 1919 and 1923—was of the *Adversus haereses* of Irenaeus of Lyons, a work of seminal paramountcy in the history

36. Karl Rahner, *I Remember* (London: SCM, 1985), 61. My inclusion of this remark is not entirely gratuitous, but heralds my chapter on Rahner's theology of deification within the sphere of the mundane and ordinary.

37. Hans Urs von Balthasar, *The Theology of Henri de Lubac* (San Francisco: Ignatius, 1991), 23.

of Christian thought for all sorts of reasons, but not least for definitively articulating God's plan in Christ to bring about a supernatural finality for human beings, who are equally created in his image and destined to attain a glorious assimilation to the Trinity.[38]

De Lubac only published his first major book in 1938 at the age of forty-two. Titled *Catholicisme: Les aspects sociaux du dogme*, his own judgments about it suggest it to be little more than a hasty and mediocre dossier.[39] It was a work, he remarks, "stitched together" from somewhat disparate materials originally given as lectures and short papers from as early as 1933, supplemented by additional chapters "extracted" (like a tooth?) from the Jesuit by his Dominican friend, Yves Congar, for the latter's new *Unam Sanctam* series. *Catholicisme* was certainly never intended to be a manual or dogmatic treatise on the Church.[40] According to de Lubac, it merely "tries to show the simultaneously social, historical and interior character of Christianity. . . ."[41] But these and similar laconic remarks mask the profound power and originality of a work that at the time signaled a different way of doing theology, and that was destined to become an acclaimed and highly influential masterpiece of the twentieth century. Karl Rahner labeled it "an outstanding book" of "considerable theological depth."[42] Joseph Ratzinger highlighted its importance as "a milestone" in his own "theological journey."[43] Hans Urs von Balthasar hailed it as "a work of genius," "seminal" and "programmatic" for all that would follow,

38. Although Irenaeus was a bishop in Gaul, and his writings mostly survive only in Latin and Armenian translations, he originally came from Asia Minor, wrote in Greek his native tongue, and is commonly counted among the Greek Apologists. See further Johannes Quasten, *Patrology*, vol. 1 (Allen, TX: Christian Classics, nd), 287–93. On the image/likeness distinction in Irenaeus, see Eric Osborn, *Irenaeus of Lyons* (Cambridge: Cambridge University Press, 2001), 211–31; Jean Daniélou, *Gospel Message and Hellenistic Culture: A History of Early Christian Doctrine Before the Council of Nicaea*, vol. 2 (London: Darton, Longman & Todd, 1973), 398–408; Gustaf Wingren, *Man and the Incarnation: A Study in the Biblical Theology of Irenaeus*, trans. R. Mackenzie (Edinburgh: Oliver & Boyd, 1959), 14–26.

39. I call *Catholicism* de Lubac's "first book," though strictly speaking it was preceded in 1936 by a lengthy essay on the same topic, *Le caractère social du dogme chrétien* (Lyon). The translation I shall be using in this chapter and elsewhere in this book is from the fourth French edition (1947): Henri de Lubac, *Catholicism: Christ and the Common Destiny of Man*, trans. L. Sheppard (London: Burns & Oates, 1950).

40. "[S]ome, believing the title to be 'Le Catholicisme,' supposed the book was intended to be a treatise on the Catholic Church. They began to reproach me for omissions that, if this had been the case, would have in fact been regrettable: not a single chapter on the papacy!" De Lubac, *At the Service of the Church*, 27–28.

41. De Lubac, *At the Service of the Church*, 27.

42. In a review published in *Zeitschrift für katholische Theologie* 63 (1939): 443–44.

43. Preface to the later English edition by Ignatius, 1988.

likening it to a great tree trunk from which would eventually branch numerous vital theological works.[44]

Throughout his life, de Lubac suffered from shellshock and the trauma of his mandatory military service in World War I. There he also lost many friends, including the remarkable proponent of affective Thomism, Pierre Rousselot (1878–1915). But it is quite arguable that he suffered even more deeply in the attacks, apparently spearheaded by Garrigou-Lagrange, which led to his temporary suspension from teaching dogmatic theology and to what he often called the "lightning bolt" of *Humani Generis*. De Lubac himself was no wimp when it came to polemics. In the opening chapter of his 1965 *Mystery of the Supernatural*, he implicitly includes Garrigou-Lagrange among those "few lazy minds" who defend the indefensible and fail to undertake a detailed exegetical and historical study of sources.[45] Or just as pointedly, he identifies Garrigou-Lagrange as representative of certain contemporary commentators who seem not to notice that, in their defense of the (Aristotelian) principle that natural desires must conform to natural ends, "they are flatly contradicting St. Thomas."[46] On the other hand, while de Lubac and Karl Rahner sometimes expressed critical differences with one another, even over weighty matters, de Lubac often drew upon various statements in Rahner's theology to corroborate his own arguments, and even confessed a "strong personal affection" for his Jesuit confrere.[47] On this score, the late Donald L. Gelpi once related how, when on a lecture tour of the USA in the 1970s, de Lubac wanted to go to Los Angeles instead of Chicago. When asked why, de Lubac replied, "Because I just got a letter from Karl Rahner . . . , and Rahner tells me that I must not die without seeing Disneyland."[48] Although in criticism he could be as bold and acute as anyone, he preserved such an irenic manner and theological even-headedness that von Balthasar proposed him as a "peacemaker" in the contest between the Neothomists on the one side and the Neocatholics on the other, a proposition this book in part undertakes to materialize.[49]

44. Hans Urs von Balthasar, *The Theology of Henri de Lubac: An Overview* (San Francisco: Ignatius, 1991), 28, 35.

45. Henri de Lubac, *The Mystery of the Supernatural*, trans. R. Sheed (New York: Crossroad, 1998, orig. 1965), 12 n. 64.

46. Ibid., 149.

47. See ibid., 107 n. 36.

48. This excerpt comes from a lengthier personal anecdote by Gelpi published on the worldwide web a few years before his death in 2011. I and no doubt some others recorded it, but the report now seems to have been lost in cyberspatial oblivion.

49. Von Balthasar, *Moment of Christian Witness*, 150.

It has been said that the difference between Rahner and de Lubac lies in the fact that while the former "proposes an attempt at a face-to-face meeting . . . between Thomism and Kantianism," de Lubac "right away has a 'dogmatic' perspective."[50] However, the real differences seem more to lie not in where their respective theologies begin (for we do not do Rahner justice by allying him too closely with an all-encompassing philosophical agenda), but in where they end up. Already during and especially after the Council, de Lubac discerned a disconcerting falling away on the part of many leading bishops and theologians from the fundamentals of the faith and a troubling penchant for revisionist interpretations ultimately subversive of the revealed objectivity of creation and incarnation, redemption and resurrection.[51] His deliberate break with this paraconciliar trend is symbolized by his dissociation from the circle of theologians connected with the *Concilium* journal, which Rahner had co-founded in 1965 and of which he remained a key representative, and his establishment with von Balthasar, Ratzinger, le Guillou, Bouyer, Lehmann, and others of the *Communio* journal in 1972, envisioned as an alternative to, and even the rival of, *Concilium*.

As an antidote to any shortsighted emptying of the Christian faith of all substance, de Lubac tirelessly counseled a return to the ever "fructifying" and timeless fecundity of the Fathers of the church, who "do not dictate our solutions to us" or "dispense us from reflecting," but who "prepare in us the movement that must not be stopped" and "initiate us to a faith that frees us as much as it engages us."[52] His doctrine of deification, which becomes more and more explicit in later works, functions as a corollary of this concern to restore to human beings—and to the church—what is essential for their being, self-understanding, and destiny. Deification is not an ideology, but a reality. As he summed it up in *The Mystery of the Supernatural*, "Our 'deification' is

50. G. Narcisse, "The Supernatural in Contemporary Theology," in *Surnaturel: A Controversy at the Heart of Twentieth-Century Thomistic Thought*, ed. S.-T. Bonino, trans. R. Williams and M. Levering (Ave Maria, FL: Sapientia, 2009), 295–310 at 300. I was unable before the completion of this book to consult the encyclopedic study by Eric de Moulins-Beaufort, *Anthropologie et mystique selon Henri de Lubac* (Paris: Cerf, 2003), in which the author offers a comparative analysis of the respective theological anthropologies of de Lubac and Rahner.

51. See, e.g., Henri de Lubac, "The Church in Crisis," *Theology Digest* 17 (1969): 312–25. Also Christopher J. Walsh, "De Lubac's Critique of the Postconciliar Church," *Communio* 19 (1992): 404–32; and the review of de Lubac's Vatican II diary by Jared Wicks, "Further Light on Vatican Council II," *Catholic Historical Review* 95 (2009): 546–69.

52. De Lubac, *At the Service of the Church*, 319.

an incredible marvel, and we can believe it only because of that even greater marvel in which it originated—the Son of God becoming a son of man."[53]

53. De Lubac, *The Mystery of the Supernatural*, 21.

PART I

Réginald Garrigou-Lagrange

3

Deification and the Person of Christ

The Christian doctrine of deification has always depended crucially on its root and foundation in christology.[1] Incarnation and deification are two sides of a single soteriological coin, structural corollaries one of the other. Early patristic formulations posit human participation in the divine nature as a gratuitous and proportionately related consequence of God's becoming human in Christ. Athanasius gives us the famous formula: "He [the Logos] became human, that we might be deified." Augustine envisages the same kind of proportionality, "To make gods those who were human, he was made human who was God," while for Maximus the terms are even more explicitly reciprocal: "For they say that God and humanity are paradigms one of another, so that to the extent that God is humanised through love for humankind, so far is humanity able to be deified through love."[2] These comments should not be taken to mean that the two elements are strictly identical: the incarnation does not amount to the actual divinization of every human being. In the incarnation, the divine and human natures are united as a single personal entity, such that to point to the man Jesus Christ is to point to the second person of the Trinity. In deification, by contrast, the human person does not enter into hypostatic union with God or with any one "member" of the Trinity, but, retaining her distinct personal and human identity, comes to be penetrated soul and body with divine activity. Following the biblical terminology (2 Pet. 1:4), deification has always been understood as a communion or "participation"—or even a kind of "dwelling" (John 14:17, 20, 23)—in the divine nature. The incarnation, even if it is efficaciously analogous, is not quite the same as that. In Christ, God does not just "participate" in

1. This chapter contains material previously published by me in the article "Criteria for Authentic Mystical Experience: Reginald Garrigou-Lagrange's Doctrine of Deification," *The Heythrop Journal* 55, no. 2 (2014): 230-43.

2. Athanasius, *De Incarnatione* 54 (PG 25, 192B); Augustine, *Sermo* 192, 1, 1 (PL 38, 1012); Maximus Confessor, *Ambigua ad Iohannem* 10 (PG 91, 1113BC).

human nature, although this is a perfectly acceptable expression.[3] According to the well-known Johannine phrase, the Word precisely "became" (ἐγένετο) flesh, "flesh" here meaning "human." This is to say that, in the Christ event, the eternal Son of the Father, without in any way ceasing to be himself, assumed human nature in its full created integrity, appropriating it to his personal identity in such a way that all its properties became his very own. But precisely because of this unique personal appropriation, the human nature of Christ—by which we mean his physical, contingent, and ongoing human existence—has been rendered the particular instrumental medium by which alone deification becomes universally accessible to human beings. Deification is indeed a participation of human beings in the divine nature, but it is so by means of the real humanity of a person who is God. To commune with Jesus is to share in the divine life of God, because Jesus is God.

In this chapter I shall try to penetrate more deeply into the way Garrigou-Lagrange envisages this fundamental relation between christology and deification. I begin by presenting a key foundational structural analogy between the hypostatic union and the deification of the justified, proposed by Garrigou-Lagrange in his 1933 classic, *Le Sauveur et son amour pour nous*.[4] Two features pertinent to the question of the theology of deification seem especially striking in this work, and will constitute a primary focus. The first is Garrigou-Lagrange's defense of the psychological integrity of Christ's human nature, a matter often found all the more difficult to understand in view of the traditional claim that Jesus' "personality" was not human but divine. The second is Garrigou-Lagrange's proposal that contemplative adherence to Jesus' humanity stands as an abiding criterion by which to distinguish authentic mystical union with God from other forms of religious experience. In both discussions it is possible to detect a clear portrayal of deification as a corollary to the incarnation. After analyzing these two themes we can turn to see how Garrigou-Lagrange applies these christological insights to the question of authentic Christian spirituality or mysticism.

3. See, for example, Heb. 2:14: "Since the children share a common flesh and blood, he [Jesus] also partook equally in the same."

4. English translation: *Our Savior and His Love for Us*, trans. A. Bouchard (St. Louis and London: Herder, 1951). A revised French edition was published in 1952.

DEIFICATION AND THE HYPOSTATIC UNION

Intelligent appreciation of development in the history of christology is often hampered by the changes in meaning acquired by certain words over time. Today all orthodox Christians confess that Jesus Christ is one person with two natures, one divine and one human. But the English word "person" does little to convey what was meant by the Greek words "hypostasis" or "prosopon," or even by the Latin "persona," with which words the early church formulated its definitive confessions of faith.

This highlights the difficulties theology faces when trying to understand what it means to say that Christ is one person. In what sense are we using that word "person"? For Garrigou-Lagrange, this was a question in need of urgent clarification before any useful reflection on the nature and purpose of the incarnation could take place. Was "person" to be taken in the positivist sense of an aggregate of phenomena united by association, or in the Bergsonian sense of an "élan vital et libre" whose successive forms are merely evolving states of consciousness? Or was it rather to be taken in the sense of the notion of person such as we find in the medieval philosophy of being: "person as subsistence, as the principle of an *id quod* which exists and operates by means of, or through, a determinate nature (*id quo*)"? Having listed these three possibilities, Guy Mansini has argued that it was this third sense alone that Garrigou-Lagrange found to be "both theologically useful and as well continuous with common sense."[5] Only the notion of person entertained in the "commonsense" philosophy of being comes close to explaining what we encounter in Jesus.

In settling for this meaning of person with its roots firmly in medieval metaphysics, Garrigou-Lagrange does not seem to consider the possibility that the reality encountered in the person of Christ might enrich or even modify existing metaphysical notions of person arrived at through traditional natural philosophy.[6] Yet precisely insofar as deification possesses a structural analogy to the hypostatic union, Garrigou-Lagrange implicitly reconfigures his "commonsense" notion of personhood with a more christocentric and even kenotic model, derived from the simple data of revelation. For one of the articles of faith accepted by Garrigou-Lagrange is that the human nature of Christ was assumed by the person of the divine Word in such a way that that human

---

5. Guy Mansini, *"What Is a Dogma?" The Meaning and Truth of Dogma in Eduoard le Roy and His Scholastic Opponents* (Rome: Editrice Pontificia Università Gregoriana, 1985), 313, paraphrasing Garrigou-Lagrange's concept of *le sens commun*.

6. On this possibility, see further Hans Urs von Balthasar, "On the Concept of Person," *Communio* 13, no. 1 (1986): 18–26; Joseph Ratzinger, "The Notion of Person in Theology," *Communio* 17, no. 3 (1990): 439–54.

nature has no "personality" of its own as such. So fully and intimately does God, who is essentially diffusive goodness, communicate himself in the incarnation that the human "personality" of Christ is effaced, without his human nature in any way being diminished. This mystery, uniquely given in the incarnation, in turn sheds light on the real meaning and vocation of human personhood. And so we will find Garrigou-Lagrange proposing that human beings are deified, or receive God's intimate self-communication, to the degree that they efface themselves or "depersonalize" their own ego. Just as the deprivation of the dimension of personal existence renders Christ's humanity more absolutely open to the deifying influence of the divine Logos, so too does the Christian realize deification in a dramatic and ecstatic self-mortification.

What is the background to these claims by Garrigou-Lagrange? Traditional dogmatic formulations and mystical treatises have long asserted in one form or another the rather unusual-sounding claim that Christ had no human personality. By this they do not mean to deny Jesus was truly human. Rather they mean to counter the old Nestorian error of thinking that there are two centers of subjectivity or conscious agency—two persons, two egos—in Jesus, one human and one divine. Instead, even though Christ has two natures, and so is essentially both human and divine, he is fundamentally one person; indeed, he is none other than the second Person of the holy Trinity. As Cyril of Alexandria's Third Letter to Nestorius had stated—and as it was reaffirmed at the fifth-century Council of Ephesus (431)—all Christ's actions, all his sufferings, are to be ascribed not to this or that nature, but to one and the same divine personal subject: the now-incarnate eternal Word and only-begotten Son of God.[7]

In the nineteenth and early twentieth centuries, however, this traditional understanding of Christ's divine "personality" came under sustained criticism. Historicist and naturalist interpretations, departing from the high christology of the Gospels and the primitive church, painted Jesus' life and self-understanding in purely human developmental terms.[8] A helpful index of the kinds of concerns presented under the rubric of the "modernist" agenda can be found in the

---

7. "For we do not divide up the words of our Saviour in the gospels among two hypostases or persons. For the one and only Christ is not dual, even though he be considered to be from two distinct realities, brought together into an unbreakable union. . . . Therefore, in thinking rightly, we refer both the human and divine expressions to the same person." *Third Letter of Cyril to Nestorius*, in, *Decrees of the Ecumenical Councils*, vol. 1, ed. N. P. Tanner (London: Sheed & Ward, 1990), 55.

8. For a brief analysis see Yves Congar, *Jesus Christ*, trans. Luke O'Neill (London: Geoffrey Chapman, 1966), 52 n. 1; Walter Kasper, *Jesus the Christ*, trans. V. Green (London: Burns & Oates, 1976), 115; Frederick Copleston, *A History of Philosophy: 19th and 20th Century French Philosophy* (London: Continuum, 1999), 245–49.

official pronouncements of the time: we may mention for example the decree *Lamentabili* (1907) under Pope Pius X and the *Decree of the Holy Office* (1918) under Pope Benedict XV, both of which address the much-disputed question of Christ's consciousness.[9] According to the more revisionist line of thought, represented for example by Anton Günther in the nineteenth century and Déodat de Basly in the twentieth, if Jesus was really human, as no one seriously seemed to doubt, then he must have had a human consciousness, a center of human subjectivity, or in other words, a human personality.[10] Moreover, it was reasoned, it is naturally the case with human consciousness that it is limited and in need of gradual development. Surely, then, if we are to do full justice to the reality of Christ's humanity, we must allow for the presence in him of the full range of psychological complexities involved in the subjective experience of having human consciousness.

As one may discern in the papal pronouncements cited, early official responses to these and similar speculations, although by no means bypassing detailed analysis of the contrary doctrines, were flatly negative, and gave little room for genuine inquiry into the nature and development of Christ's humanity. Later an attempt was made by Pope Pius XII in the encyclical *Sempiternus Rex* (1951) to state the orthodox case with more subtlety. Pius affirmed the legitimacy of studying the humanity of Christ from the perspective of psychology, "yet in this difficult matter there are some who too rashly set up novel constructions which they wrongly place under the patronage of the Council of Chalcedon."[11] The pope especially had in mind the so-called *homo assumptus* ("assumed human being") christology of the fifth century, rejected not only by the great Cyril of Alexandria but also later by Severus of Antioch, regarded by many of his contemporaries and later conciliar orthodoxy as a leading monophysite. The *homo assumptus* formula implies the existence of an already-existing human being who, in the *henosis* achieved in the incarnation, is subsequently assumed into the unity of the person of the Logos.[12] Christ's humanity in this way is virtually accorded, in Nestorian-like fashion, an

---

9. See Heinrich Denzinger, *Compendium of Creeds, Definitions, and Declarations on Matters of Faith and Morals*, rev. and ed. by Peter Hünermann et al. (San Francisco: Ignatius, 2012, 43rd ed.) [=DS], 3427–38; 3646–47.

10. Anton Günther (d. 1863) defined personhood in terms of self-consciousness. Christ is thereby a moral unity of two self-conscious persons. His christology was condemned by Pope Pius IX. Déodat de Basly (d. 1937) similarly asserted a moral union in Christ between the Logos and Jesus, the assumed man.

11. DS 3905.

12. See Aloys Grillmeier, *Christ in Christian Tradition*, vol. 2, part 2: *The Church of Constantinople in the Sixth Century*, trans. P. Allen and J. Cawte (London: Mowbray, 1995), 41 and 76–78.

autonomy equivalent to a personal subject in its own right.[13] But if this is ruled out in view of the absolute temporal coincidence of the creation of Christ's humanity and its union with the Word, what kind of "personality" can in fact be predicated of Christ that does full justice to his real humanity yet does not suggest some kind of divine-human hybrid, in other words, some kind of *tertium quid*?

CHRIST'S "ONTOLOGICAL" PERSONALITY

With these kinds of theological sensitivities at large, Garrigou-Lagrange sets out to define Christ's personhood by determining a rationally coherent definition of the concept "person" that can be applied also in the unique case of Jesus Christ, the incarnate Word and Son of God. Accordingly, we shall see that Garrigou-Lagrange proposes an understanding of personhood or personality that does not locate it at the level of psychological consciousness or moral experience but has it constituting the ontological "presupposition," as it were, of both these dimensions. Aidan Nichols has described this as Garrigou-Lagrange's "concept of ontological personhood," identifying it as the self-same concept "that enabled Chalcedon in 451 and the subsequent ecumenical councils of the Church to affirm that in the Word Incarnate a single subject is indeed single, one."[14]

---

13. We leave aside here the discussion of Nestorius' real mind on the matter, except to mention that it has been the general consensus for some decades that he was more orthodox than his contemporaries allowed. See J. S. Romanides, "Highlights in the Debate over Theodore of Mopsuestia's Christology and Some Suggestions for a Fresh Approach," *Greek Orthodox Theological Review* 5 (1959–60): 140–85; Aloys Grillmeier, *Christ in Christian Tradition: From the Apostolic Age to Chalcedon (451)*, trans. J. S. Bowden (London: Mowbray, 1965), 496–505.

14. Aidan Nichols, *Reason with Piety: Garrigou-Lagrange in the Service of Catholic Thought* (Ave Maria, FL: Sapientia, 2008), 84. Garrigou-Lagrange seems to have derived the term "ontological personality" from Cajetan; see his *Reality: A Synthesis of Thomistic Thought*, trans. P. Cummins (London: Herder, 1950) (reprinted by Ex Fontibus, 2007), 335. Whether this notion is in fact what the Council Fathers had in mind when they formulated the famous Chalcedonian definition is a debatable question, but one I cannot pursue in any detail here. My own sense is that rather too much conceptual content from later in the history of personalism often tends to be read into the Fathers' use of the relevant terms. See the critical analysis by André de Halleux, "Personalisme ou essentialisme trinitaire chez les Pères cappadociens?," *Revue théologique de Louvain* 17 (1986): 129–55, 265–92; idem, "La définition christologique à Chalcédoine," *Revue théologique de Louvain* 7 (1976): 3–23, 155–70; also Andrew Louth, *St John Damascene: Tradition and Originality in Byzantine Theology* (Oxford: Oxford University Press, 2002), 47–53; L. Turcescu, "'Person' versus 'Individual,' and Other Misreadings of Gregory of Nyssa," in, *Re-Thinking Gregory of Nyssa*, ed. Sarah Coakley (Oxford: Blackwell, 2003): 97–109.

In any case, it is possible to show how Garrigou-Lagrange's attempt to elaborate and defend traditional christology in terms of this "ontological" understanding of personality or personhood involves him in laying down a clear substructure for a dynamic that takes place when any human person—in a way analogous to the hypostatic union—is intimately united to God. The full blossoming of human personality only takes place in a deifying union in which the human ego is effaced and subsumed beneath a divine *alter ego* more intimate to one's being than one's very own self. To that extent perhaps even Garrigou-Lagrange would have to allow that the divine person we meet in Christ, acting like a catalyst, makes possible and actually brings about a human reality qualitatively new and unprecedented in human history.

How does Garrigou-Lagrange begin? As we might expect, he starts with St. Thomas. From him he draws a definition of personality as that which makes possible the independent subjectivity, self-possession, and self-mastery we normally associate with conscious human activity and which we attribute to distinct human individuals.[15] While personhood is manifest in these acts, as well as in other species- or individual-specific attributes, it is not reducible to them. It stands behind them, distinct from them. All of them may presuppose personality, a particular existing subject or "I" to whom they can be attributed, but none of them constitute it, for it is their very root. In this way, says Garrigou-Lagrange, a person is "a subject of attribution," "a totality," an "independent subject," an "entity" differentiated not only from other persons but from all that is fittingly attributed to him as to an "I."[16] Personhood is therefore quite distinct from nature. Nature is that *by which* a subject exists. It is also distinct from existence. Existence is what an existing subject *has*.[17] Person is the subject that exists, that to which or to whom existence and a nature of a certain kind and all the particular actions peculiar to that existing subject are predicated. Personality is neither psychological nor moral, still less a developmental or historical accomplishment, but "basic" or ontological, that is, belonging to the order of being.[18]

15. Garrigou-Lagrange, *Our Savior and His Love for Us*, 83.

16. Ibid., 92–99.

17. This applies of course only in the case of finite creatures. God does not *have*, but *is* his own existence.

18. Garrigou-Lagrange, *Our Savior and His Love for Us*, 83. Nichols's statement that "personhood is the radical principle of our actions" is a little misleading, even though it echoes the Latin "radix" which Garrigou-Lagrange indeed uses. Strictly speaking it is human nature, not personhood, which is the principle of human actions. What Nichols seems to want to say is that it is ultimately the person who

Garrigou-Lagrange goes on to explain the implications of this concept of personhood for traditional one-person, two-nature christology. Even if we attribute to Jesus two intelligences, two wills, two freedoms (in each case one divine, the other human), it does not follow that there are in him two persons, for such attributions are made to him as to "a single independent subject."[19] At the root of Jesus' human intelligence and will, at the root of his soul itself, "in the order of being," stands "the divine Person of the Word" who has assumed concrete humanity.[20] Thus in Jesus "there is no human personality, no human ego, and yet He is truly a man."[21] This is possible because the actual existence that his human nature comes to possess in coming to be is none other than the already-actual personal existence of the divine Word and Son of God. The old argument that Christ's having two natures implies his having two existences does not hold. According to Thomas, existence (*esse*) is relative to nature and hypostasis in two quite different ways. It is relative to nature inasmuch as nature is *that by which* a thing exists as it does. It is relative to hypostasis inasmuch as hypostasis is *that which* exists.[22] Thus Christ's existence is perfectly singular inasmuch as it is relative to the one hypostasis *which he is*, even if after the incarnation *that by which* he exists as this singular existence is dual. As Garrigou-Lagrange summarizes, "in Jesus there is only one existence," for "the unity of existence follows from the unity of the person."[23]

Garrigou-Lagrange acknowledges that all this "contains a great mystery which we cannot understand," though he is quick to deny that it is "unintelligible or absurd."[24] In fact he has said nothing of *personalitas* beyond the traditional meaning of *suppositum* (= *hypostasis* or subsisting subject) or *subsistentia* (perfect existence).[25] Still, aware of the difficulties faced by his readers, he advances what traditionally is known as an argument from congruity (*ex congruentia*),[26] an explanation aimed at demonstrating the aptness or suitability of the contingent realities set forth in the christological doctrine in

---

performs them. Natures do not act. Persons act, by virtue of their nature/s. See Nichols, *Reason with Piety*, 86.

19. Garrigou-Lagrange, *Our Savior and His Love for Us*, 84.

20. Ibid., 87.

21. Ibid., 88.

22. *Summa theologiae* III, 17, 2.

23. Garrigou-Lagrange, *Our Savior and His Love for Us*, 94.

24. Ibid., 84.

25. Ibid., 97–98.

26. See Nichols, *Reason with Piety*, 81.

question. It is here that the christo-form substructure of deification mentioned earlier is laid out in clearer lineaments.

In the mystery of the incarnation can be glimpsed a certain coming together of two related facts. On the one hand, it is God's "tendency" to communicate himself as much as possible to man. Why? "Because," in keeping with the oft-quoted saying of Dionysius the Areopagite,

> ... goodness is essentially communicative. The good naturally tends to pour itself out, to share the riches within it. And the more perfect a good is, the more it tends to communicate itself fully and intimately. ... Thus, since God is the Sovereign Good, it is highly fitting that He communicate Himself in the highest degree possible to His creatures, both intimately and fully.[27]

If this is the case, why could God not realize this principle and give himself to us "intimately and fully" in person? It seems it would be entirely in keeping with his infinite goodness and gratuitous love for God to give himself in this way "to a privileged soul, in such a manner that the Word, this soul and its body would form only one person, a single self, that of the Word made flesh, in whom would dwell divine perfections and human properties, a person who could truthfully say: 'I who speak to you am the way, the truth, and the life.'"[28]

Similarly, and here is the other side of the coin, it is the innate human tendency to incline as much as possible toward union with God. In fact, says Garrigou-Lagrange, human personality develops and reaches its full moral and psychological perfection precisely to the degree that it becomes more and more dependent upon God, that is, to the degree "that it tends to become more intimately united to God, obliterating itself before Him. This union in self-effacement, far from being servitude, is a glorification."[29] What is true here at the contingent level for every graced human being, argues Garrigou-Lagrange, is realized absolutely and ontologically in Christ.[30] So intimate is his soul's union with God, so total the self-effacement involved, that from the very moment

27. Garrigou-Lagrange, *Our Savior and His Love for Us*, 80–81.

28. Ibid., 81.

29. Ibid., 84.

30. Karl Rahner also refers to this two-dimensional, ontological self-communication between God and man in Christ: "the mystery of the Incarnation fundamentally lies on the one hand in the mystery of the divine self-communication to the world, and on the other in the fact that it took place in Jesus Christ. The former aspect, however, is 'thinkable' through man's fundamental tendency towards absolute closeness to God, a tendency based in fact on God's self-communication. This preserves the mystery of the Incarnation from giving the impression that it is a sort of marvel or something heteronomous." Karl

of his temporal generation he has no human personality at all. Garrigou-Lagrange realizes how this offends against contemporary notions of personality. He reasons that this is because

> it is forgotten that the full development of the human personality consists in being effaced before that of God, by becoming as united as possible to Him. We must consider this fact most carefully that we may begin to understand how it is that the humanity of Jesus is in no sense diminished because in Him human personality has made way for the divine personality of the Word. This is the culminating point of the lofty law: Human personality grows by effacing itself before that of God.[31]

The Depersonalized Ego

It is worth pointing out how closely Garrigou-Lagrange here echoes a long tradition of christological mysticism as we might find it represented for example by the French Cardinal Pierre de Bérulle (1575–1629). The Berullian school repeatedly emphasized the need for a kind of "depersonalization," the annihilation or negation of our individual personality in surrender to the divine will. In this way it was thought that we come closer to imitating Christ, whose human subsistence was effaced to the extent of actually being substituted by the subsistence of the divine Son of God.[32] Being deprived of its native personal existence rendered Christ's humanity more potently and absolutely open to the deifying activity of the Word. Its deification is at once utterly unique and universally paradigmatic:

> For everything in Jesus Christ has its foundation in the hypostasis of his divinity. The eternal Word, as the substance and divine

Rahner, "Incarnation," in *Encyclopedia of Theology: A Concise Sacramentum Mundi*, ed. Karl Rahner (London: Burns & Oates, 1975), 690–99 at 697.

31. Garrigou-Lagrange, *Our Savior and His Love for Us*, 85–86. In this respect the Dominican would seem to agree with Rahner ("Incarnation," 695) that union with God and personal human fulfillment—which Rahner calls "independence"—are "realities that grow in direct, not inverse, proportion" to one another. Garrigou-Lagrange (*Our Savior and His Love for Us*, 85) also refers to personality in terms of independence, though he means "independence with regard not to all things, but to those which are inferior to us and which we dominate by our reason and our liberty. . . ."

32. See Louis Cognet, *Post-Reformation Spirituality*, trans. P. J. Hepburne-Scott (London: Burns & Oates, 1959), 56–115.

suppositum of this human nature, is the proprietor of all its actions and sufferings. He sustains them, elevates them, deifies them in his own person, by sustaining, elevating and deifying the substance of this humanity. . . .[33]

Union with God in this light is seen to affect the human person at the most radical level, the level at which a person says "I." The new situation toward which the path to deification leads is exemplified by St. Paul's negation of the "I": his "no longer I, but Christ living in me" (Gal. 2:20). A dramatic and ecstatic mortification is called for in which "the ego composed of self-love and pride," the "I" which the saints invoke only "to accuse themselves of their faults," is replaced by a truly divine *alter ego*, the *ego* of the Word made flesh, the *ego* through which it becomes clear that God himself is here living and speaking in person.[34] It is not a matter of being converted or changed into the divine nature. That was not even the case with Christ's human nature. It is more a matter of a radical, voluntary shift in the energizing center of one's existence, a kind of kenotic, personal *ecstasis*. It has been pointed out that in emphasizing this aspect in the mystical interpretation of christology and the Christian life, Garrigou-Lagrange was basically running with the "ecstasy of being" thesis developed by Cajetan according to which, in Christ, the entire human existence is virtually overwhelmed and supplemented by the divine existence.[35] It is now generally agreed among scholars that the mature Thomas, by contrast, did not exclude from Christ a certain existential duality attributable to the fact that in him the divine and a human nature are inseparably united without confusion. While it is true that Christ possessed only a single, primary *esse*, that is, the infinite *esse* which he is as the eternal Logos, there was also, says Thomas in his late work *Quaestio disputata de unione Verbi incarnati*, "another existence" (*aliud esse*) in him, a "secondary" one (*secundarium*), such that the word "human" is predicated of him not as some kind of accident, but properly.[36]

33. Pierre de Bérulle, "Discourse on the State and Grandeurs of Jesus," in *Bérulle and the French School: Selected Writings*, ed. W. M. Thompson (New York: Paulist, 1989), 124.

34. Garrigou-Lagrange, *Our Savior and His Love for Us*, 86–88.

35. See M.-H. Deloffre, "La Question disputée: L'union du Verbe incarné de saint Thomas d'Aquin," http://www.thomas-d-aquin.com/Pages/Articles/PresDeUnion.pdf, accessed August 2010; M.-H. Deloffre and G. Delaporte, "Le 'esse secundarium' du Christ," http://www.thomas-d-aquin.com/Pages/Articles/EsseSecundarium.pdf, accessed August 2010.

36. See ibid. Ever since the importance of this passage was highlighted by Herman Diepen in the 1950s—see H. M. Diepen, "L'existence humaine du Christ en métaphysique thomiste," *Revue Thomiste* 58 (1958): 197–213—it has been the subject of renewed study. It has been dated to 1272, and thus to a time postdating the *Tertia Pars* of the *Summa theologiae*. For a critical edition with introduction, translation,

In this way Aquinas echoes the teaching of the later Greek Fathers when they predicated of the incarnate Logos a hypostasis that is no longer simple but "composite" (*synthetos*).[37] Citing St. John of Damascus as his decisive authority, Aquinas acknowledges that there is only one subsisting being in Christ, "yet there are different aspects of subsistence, and hence he is said to be a composite person [*persona composita*]."[38] How one goes about applying this christology to questions concerning the mode of Christian transformation obviously depends on what one makes of the term "composite person." Insofar as one understands *persona* chiefly in psychological terms, one will find the concept of "composite person" or "composite hypostasis" tending either toward psychological dualism or else toward a kind of Apollinarian spirituality in which the human soul is effectively supplanted by the divine Logos.[39] These are clearly problematic possibilities that Garrigou-Lagrange scrupulously sought to avoid. Still, he was rightly convinced that personal transformation correlates structurally to the incarnation. To the human nature of Christ belongs perfect dignity because it exists not in itself but in the person of the Word. In a similar way, even though our human nature has its own personality by its existing in us, an even greater dignity is available to it by our giving way to the divine will, by our coming to exist increasingly in Christ through love.[40]

and commentary, see M.-H. Deloffre, *Thomas d'Aquin: Question disputée: L'union du Verbe incarne (De unione Verbi Incarnati)* (Paris: Vrin, 2000). Citing this reference to the *secundarium esse* in Thomas's mature thought, J.-P. Torrell points out that it essentially expresses the Chalcedonian concern to uphold the complete integrity of Christ's humanity. See idem, "Le thomisme dans le débat christologique contemporain," in *Saint Thomas au XXe siècle. Colloque du centenaire de la "Revue thomiste" (1893-1992)*, Toulouse, 25–28 mars 1993, ed. T. Bonino (Paris: Éditions Saint-Paul, 1994): 379–93 at 386.

37. See Aloys Grillmeier and Theresia Hainthaler, *Christ in Christian Tradition*, vol. 2, part 3: *The Churches of Jerusalem and Antioch* (Oxford: Oxford University Press, 2012), 336–38; Nicholas Madden, "Composite Hypostasis in Maximus the Confessor," *Studia Patristica* 27 (1993): 175–97.

38. *Summa theologiae* III, 2, 4. Notably, the *Tertia Pars* exhibits a profound increase in the number of (especially Greek) patristic citations.

39. "Reading a psychological notion of the person into Christology inevitably leads to some form of Apollinarianism in which Christ's human soul or intellect (as being the 'person') is annihilated and replaced by the Logos. In brief, modern personalism, it seems to me, could hardly accommodate the concept of 'composite hypostasis.'" This instructive judgement comes from the British-based Orthodox monk M. Törönen, *Union and Distinction in the Thought of St. Maximus the Confessor* (Oxford: Oxford University Press, 2007), 99.

40. See *Summa theologiae* III, 2, 2, cited by Garrigou-Lagrange, *Our Savior and His Love for Us*, 100 n. 17.

AUTHENTIC MYSTICISM

A second dimension of Garrigou-Lagrange's christological doctrine opens the way for us to see more clearly his understanding of the Christian spiritual life as a progression toward final deification. It concerns the question of mystical experience, a subject to be developed more fully in the next chapter on the divine indwelling, but about which some preliminary comments may be made here. Toward the end of *Our Savior and His Love for Us*, Garrigou-Lagrange devotes the penultimate chapter to a critical consideration of an increasing number of contemporary studies whose authors purport to have found fundamental correspondences between the mystical experiences of catholics and adherents of other, non-Christian religions. These correspondences are said to testify to a superior and more universal form of spirituality beyond the strictures of any particular creed or historical religion. Garrigou-Lagrange offers an example of such sentiments by quoting from a 1930 essay by the celebrated orientalist Emile Dermenghem on Islamic mysticism:

> All these *çoufis*, thinkers, poets, or saints, have given expression to the great mystical experience: to die to the world in order to live in God, in compelling formulas analogous to those of the Christian Fathers, doctors, and mystics. . . . They repeat incessantly with the Scholastics that creatures have no being except that which they receive from God, and with St. Paul that it is in Him that we have our life, our movement, and our being.[41]

In addition to such claims, advanced in the main by missionary-priests and scholars of comparative religion, Garrigou-Lagrange cites "certain rationalists and surviving Modernists" who interpret the "supernatural mysticism" of the Carmelite tradition in terms that understand it simply as another form of the natural mysticism found in varying degrees in all religions. "According to this approach," he writes, "the revelation of the mysteries of salvation as proposed by the Church, the person of our Lord, His example, the sacraments instituted by Him, bring nothing essential to the Catholic but merely a greater security."[42] In other words, the going claim is that the different forms of religious mystical experience derive essentially from one and the same source. If there is something that distinguishes the mystical experience of the Christian from that of the pagan, Hindu, Buddhist, Jew, or Muslim, it is only that its subjective features are open to more positive and vivid objective description.

41. Ibid., 355–56.
42. Ibid., 356.

In tackling these problems, Garrigou-Lagrange does not deny that God may extend sanctifying grace and salvation to those who, explicitly knowing nothing of Christ, "do what lies within them" (with the help of actual grace). Nevertheless he identifies three kinds of mysticism between which it is necessary to distinguish in order to make accurate theological judgments about this or that particular mystical experience: (1) false or diabolical mysticism; (2) natural pre-mysticism; and (3) supernatural mysticism. The second of these, natural pre-mysticism, is the most ambiguous and difficult to appraise, for it shares a vocabulary more or less in common with supernatural mysticism, all the while lying open to being ordered toward the truth or to being corrupted by falsehood. In its positive form, it involves a certain natural, "inefficacious" love for God in the form of love for art or philosophy or even love for God as the author of nature. "Although this love does not make us renounce mortal sin, that is, does not fundamentally rectify our will and our life, it prompts us to admire God's perfections that are naturally knowable, His infinite wisdom and His goodness." It is the kind of pre-mysticism found powerfully in Plato and Plotinus. Yet this natural love is prone to lapsing toward "a sentimentalism full of deceiving fluctuations, one whose fires soon flicker out." If it does not lead eventually to God, it necessarily leads away from him. "There is no middle ground."[43]

A few pages on, this assertion gives rise to a suggestive and important qualification by Garrigou-Lagrange with respect to the category of "pure nature," which within the next decade or so was to become the subject of vigorous contestation. Garrigou-Lagrange acknowledges that the so-called state of pure nature is an abstraction, a hypothesis contrary to fact. "In the actual plan of Providence in which the state of pure nature does not exist, every man is either in the state of grace or in the state of mortal sin. There is no middle ground." That is, as things actually stand in history, there cannot in fact be two integral ends for man, one natural and one supernatural, juxtaposed without any intrinsic relation. Rather human beings live always and actually in an accountable relation to their ultimate end, toward which they either are or are not decisively oriented by their concrete acts of will. "In the actual state of things, man is born a sinner, turned from his last supernatural end and indirectly from his final natural end, for every sin against supernatural law transgresses natural law at least indirectly. . . . Indifference properly so called or absolute neutrality is not possible with regard to the ultimate end."[44]

43. Ibid., 368–70.
44. Ibid., 378.

Returning to the question of how to determine the authentic shape of mysticism, Garrigou-Lagrange seems to suggest that as long as the analysis remains at the level of subjective experience, it will remain difficult to distinguish accurately between the three kinds of mysticism: diabolical, natural, or supernatural. Attention must instead be turned toward the formal object of mystical experience. The question must be asked: What or who is it that the contemplative knows or experiences? The formal object of supernatural mysticism is properly none other than the divine essence, God as God is in himself, an object that infinitely surpasses the knowing capabilities of any intelligent creature, whether human or angelic. But this raises a profound problem. It is axiomatic of realist epistemology that the knower and the object known be proportionate to one another, that they be somehow similar or akin. How then can a finite creature know an infinite God? To know God in his works is one thing. To know God as God is in himself is another. The necessary proportionality or connaturality that this "quasi-experimental" knowledge of the divine essence presupposes can only be supernaturally and gratuitously wrought from the divine side. Only the Spirit of God knows "the deep things of God" (1 Cor. 2:10), and so only the Spirit can make God known in such a way that knower and known become one. As Garrigou-Lagrange has it:

> There is a difference in formal object between the dim natural intuition of God known from the outside in the mirror of sensible things without the grace of faith and, on the other hand, the supernatural and quasi-experimental knowledge of God founded on divine revelation and infused faith united to charity and enlightened by the gifts of the Holy Ghost. Only supernatural knowledge can ultimately attain "the deep things of God," as St. Paul says. In other words, it alone attains the intimate life of God, the Deity. First it succeeds in doing this dimly through faith and then it does so clearly through the beatific vision.[45]

It is striking to note the terms that Garrigou-Lagrange uses to describe this encounter with the divine essence. It is a "quasi-experimental knowledge of God,"[46] an "intimate experience,"[47] a "participation in the divine nature,"[48] a "mystical" and "intimate union"[49] by which the soul, "totally transformed into

45. Ibid., 371.
46. Ibid., 371, 377, 383.
47. Ibid., 373.
48. Ibid., 382.

its Beloved has become God by participation."[50] Here is all the language of the nuptial mystical tradition, used by a theologian for whom language is no empty rhetorical instrument, but a heavy-laden bearer of reality. Yet we have still not indicated the specifically christological character of this knowing and unifying experience. What for Garrigou-Lagrange constitutes its fundamental litmus test? What in this life is the characteristic mark or criterion indicating authentic union with God?

The answer is: cruciform humility, or loving suffering with Christ. If the final object of contemplation is the infinite essence of God, that essence is rendered accessible to creatures in no other way than in and through Jesus Christ, the divine Word made flesh, and his indwelling Spirit. Final union with God by direct vision is therefore anticipated and embodied in this life in the mode of union with Christ by love-formed faith. And since by love one becomes the object of one's love, such union with Christ will increasingly impart to the believing subject a peculiarly christo-form character. But this is exactly what sinful human pride so actively resists. Quoting St. John of the Cross, Garrigou-Lagrange claims that the high failure rate among Christians in reaching loftier stages of mystical experience is largely due to the fear of suffering, the refusal "to bear the slightest dryness and mortification."[51] The restless search for a comfortable, private spirituality—or for more extraordinary experiences of supernatural phenomena—that bypasses the path of discipleship and mortifying union with the crucified Lord amounts to disrespect for him. Even the most mystically "experienced" saints, such as Theresa of Avila and John of the Cross, emphasize the need to adhere closely to the incarnate God. They stress the significance of the divine command to "listen to him" spoken on the mountain of transfiguration, maintaining "that the contemplative must not of his own initiative turn away from the consideration of Christ's humanity."[52] Inspired as it may appear, the natural pre-mysticism of a Proclus or Plotinus is decisively lacking in just this respect. The way that leads to the transcendent end in the *visio Dei* "must pass by the adorable life and passion of our Lord Jesus Christ," as another mystic, the German Dominican Johann Tauler, preached. "We must pass through this beautiful door by doing violence to nature, by practicing virtue with humility, gentleness, and patience. Know this in truth: he who does not follow this path will lose his way."[53] Perhaps it is on this basis

49. Ibid., 364.
50. Ibid., 361.
51. Ibid., 380.
52. Ibid., 363 n. 14.
53. Quoted in ibid., 382.

that Garrigou-Lagrange is willing to admit "a certain intimacy with God and genuine inspirations of the Holy Ghost" among those Muslim contemplatives and Indian Vedanta whose veneration for Jesus, according to one authority, exposed them to "the calumnies and persecutions of the literalist theologians, to the point of having their own martyrs. . . ."[54] All this is possible because the graced, adopted sonship of the human being is effectively identical to the natural, divine sonship of Christ. But if our filial life really images his, then it is bound to follow the path traced out by his humanity through self-emptying docility, obedience, suffering, and death.

In these ways we can see how christological concerns lie at the heart and center of Garrigou-Lagrange's doctrine of deification. Both structurally and experientially, the hypostatic union and the cross of Jesus effactually determine in Garrigou-Lagrange's theological vision the characteristic shape of final human union with God. This fact would suggest that the more usual accounts of Garrigou-Lagrange's theological anthropology that focus only on his problematic defense of the "two ends" and "pure nature" theories of Baroque scholasticism stand in need of some kind of supplementation. Insofar as he lets christology inform his understanding of the human vocation, Garrigou-Lagrange propounds a profoundly mystical theological anthropology. In making use of the concept of "ontological personality" to explain the data of christology, Garrigou-Lagrange tries to articulate a coherent synthesis in which the elements of his christocentric doctrine of deification dovetail with certain givens in his philosophical worldview. While the metaphysical conception of Christ's nonhuman "personality" advanced by Garrigou-Lagrange has since fallen into virtual disuse in favor of more historically and existentially accessible forms of description, such as we shall find for example in Karl Rahner's evolutionary christology, his recognition that Christ's person and mode of being definitively and abidingly constitute the locus of human self-transcendence remains one of the central insights of catholic Christianity. We shall turn now to consider the closely related aspect in Garrigou-Lagrange's doctrine of deification, namely, the indwelling of the holy Trinity.

54. Ibid., 379 n. 51.

4

Deification and the Divine Indwelling

Although today we generally do not hesitate to speak of such matters as mysticism, spiritual experience, and personal union with God, there was a period lasting almost three hundred years in French Catholic history when such language was felt to be only marginally Christian and even doctrinally suspicious. The Quietist condemnation in the papal brief *Cum alias* of 1699 eventuated as the culmination of a bitter controversy between Bossuet, then Bishop of Meaux, and Fénelon, Archbishop of Cambrai and defender of spiritual writer Madame Guyon, over the relative normality of mystical experience in the Christian life. It was followed by a long spiritual drought during which Bossuet's conception of union with God as an unusual and quite exceptional experience predominated, and all forms of subjective spiritual experience became suspect.[1] Catholic mysticism in France thereafter suffered a "complete rout," to quote the study on post-Reformation spirituality by Louis Cognet. "Deprived of the living source of inner experience, the literature of devotion went on drying up, retaining no more than a distant memory of the magnificent flowering it had known on French soil." With the arrival of the Age of Reason, French spirituality came "to the end of its history."[2] The sweeping influence of a multitude of forces—Jansenism, Ultramontanism, Gallicanism, rationalism, manualism, extrinsicism—saw the French church arrive at the turn of the twentieth century with deep internal rifts between thought and feeling, dogma and experience, nature and grace.

---

1. See Michael de la Bedoyere, *The Archbishop and the Lady: The Story of Fénelon and Madame Guyon* (London: Collins, 1956), 215–23.

2. Louis Cognet, *Post-Reformation Spirituality* (London: Burns & Oates, 1959), 136.

THE QUESTION OF EXTRINSICISM

Whoever studies the writings of Garrigou-Lagrange can't help but notice the odd and sometimes uneasy coexistence of various of these contrasting trends. His tirade against "pragmatism" offers a good case in point. In numerous of his works Garrigou-Lagrange found pragmatism exemplified in the new definition of truth suggested by Blondel as the conformity of the intellect, not to reality, as the traditional definition has it, but to life. In altering the definition in this way, Blondel's concern had been to arrest the increasing disconnect between Catholic apologetics and the emerging mindset of western culture. The dominant apologetic method emphasized the conformity of the contents of Christian revelation and Catholic dogma and moral teaching to the requirements and deductions of rational philosophy. Blondel saw this emphasis running into two main problems. First, it risked naturalizing the supernatural: revelation ends up being weighed and judged at the bar of human reason. Second, it placed the supernatural apart from life and action as a mere postulate of thought. And thus,

> for those who have not the truth, while believing themselves to have it, for those above all who are honestly seeking it, for the beggar and the hungry who stand at the door of the feast, there is something meaningless and even irritating about such an inventory of spiritual treasures, of which they know nothing, or which they consider imaginary, and about the use of unfamiliar language full of complacent sentiments which wake no echo in their own hearts.[3]

In his characterization of so much Thomistic philosophy as "extrinsicist," by which he meant the tendency to divorce questions of credibility from questions of meaning and desirability, Blondel's concern had been to draw discussion about what is true away from disinterested speculation and abstract generalizations and into the sphere of human action and commitment. With reference to the realm of the supernaturally revealed realities of faith, "it is not sufficient to establish separately the *possibility* and the *reality*, but one must show further the *necessity for us* (*nécessité pour nous*) of adhering to this reality of the supernatural."[4] What is needed in our time therefore, Blondel argued, is less a

---

3. Maurice Blondel, *The Letter on Apologetics & History and Dogma* (Grand Rapids: Eerdmans, 1995), 140.

4. Blondel, "Lettre sur les exigences de la pensée," 107, quoted by Michael A. Conway, "Maurice Blondel and *Ressourcement*," in *Ressourcement: A Movement for Renewal in Twentieth-Century Catholic Theology*, ed. Gabriel Flynn and Paul D. Murray (Oxford: Oxford University Press, 2012): 63–82 at 72.

watertight, untouchable system of abstract rational truth inexorably extruded from first principles, and more an integrated witness of life and thought, as one finds, for example, in the saint.

> Steeped as he is in revealed truth and enriched by its fullness, he has made it a part of his own substance, and this has passed from his life into the expression of his thought. The evidence for what he thinks shines out from what he is, and his thought clarifies and justifies his living faith by all the harmony and beauty which it manifests and communicates. Nothing is more decisive or irrefutable than such a witness.[5]

In seeking to develop and propose an adequate apologetics that results in just this kind of saintly Christian existence, one cannot just make do with metaphysical principles and mathematical certainties. "No intellectual evidence, even that of absolute and ontologically valid principles, is imposed on us with a certitude that is spontaneous and infallibly compelling. . . ."[6] On the contrary, the truth often only appears in its full light as a consequence of personal action and the risk of venturing into the unknown. "I cannot put off acting until all the evidence has appeared. . . . Pure knowledge is never enough to move us because it does not take hold of us in our entirety."[7]

Against all this, however, Garrigou-Lagrange trenchantly advanced the axiomatic principle, old as Augustine: "nothing can be loved unless it is known." If there are to be good lives, if there is to be rectitude in the will, there must be right judgment in the intellect, the conformity of mind to reality.

> Let us, then, return to the traditional definition of truth. Action can never be the first criterion. The first criterion must be ontological, must be that objective reality from which reason draws first principles. . . . The exigencies of life, far from making our thoughts true, derive their own truth from the thoughts that conform to reality and to divine reality.[8]

5. *The Letter on Apologetics*, 140, with actual reference to Blondel's former teacher at the École Normale Supérieure, the nineteenth-century philosopher Léon Ollé-Laprune (1839–1898).

6. From Blondel, *L'Être et les êtres* (1935), quoted by Garrigou-Lagrange in *Reality: A Synthesis of Thomistic Thought*, trans. P. Cummins (London: Herder 1950), 331.

7. Blondel, *Action (1893): Essay on a Critique of Life and a Science of Practice*, trans. Oliva Blanchette (Notre Dame: University of Notre Dame Press, 2003), 4.

8. Garrigou-Lagrange, *Reality: A Synthesis of Thomistic Thought*, trans. P. Cummins (London, Herder 1950), 332.

Clearly Garrigou-Lagrange is anxious to ward off any kind of relativizing influence. Yet in such a system, revelation tends almost entirely to be understood as a body of transcendent truths proposed to the intellect, which appear as a kind of supplementary layer additional to what the mind can already know on its own terms. This is in fact the way Garrigou-Lagrange expresses the relation between the two orders of nature and grace: natural certainty derived from philosophy "is supplemented" by supernatural certainty derived from revelation.[9] On this basis it is no surprise that becoming a Christian could appear to the outsider and uninitiated as little more significant than acquiring a postgraduate degree in some esoteric and rather clever branch of knowledge.

On the other hand, we have already had occasion to mention how his early contact with the writings of Ernest Hello and Juan Arintero contributed to a dramatic spiritual renewal in Garrigou-Lagrange's life in which he was gripped by the Christian mystery as by a life-changing and efficacious call to live totally and radically in God. In his spiritual writings in particular it becomes clear that being a Christian is for him ultimately about becoming more fully human, a living journey involving an increasingly more perfect communion between the human person and God. Just as our very existence depends utterly on God, so the first beginning of the Christian life right through to its final fulfillment depends utterly upon the intimate and personal indwelling of the holy Trinity in the human soul. Shaped by such convictions, his spiritual theology came to be dominated by a number of prominent themes. Christ's mission was not simply to redeem humanity from sin, but to elevate it to participate in the life of the triune God. The soul achieves union with God by docility to the Holy Spirit, by prayer, and by bearing sufferings with patience, gratitude, and love. Union with God is an unfolding process that begins already in this life and is not just a goal. The human being relies utterly upon the prevenient and operative grace of God, whose merciful power underlies all one's undertakings and assimilates one to God's own self. One may be struck in these sentiments by the apparently individualistic emphasis upon the soul and God. Yet Garrigou-Lagrange never envisions the spiritual life in isolation from the church, its saints, and its sacramental life. Every aspect of the spiritual life always implies a network of vital human relations.

Two additional themes also find repeated exposition in Garrigou-Lagrange's spiritual theology that lifts it out from the purely rational and abstract. The first is the doctrine of the mutual indwelling of God in the believer and the believer in God. The second is the notion of a "quasi-experimental" knowledge of God, a term much debated in Thomistic circles in the first half

9. Ibid., 329.

of the twentieth century. Just what these two themes mean and how they shed light on Garrigou-Lagrange's understanding of the way deification unfolds in the actual contours of the Christian life call for closer attention.

THE INDWELLING OF THE TRINITY

In his so-called farewell discourse, Jesus tells his apostles that his goal for them is not simply that they will come to dwell in his heavenly "mansions" (μοναί; John 14:2), but that they themselves shall become a "home" for God: "If anyone loves me, he will keep my word. My Father will love him, and we will come to him and make our home [μονήν] with him" (John 14:23). A little earlier on in the same discourse, Jesus had spoken in a similar way about the Holy Spirit, the promised paraclete. "The world cannot accept him, because it neither sees him nor knows him. But you know him, for he lives with you and will be in you" (John 14:17). The believer thereby becomes a dwelling place, a home, a living temple, for the triune God. Just as the Son is in the Father and the Father in the Son, so God is in the believer and the believer in God.

The doctrine of this mysterious mutual indwelling is developed in other New Testament passages. Both collectively and individually, Christians are bodily temples of the Holy Spirit (1 Cor. 3:16; 6:19). St. Paul summarizes the great mystery which God has hidden for ages and generations past but has now revealed in Jesus' life, death, and resurrection: "it is Christ in you, the hope of glory" (Col. 1:27). Or again, in words closer to Paul's own experience, "It is no longer I who live, but Christ in me" (Gal. 2:20). By deliverance from slavery to sin and through filial adoption in baptism, the believer has received the self-same Spirit of the Son who knows God as "Abba, Father" (Rom. 8:15). Insofar as participation in the divine nature takes the form of filial adoption as sons of the eternal Father, "deification has an irreducibly Trinitarian structure."[10]

In reflecting on these passages in the light of Trinitarian dogma and Christian experience, the Fathers highlighted the asymmetry of the interpenetration, the special character of God's indwelling presence in comparison with his general omnipresence in creation, and the historical specificity of the Trinitarian missions. Commenting on the John 14 passage, St. Augustine wrote, "God the Trinity, Father, Son, and Holy Spirit come to us, even while we come to them; they come by answering our call, we by obeying theirs; they come by giving light, we by employing sight; they come

---

10. See Bruce D. Marshall, "*Ex Occidente Lux?* Aquinas and Eastern Orthodox Theology," *Modern Theology* 20, no. 1 (2004): 23–50 at 26.

by filling us with themselves, we come by being filled with them. . . ."[11] In this relation God is the main agent, whereas the believer is the recipient. One "enters" God by receiving him. The union is real yet asymmetrical. When it comes to the question of what it means to say that the Trinity comes to be "in" a person, Augustine distinguished between "the presence of divinity," by which God is everywhere, and "the grace of inhabitation," by which his presence is realized in a restricted and specific mode, and which depends in some part on the perception of divine love by the one in whom he dwells:

> For because of this inhabitation, where beyond doubt the grace of his love is perceived, we do not say "Our Father who is everywhere" (even if this is true), but "Our Father in heaven," so that in the prayer we should bring to remembrance his Temple, which we ourselves should be, and in so far as we are, so far do we belong to his fellowship and his adoptive family.[12]

The third feature in patristic reflection on the mutual indwelling of the Trinity and the believer relates to the way the Trinitarian missions bear upon Christian experience. All the terms predicable to the divine missions—both *ad intra* and in the creative and salvific economies—are preserved in the Trinitarian interactions within the Christian. It is not just God in general who comes to indwell the Christian, but the persons of the holy Trinity, one in their divine causal activity, distinct in the modalities of their action, modalities proper to each person. Most basically, "to be sent" means "to be known or perceived." So when the Son says he is "sent" from the Father, or that he will "send" the paraclete, he is not just speaking of the Trinitarian missions in the incarnation and at Pentecost, but is describing the way in which the divine persons are subjectively communicated, manifested, known, and enjoyed in the mind, heart, and affections of the Christian.[13]

Down through the ages this doctrine of the indwelling Trinity was elaborated upon by proponents of both the scholastic and mystical

11. Augustine, *Hom.* 76 (on John 14), ET: idem, *Thirteen Homilies of St Augustine on St John XIV*, trans. H. F. Stewart (Cambridge: Cambridge University Press, 1902), 77.

12. Augustine, *Ep.* 187 *ad Dardanum* 5.16 (PL 33, 837–38), ET: idem, *The Works of Saint Augustine: A Translation for the 21st Century* Part II—Letters, vol. 3, Letters 156–210, ed. B. Ramsey, trans. R. Teske (New York: New City, 2004), 237–38.

13. Augustine, *De trinitate* 4.20–21; a similar idea is found in Maximus Confessor, *Ambigua ad Thomam* 1 (PG 91, 1033D–1036C). On the distinct modes of Trinitarian action in the theology of Aquinas, see Gilles Emery, "The Personal Mode of Trinitarian Action in St. Thomas Aquinas," in idem, *Trinity, Church, and the Human Person: Thomistic Essays* (Naples, FL: Sapientia, 2007), 115–53.

traditions—from Irenaeus and Augustine and Aquinas to Scheeben and Mersch and von Balthasar—and it certainly "plays a central role in the spirituality" of Garrigou-Lagrange.[14] In union with Father, Son, and Holy Spirit the human person discovers the summit of being, thought, and love. Only in assimilation to and intimate fellowship with this holy triad are the specific longings of a human being fulfilled. Since humans are made in the image of the Trinity, they only come to their completion through unifying conformity to their template. Thus the "structure" and form of the indwelling and assimilation are determined by the mode of intra-Trinitarian relations. The Father generates the Son as his Word; the Father and Son issue forth the Holy Spirit as love. Love assimilates believers to the Holy Spirit, while knowledge assimilates them to the Word, who is the image of the Father. In this way human beings are drawn into the very inner circle of the life of the holy Trinity.

> The elect will become part of the very family of God as they enter into the circle of the Holy Trinity. In them the Father will generate his Word; the Father and the Son will issue forth Love. Charity will assimilate them to the Holy Spirit and meanwhile the vision will assimilate them to the Word, who in turn will make them similar to the Father whose expression He is. At that time we will be able to say truly that we know and love the Trinity that dwells in us as in a temple of glory, and we shall be in the Trinity, at the summit of Being, Thought, and Love. This is the glory; this is the goal to which our spiritual progress tends—configuration to the Word of God.[15]

A SPECIAL PRESENCE

Garrigou-Lagrange similarly draws a distinction between God's general or universal presence, and his special presence in the just. God is in all things—including "plants, men, angels, and devils"—as cause in effect. "He is the burning hearth from which the life of creation flames up, the center of gravity drawing all things to Himself. . . ."[16] By contrast, God's special presence in the just comes about not only in the form of created grace, but by the

14. Richard Peddicord, *The Sacred Monster of Thomism: An Introduction to the Life and Legacy of Reginald Garrigou-Lagrange* (South Bend, IN: St. Augustine's, 2004) 203.

15. Garrigou-Lagrange, *The Last Writings*, quoted by Peddicord, *The Sacred Monster of Thomism*, 178.

16. Garrigou-Lagrange, *The Love of God and the Cross of Jesus*, vol. 1, trans. J. Marie (St. Louis: Herder, 1947), 136–38.

actual indwelling of the three divine persons themselves. Garrigou-Lagrange has recourse to the Johannine text quoted above: "If anyone loves me, he will keep my word. And my Father will love him, and we will come and make our home in him." Garrigou-Lagrange fixes upon the personal and communional nature of this marvelous and mysterious indwelling: *we* will come. What does this "we" refer to? "Created effects? Supernatural gifts? No. Those who love and those who come are the same, the divine Persons, Father, Son and inseparable Spirit promised us by our Lord and sent visibly to His Church on Pentecost."[17] And they will come not just temporarily, but to establish their abode, their dwelling, their home. St. Ignatius of Antioch had this indwelling in mind when he taught that all true Christians are *theophoroi*: Godbearers. A Christian is a temple of the Holy Spirit. To the Spirit belongs the

> special mission as the One sent by the other two Persons from whom He proceeds and because charity likens us to the Holy Ghost just as the intellectual gifts liken us to the Word—although only in heaven will He make us perfect likenesses of Himself, assimilating us to the Father, whose splendor He is.[18]

Garrigou-Lagrange's insistence upon the personal character of the divine indwelling in the elect was directed in particular against the view that God's presence in the soul of the faithful is qualitatively no different from the divine presence in all people and all things. Referring to the "new and profound" study by Ambrose Gardeil, *La structure de l'âme et l'expérience mystique* (1927)—from which Henri de Lubac also drew favorably in his *Sur les chemins de Dieu* (1956)[19]—Garrigou-Lagrange criticizes any reduction of the special presence of God in us to a particular mode or effect of his general presence in all things, that is, to the nonsubstantial "presence of immensity" whereby God maintains all things in existence.

> This amounts to saying that God is not really present in the just as an object known and loved but only as absent loved ones are represented in minds and hearts that hold them dear. [This] conception seems to rob the Gospel and Pauline texts relative to the indwelling Trinity of much of their wealth.[20]

17. Ibid., 138.

18. Ibid., 140.

19. ET: Henri de Lubac, *The Discovery of God*, trans. A Dru (Edinburgh: T. & T. Clark, 1996), 13.

Garrigou-Lagrange finds the rationale that best preserves the obvious sense of Scripture in the explanation of St. Augustine and St. Thomas, summarized as follows:

> [I]n those who possess grace the three divine Persons are present as an object known in the knower, as an object loved in the lover; no distance divides Them from Their host who really possesses Them and enjoys a quasi-experience of Their presence.[21]

The gifts, in other words, are not divided from the giver.

The corrective outlined above had been especially directed at Gabriel Vasquez (1549–1604). Next, Garrigou-Lagrange relates Gardeil's discussion of the opinion of Vasquez's rival, Francisco Suarez (1548–1617). Suarez bases the union between God and human beings on the moral ground of their mutual spiritual friendship. The problem with this, Garrigou-Lagrange contends, is that it still does not imply a *substantial* presence. "After all, separated friends are bound together with ties of affection, yet distance lies between them just the same; for friendship as such makes us desire the real presence of the one we love, but it cannot bring him to us."[22] He gives another example: loving devotion to the blessed Virgin does not render her substantially present within the heart. Affection or desire must precede, but does not itself constitute, the union established by mutual possession or indwelling. Love tends toward this union, and certainly accompanies it, but only *actual presence* effects it. Garrigou-Lagrange goes on to expound Gardeil's take on the matter, which Gardeil himself drew from John of St. Thomas's exposition of Aquinas. The special indwelling presence of God is distinct from, yet presupposes, the general presence by which God is in all things. By sanctifying grace, God becomes present in a new way, so that there arises an "experimental" knowledge and affective delight. Those in a state of mortal sin, even if baptized, can have no such knowledge or delight. If they know God, it is as one absent from them. "[I]n this life we do not see God, but believe in Him and, in the obscurity of faith, we can have a quasi-experimental knowledge of Him such as the Scriptures frequently describe, and sometimes, by a gift of His good pleasure, we may experience Him in us through the gift of wisdom."[23] The gift of

---

20. Garrigou-Lagrange, *The Love of God and the Cross of Jesus*, 141 (recalling especially Rom. 5:5 and 1 Cor. 3:16).

21. Ibid., 142.

22. Ibid., 143.

23. Ibid., 144–46.

wisdom (*sapientia*) brings about a connatural affinity between the human person and God, so that the person as it were savors or tastes (*sapit*) the goodness of God present as he really is.

QUASI-EXPERIMENTAL KNOWING

We have now a number of times come across the term "experimental" or "quasi-experimental" knowledge. Garrigou-Lagrange makes it clear that this form of knowing is distinct from conscious, discursive understanding. One determinative text in the Johannine writings seems uppermost in his mind: "God is charity: and he that abideth in charity abideth in God, and God in him" (1 John 4:16). The subjective experience of love, it seems, more than objective knowledge, is the glue or uniting force in this union of mutual indwelling. True, one cannot love what one does not somehow know, yet Garrigou-Lagrange concedes that the indwelling of God begins "generally without any consciousness of it on our part. . . ."[24] "At the moment of justification, without any consciousness of our own, our spiritual life begins with God's indwelling. . . ."[25] But here Garrigou-Lagrange is speaking of a seminal beginning, far from actualized perfection. The grace given by and with the Holy Spirit constitutes a proximate power or principle that needs to be actualized, such that one can say that the intimate contact implied in knowing and loving God comes about *per operationem creaturae.* In Aquinas's words, "The rational creature by its own operation of knowledge and love attains to God Himself. . . . By the gift of sanctifying grace the rational creature is perfected so that it can freely use not only the created gift itself, but enjoy also the divine Person Himself."[26] The divine persons present themselves, give themselves, to be known and possessed in just this way.

While the idea of an experimental or experiential knowledge of God was commonplace in medieval sources, the qualification "quasi" seems to be a unique contribution by Aquinas.[27] Quasi-experimental knowledge is not discursive or inferred knowledge or knowledge that one comes to by reasoning.

---

24. Ibid., 136.

25. Ibid., 153.

26. *Summa theologiae* I, 43, 3.

27. For a closer analysis of texts, see J. F. Dedek, "*Quasi Experimentalis Cognitio*: A Historical Approach to the Meaning of St. Thomas," *Theological Studies* 22 (1961): 357–90; Albert Patfoort, "Missions divines et expérience des Personnes divines selon S. Thomas," *Angelicum* 63 (1986): 545–59; J.-P. Torrell, *Saint Thomas Aquinas*, vol. 2: *Spiritual Master*, trans. R. Royal (Washington, DC: Catholic University of America Press, 2003), 90–100.

It is rather the knowledge that rises from "a certain connaturality or conformity to divine things. . . ."[28] This connaturality of the soul to divine things is "a means prepared by charity" and used by the Holy Spirit. The Spirit "uses our interior disposition of love for the divine Persons, which He Himself has aroused, to make Their presence manifest to us."[29] Importantly, the affection precedes the manifestation. The manifestation arises from and depends upon the affection aroused in us by the connatural affinity, which is itself wrought by the indwelling presence of the Spirit.

Garrigou-Lagrange asks why this knowledge should be deemed *quasi*-experimental and not properly experimental. First, because in this life we do not experience God immediately but only through the filial love which he works in us. Second, because it is not always possible to distinguish between the delight produced by grace and the delight produced by natural causes.[30] Yet in his insistence on the importance of the word "quasi," it seems Garrigou-Lagrange may have been going beyond Aquinas. Citing the research of Albert Patfoort, Torrell argues that Thomas also speaks about an experimental knowledge of God without using the qualifying word "quasi."[31] The passages in question come from his commentary on the Sentences of Peter Lombard: "Although the knowledge is appropriated to the Son, the gift by which this experiential knowledge (*experimentalis cognitio*) is assumed, necessary for there to be a mission, is not, however, necessarily appropriated to the Son, but it could be appropriated to the Holy Spirit, in so far as he is love."[32] And citing Augustine's comment, mentioned earlier, that for the Son to be "sent" means that he is known and perceived by us, Thomas writes: "The word *perception* means a certain knowledge through experience. This is, properly speaking, the 'wisdom' or 'savoury knowledge' according to the words of Sirach (6:23)."[33] Here Aquinas refers to "a certain" knowledge by experience, suggesting that he wants to stretch what we ordinarily take "knowledge" to mean, without detracting from the fact that it still involves a correspondence and unifying assimilation between knower and known. Patfoort further points out that in one place where Thomas does use the term "quasi" he goes on to use the word "properly." "Since Thomas would certainly not contradict himself within

---

28. Garrigou-Lagrange, *The Love of God and the Cross of Jesus*, 154, with reference to *Summa theologiae* II-II, 45, 2.

29. Ibid., 155–56.

30. Ibid., 156–57.

31. Patfoort, cited by Torrell, *Saint Thomas Aquinas*, vol. 2: *Spiritual Master*, 94.

32. Thomas Aquinas, *In I Sent* d. 15, q. 2 ad 5; also *In I Sent* d. 16, q. 2.

33. *Summa theologiae* I, 43, 5.

a matter of two lines, we have to conclude that the 'quasi' does not have the meaning of an experience that costs little, but that he wishes to distinguish it from another kind of knowing that is merely intellectual."[34]

What Thomas seems to indicate by his use of the term experimental or quasi-experimental knowledge is the unity of the intellectual and affective dimensions of the human person in his fellowship with God. Knowing the Trinity through connatural union and mutual indwelling entails a real enjoyment and delightful possession on the part of the knower and known, possessor and possessed. Torrell concludes: "Basically, the word *experience*, borrowing from the vocabulary of the senses, suggests something of direct contact with reality transposed into the realm of divine things."[35] We are here close to the Dionysian and patristic doctrine of knowledge not by learning but by "suffering divine things."[36] In fact Thomas quotes this very phrase to make the point that by means of affective or experimental knowledge one tastes and proves the goodness of God in one's own living experience:

> There are two ways of knowing the goodness or will of God. One is speculative, and from that point of view, we are allowed neither to doubt the divine goodness nor to put it to the test. . . . The other is an affective or experimental knowing (*affective seu experimentalis*) of the divine goodness or will, when one personally experiences the taste of the divine sweetness and the delight of his will, after the fashion of Hierotheos, whom Dionysius says "learned divine things through experiencing them." It is from this point of view that we are told to "prove" the divine will and "taste" his sweetness.[37]

Although we have so far studied the two themes of divine indwelling and quasi-experimental knowledge separately, it will hopefully have become clear that the two are intimately related. For Garrigou-Lagrange this fact confirms his conviction that "infused contemplation of the mysteries of faith belongs to the normal progress of sanctity." The indwelling of the holy Trinity "is explicable only so far as God can be known and loved as the object of quasi-experimental knowledge," that is, a knowledge that transcends discursive analysis and that involves the affective and connatural assimilation of the soul to God.[38]

34. Torrell, *Saint Thomas Aquinas*, vol. 2: *Spiritual Master*, 94–95.

35. Ibid., 95–96.

36. Dionysius Areopagite, *Divine Names* 2.9.

37. *Summa theologiae* II-II, 97, 2.

38. Garrigou-Lagrange, *The Love of God and the Cross of Jesus*, 159.

Active Receptivity

But we have not yet got to the bottom of the matter. What is the relationship between the divine presence, the uncreated grace which is the Holy Spirit, and created, sanctifying grace? Can we speak with Maurice de la Taille of a created actuation by the uncreated act, or with Emil Mersch and Karl Rahner and others of a "quasi-formal causality" whereby God, or perhaps specifically the Holy Spirit, by his own self-donation, becomes as it were the formal, actuating principle of the deified soul? And another question: If one can only love what one knows, is it not still the case that the human intellect plays the primary role in this unifying relation, so that the knowledge granted through infused faith, however obscure, remains the primary mode of experiential indwelling?

We may observe at this point that Garrigou-Lagrange does not seem to answer the third question directly. However, in his enthusiastic exposition of the undeservedly little-known work of seventeenth-century Thomist Louis de Chardon (d. 1651), we sense a modification of a purely intellectualist mysticism in the direction of a more affective, performative mysticism of love. Writing before the crisis between Bossuet and Fénelon, Chardon in his spiritual masterpiece *La Croix de Jésus* (1647) posited the divine persons not only as objects known and loved but as the principles of supernatural operation in the soul.[39] "They are no longer present to us simply as objects powerfully attracting our operations but as actualizing, effecting, applying, and directing our operations. . . ."[40] Chardon also drew a close parallel between the "internal/eternal" (= *ad intra*) and "external/temporal" (= *ad extra*) processions in the divinity:

> The temporal mission of a divine Person is only an extension of the eternal procession in God. . . . Thus the Word, begotten by the Father from all eternity, and with Him the Holy Ghost, are invisibly sent to the just at the moment of conversion.[41]

So far Chardon has said nothing peculiar; nothing, that is, that runs at odds with Garrigou-Lagrange's own account to this point. Yet Garrigou-Lagrange goes on to reflect positively upon an emphasis in Chardon's spiritual theology upon the passivity of the soul in respect to the deiform life:

---

39. Ibid., 161. The English translation of Chardon's work is *The Cross of Jesus*, trans. R. T. Murphy (St. Louis: Herder, 1957).

40. Garrigou-Lagrange, *The Love of God and the Cross of Jesus*, 162.

41. Ibid., 162.

Charity may at times act with such efficacious strength that it reduces souls to a passive state in regard to divine things; they are no longer conscious of their cooperation and concurrence in supernatural and Godlike acts. They do not so much live the life of God as the life of God lives in them; they are more loved than loving; and even when they love, they receive rather than give.[42]

On this passivity, or as we might prefer to call it, active receptivity, Garrigou-Lagrange comments: "[I]n the passive state which Chardon refers to here, God accomplishes in us and for us a much more perfect and complete giving of ourselves than we could ever achieve by our own efforts with ordinary actual grace."[43] Citing Chardon further, Garrigou-Lagrange states that God in indwelling the soul "penetrates all and destroys nothing, making us participants of His divine society and sharers, by imitation, in His own natural life that we may be caught and embraced by the fullness of Divinity."[44] Garrigou-Lagrange's final comments suggest that with Chardon's theory of passive deification, we have arrived at the essence of mystical experience. Here, he says, "in a really vital way, [Chardon] brings us back to the very source of theology, the truths of Scripture and tradition."[45]

Chardon's spiritual theology, a key aspect of which clearly meant something very important for Garrigou-Lagrange, has not gone without its critics. But what is interesting to note, especially in light of criticisms directed toward Garrigou-Lagrange in our own time, is what it is those critics fasten upon who are anxious to prove faithful to Thomas Aquinas. Yves Congar, in a review essay on Chardon's theology, once summarized the gist of their concerns:

His critics said that he [Chardon], and those who followed him, had added to St Thomas and to unalloyed theological intellectuality, an element that belongs to the sphere of "affectivity" which is that of "mysticism" and the mystics, and not to theology as normally understood or to St Thomas himself.

Congar goes on to quote Chardon's own defense:

42. Ibid., 163.
43. Ibid., 163.
44. Ibid., 163–64.
45. Ibid., 165.

> In these discussions I am enquiring about the knowledge of God and of the things of God. My object is to love them and through loving them to try and unite myself to them and to transform myself into them. . . . I know only one theology. . . . Knowledge of God without charity is lifeless; love is its centre. Without love it is out of orbit.[46]

Arriving with these words at the end of this chapter, one might not think to call Garrigou-Lagrange a theologian of love. But his spiritual theology is without doubt a theology of grace, and for Garrigou-Lagrange, sanctifying grace is nothing else than the effective fruit of the indwelling presence of uncreated love itself, the real and substantial communication of the divine nature, the principle for living human life as it is meant to be lived: in full and intimate communion with the holy Trinity.

---

46. Yves Congar, "'The Cross of Jesus' by Fr Louis de Chardon, OP," in idem, *The Revelation of God,* trans. A. Manson and L. C. Sheppard (London: Darton, Longman & Todd, 1968), 116–28 at 126.

5

Deification and Divine Causality

In an essay published in 2004, Bruce D. Marshall took up criticisms by a number of modern Orthodox theologians directed at alleged failures on the part of western theology in general and of Thomas Aquinas in particular to give adequate expression to the mysteries expressed by the patristic doctrine of deification.[1] Allegedly burdened by an overly juridical conception of the human relation to God bequeathed to the Latin tradition by Anselm, Aquinas is specifically charged with ultimately rendering the Trinity "remote from human life and history."[2] With his notion of "created grace" serving as a kind of interposed medium between God and human beings, Aquinas is said to have depersonalized and reified divine grace in such a way as to deprive human beings of any real and direct contact with the Persons of the Trinity. In contrast to the Palamite doctrine of uncreated grace, the purportedly faulty notion of created grace "leaves us not with deification, but with a sort of creaturification."[3]

Marshall responds with a number of compelling rebuttals drawn from a wide range of primary evidence in Aquinas's many works, significantly including his biblical commentaries. He shows how deification plays an important role in Aquinas's understanding of the human being's return to God. Through communion in the humanity of Christ, who is true God, we receive "full participation in divinity, in which the happiness of the human being and the end of human life truly consist." Moreover, this participation in the divine nature "has an irreducibly Trinitarian structure," inasmuch as it takes the specific form of our adoption as sons of the Father. While the Holy Spirit is the actualizing agent directly responsible for this adoptive assimilation, it is to the Son in particular that his deifying activity conforms us. "We are conformed

---

1. Bruce D. Marshall, "*Ex Occidente Lux?* Aquinas and Eastern Orthodox Theology," *Modern Theology* 20, no. 1 (2004): 23–50.

2. Ibid., 25.

3. Ibid., 28.

specifically to the *filiatio* of Jesus Christ, to the characteristic and relationship eternally constitutive of his personal identity as the Son, in distinction from the Father, the Son, and everything else."[4] When it comes to grace, Marshall again demonstrates the coherence and luminosity of Aquinas's account. The term grace signifies God's free and unmerited love for human beings; in that respect one may speak of uncreated grace. But grace also signifies the resultant good in the creature that follows from this love. In the human creature, grace is present and active as a form: a habit or stable configuration that qualifies the human substance, enabling the person to perform actions of which he would otherwise be incapable. But even though this form has a divine origin and enables activity akin to God, even though it is congruent to God, it is not itself divine. God cannot be the form of a creature: to have God's "form," in strict metaphysical terms, would be to be God by nature, which by definition no creature can be. Thus if God is really to communicate himself, if his indwelling in the human creature is to be a matter of fact and not simply a nominal attribution, then he must also produce in the creature a commensurate quality or participatory entity, in short, "he must . . . give us the created means to receive him." Grace is that means. It is that dynamic power by which human beings are created anew and, in Thomas's words, "established in a new existence—*ex nihilo*. . . ." It is really created because, like anything created, it is caused by, yet distinct from God. It is nevertheless really deifying because it really joins the creature to God. While it is not false to call it a medium, the term can be misleading, for the contact between the human being and God that it brings about is direct and immediate. Through the connatural knowledge and love of God that come about by grace, "the rational creature . . . touches God himself," as Thomas puts it, "with nothing created intervening."[5]

Grace and Divine Causality

The themes elaborated briefly here and in greater depth in Marshall's essay help us to pose a question implicit in the doctrine of deification, a question which in this chapter we shall attempt to explore more deeply through one last analysis of the thought of Garrigou-Lagrange. That question concerns the role of divine causality in the whole deifying transformation of the human creature. Already in the 1920s, perhaps due in part to the widening dissatisfaction with Aristotelian metaphysical categories to account adequately for the mystery of

4. Ibid., 25–27.
5. Ibid., 28–29.

human deification in Christ, and due also to a conscious interest in conforming theology more closely to the language of Scripture and concrete human experience, it is possible to detect in Catholic theology the development of a more fluid and sometimes even loose terminology to describe the dynamics involved in conversion, faith, love for God, and the passage to final beatitude. In the judgment of Emil Mersch, "Aristotle's categories are too narrow for this mystery of the Most High that comes to elevate and enlarge infinitely the natural universe. . . ."[6] Specifically we may notice increasing dissatisfaction with the notion of efficient causality to describe God's activity with respect to what happens in the human person. Efficient causality implies the production of an entity extrinsic to the producer. It suggests an influence which in the context of intimate divine/human communion seems too external and coercive, and not enough intrinsic and immanent. It is significant in this regard to note that Aquinas insists that in fact nothing operates on the human will with efficient causality, that is, by means of some external principle. "Rather, every motion of the will proceeds from some interior principle."[7] On the one hand, God's efficacious or permissive will is the transcendently interior cause of all things, right down to the minutest contingency.[8] On the other hand, "God moves everything in accordance with its own manner," in which case he seems bound to move human beings not coercively or exteriorly—from the outside, as it were—but in a manner in keeping with their intelligent and volitional constitution.[9]

On the basis of renewed reflection on precisely what happens in the human being in deification, theologians began to explore new ways of articulating the causal dynamics at work in the creature's transformation. In his study *The Theology of the Mystical Body* composed mainly in the 1930s, Mersch did not reject but somewhat modified the application of traditional Aristotelian categories by developing the notion of a "quasi-formal" causality, applicable both to Christ in the incarnation and to the believer in deification. According to classic Thomistic metaphysics, formal causality consists in "the communication of the entire act or perfection of the form, formally as such, to its perfectible term, when it is united intrinsically and immediately, formally as such, to that term."[10] Mersch adapted this concept first of all to account for the perfection

6. Emil Mersch, *The Theology of the Mystical Body*, trans. C. Vollert (St. Louis: Herder, 1952), 473.

7. *Summa contra gentiles* III, 88.

8. *Summa theologiae* I, 14, 8; I, 19, 4.

9. *Summa theologiae* I-II, 113, 3.

10. Kevin F. O'Shea, "Pure Uncreated Unity," *Irish Theological Quarterly* 30, no. 4 (1963): 347–53 at 350.

of the assumed human nature in the Son's incarnation. He stressed the utter newness of the kind of divine causality that occurred there and its distinctness from the "efficient" causality involved in creation:

> By creation God establishes beings in themselves, outside the Godhead. By the Incarnation considered *in facto esse*, God establishes a being in the Godhead and above the being's own nature, by suppressing all distance and by becoming strictly immanent in that being. Creation, in the thing created, consists in having the cause of being outside the being; the Incarnation, considered in the assumed nature, consists in having the cause of being in the being itself, as its sole personality. Hence this is a new kind of action. . . .[11]

According to Mersch, the hypostatic union perfects the assumed human nature of Christ not by way of efficient cause but by way of "quasi-formal" cause.[12] By this, Mersch meant to say that the human being constituted by that union is truly God yet without his human nature undergoing substantial alteration or losing its characteristic properties. This negative qualification is crucial. "Natures are like numbers or definitions: the slightest addition or subtraction makes them cease to be what they were. . . ."[13] But the reality we meet in Jesus Christ cannot adequately be described by the strict application of mathematical formulae. In order to avoid reducing the union

> to a local juxtaposition, to a mechanical juncture, or to a juridical fiction, we have to admit something in the assumed humanity that makes it an assumed humanity, something that is human because it pertains to Christ's humanity but that is also divine because it makes the humanity the humanity of God.[14]

That something, says Mersch, is grace, "by which the gift that God gives in a divine way exists in a man in a human way; it is that which makes man formally what the coming of God makes him effectively."[15]

Having explored the christological mystery in this way, Mersch went on to suggest an analogous relation between this causal dynamism in the incarnation and that which takes place in deification. The operation of divine grace in

---

11. Mersch, *The Theology of the Mystical Body*, 471.

12. Ibid., 208.

13. Ibid., 213.

14. Ibid., 602.

15. Ibid., 610.

Christ is not far removed from its operation in the Christian, for the divinization of Christ "is radically the divinization of all humanity."[16] Of course some distinction must be observed: Christ's humanity "must be truly, intrinsically, and objectively the humanity of God." Its divinization is achieved not by efficient or instrumental means, but quasi-formally. By contrast, "as far as its mode of existing is concerned," grace "can be nothing else than an accident in man." Yet it is a truly supernatural and divine accident,

> because it is an "entity of union" modeled on the hypostatic union.
> . . . Therefore divinization, and consequently grace, is something essentially ontological. It does not merely confer this or that new perfection, but makes the recipient exist in a different way, by actuating the remotest capacities of finite being.[17]

Two other well-known theologians in the 1920s and 1930s adopted the language of quasi-formal causality to express what takes place in deification, namely Maurice de la Taille and Karl Rahner, although they arrived at the notion independently of one another's research.[18] Like Mersch, both thinkers were trying to account for the distinctly *immanent* character of the divine indwelling in the Christian and the operation of grace. Once again the notion

---

16. Ibid., 618.

17. Ibid.

18. Maurice de la Taille, "Actuation créée par Acte incréé," *Recherches de Science Religieuse* 18 (1928): 753–68. ET in idem, *The Hypostatic Union and Created Actuation by Uncreated Act*, trans. C. Vollert (West Baden, IN: West Baden College, 1952), 29–41. Karl Rahner, "Zur scholastischen Begrifflichkeit der ungeschaffenen Gnade," *Zeitschrift für katholische Theologie* 63 (1939): 137–71, reprinted in idem, *Schriften zur Theologie* 1 (1954): 347–75. ET: "Some Implications of the Scholastic Concept of Uncreated Grace," in idem, *Theological Investigations* [=TI], vol. 1, trans. Cornelius Ernst (London: Darton, Longman & Todd, 1965): 319–46. Rahner refers to de la Taille's work, published some ten years earlier, in support of the probability of his thesis (ibid., 340 n. 2). These works gave rise to a series of articles debating the question in some detail. In support of the notion of quasi-formal causality, see P. de Letter, "Created Actuation by the Uncreated Act: Difficulties and Answers," *Theological Studies* 18, no. 1 (1957): 60–92; "Divine Quasi-Formal Causality," *Irish Theological Quarterly* 27, no. 3 (1960): 221–28; "'Pure' or 'Quasi'-Formal Causality?," *Irish Theological Quarterly* 30, no. 1 (1963): 36–47; "The Theology of God's Self-Gift," *Theological Studies* 24 (1963): 402–22. More critical are: Kevin F. O'Shea, "Pure Formal Actuation," *Irish Theological Quarterly* 28, no. 1 (1961): 1–15; B. Kelly, "Divine Quasi-Formal Causality," *Irish Theological Quarterly* 28, no. 1 (1961): 16–28; Kevin F. O'Shea, "Pure Uncreated Unity," *Irish Theological Quarterly* 30, no. 4 (1963): 347–53; "Divinization: A Study in Theological Analogy," *The Thomist* 29, no. 1 (1965): 1–45. For a general summary of the issues from a contemporary systematic theological perspective, see Ralph Del Colle, *Christ and the Spirit: Spirit-Christology in Trinitarian Perspective* (New York: Oxford University Press, 1994), 64–90.

of efficient causality was found to be inadequate: by it one produces a being without oneself being a part of it. In the case of Christian transformation, the notion of efficient causality does not call for or imply any connatural community between God and humanity; it does not require any kind of intimate, ontological self-communication. Yet on its own, the notion of formal causality, properly speaking, implies too much: God cannot have any immediate, formally causal relation with a creature, since that would be to enter into composite, essential relation with it, to become its very form and act. There would arise not an ontological *union*, but, impossibly, an ontological *fusion*. By means of his now-famous formula "the created actuation by the uncreated Act," Maurice de la Taille coordinated three key realities—the incarnation, sanctifying grace, and the beatific vision—into a single harmonious economy. Each embodies a distinct yet intrinsically related instance of God's real self-donation, his utter self-communication in such a way that there necessarily follows some concomitant enriching and substantially perfecting actuation in the creature.

While de la Taille never used the term "quasi-formal" per se, Karl Rahner explicitly adopted the language of quasi-formal causality to designate the self-same dynamic. While we shall examine Rahner's theology of grace and deification in closer detail in due course, it is appropriate at this point in our discussion to touch briefly on his proposal of the notion "quasi-formality" as a means of understanding the ontology of grace. According to Rahner, the schools tended to posit uncreated grace as a consequence of created grace, so that modifications in the human soul by virtue of created grace are made the basis for the union constituted by the divine indwelling. In the Scriptures and the Greek Fathers, by contrast, the created gifts are seen to be the consequence of God's "substantial" self-communication. For the New Testament, the Holy Spirit is himself the inchoate seed, the homogeneous commencement of the beatific life. Echoing this emphasis, Thomas Aquinas called the Holy Spirit the *causa formalis inhaerens* of our adoptive sonship.[19] If this is true, Rahner argues, then it is not inappropriate to apply to the life of earthly Christian pilgrimage "the concepts of formal ontology relating to the possession of God in the *visio beatifica*. . . ."[20] In this connection Rahner invokes the approval of the encyclical *Mystici Corporis* of Pius XII, which determined that the essence of grace in this life, being as it is the *inchoatio gloriae*, is properly known as it is by reference

19. *In III Sent.* d. 10, q. 2, a. 1 sol. 3. Cited by Karl Rahner, "Some Implications of the Scholastic Concept of Uncreated Grace," TI, vol. 1, 338.

20. Rahner, "Some Implications of the Scholastic Concept of Uncreated Grace," TI, vol. 1, 334.

to the beatific vision.[21] Importantly, this must include reference to the act of knowing that comes about in the beatified person according to which God's own essence takes the place of the impressed species. Such would mean that, insofar as in the act of knowledge knower and known are the same thing, the beatified human may be said to be, or to have in herself, the form or essence of God.

Accordingly, this dynamic state of supernatural union with God, says Rahner, should be considered not under the category of efficient causality, that is, a production *out* of a cause ("ein Aus-der-Ursache-*Heraus*-stellen"), but under the category of formal causality, that is, a taking up *into* the ground or *forma* ("ein In-den-Grund[forma]-*Hinein*nehmen").[22] Rational considerations in themselves pose no legitimate objections to this as a general possibility since "it is indubitably given for every Catholic theologian at least in the special case of the hypostatic union."[23] What distinguishes the graced state of glory from the case of the hypostatic union is indicated by Rahner by the prefix "quasi," so that one may speak of God exercising a quasi-formal causality. "All this 'quasi' implies is that this 'forma,' in spite of its formal causality, which must be taken seriously, abides in its absolute transcendence (inviolateness, 'freedom')."[24] The metaphysical elements present in this claim are strikingly bold: in the beatitude that constitutes final deification, God stands in relation to the believer not simply as creator to a removed and distinct creature, but as God to his own self, as it were, that is, as a sort of formal cause. If the perfectly graced life is truly supernatural, and if by "supernatural" we mean something "absolutely mysterious," then, concludes Rahner, "God himself must belong to what constitutes it, i.e., God in so far as he is not merely the ever transcendent Creator, the efficient cause of something finite which is distinct from him, but in so far as he communicates himself to the finite entity in quasi-formal causality."[25]

Rahner never rescinded this teaching on the primacy of uncreated grace as a quasi-formal act of divine causality. In his article on grace in the widely studied seminary textbook *Encyclopedia of Theology*, he reiterated the claim that "God does not confer on man merely created gifts as a token of his love. God communicates *himself* by what is no longer simply efficient causality. He makes man share in the very nature of God."[26] But "share" is perhaps too weak a word.

21. Ibid., 340.
22. Ibid., 329.
23. Ibid., 330.
24. Ibid.
25. Ibid., 333–4 n. 3.

What Rahner really wanted to say concerning grace, causality, and deification is finally that God "in his own most proper reality makes himself the innermost constitutive element of man."[27] But let us leave off further discussion of Rahner's thought until later.

THE SEED OF DEIFICATION

So far we have barely mentioned Garrigou-Lagrange. Yet it is our purpose in this chapter to ask what he made, or would have made, of this notion of quasi-formal causality and the nature and function of grace in the deification of the justified. We know from our analyses so far that Garrigou-Lagrange tended not to depart too far, either in subject matter or terminology, from Thomas and the scholastic commentatorial tradition. Thus it may seem that he has little to contribute to a conversation that turns on the development in theology of a new terminology deemed more suitable for giving expression to the interpersonal profundities of deifying union. Yet we know also that Thomas habitually spoke of sanctifying grace as the *inchoatio gloriae*, that is, as the already-present yet hidden dynamic of a transfiguring activity in which the human being grasps in an act of intellectual and affective assimilation the infinite essence of God. We know too that Garrigou-Lagrange in his turn emphasized the definitively supernatural character of created, sanctifying grace, its essential character as "a real and formal participation" in the divine nature. Garrigou-Lagrange's metaphysics of grace is therefore not without roots in the biblical and patristic doctrine of deification, nor without relevance for the discussion in our day concerning the capacity of the western Catholic conceptual tradition to go some way toward accurately delineating the mystery of the creature's participation in God.

In 1946 Garrigou-Lagrange published his most complete and systematic book on grace in the form of a rolling commentary on Aquinas's treatise on the subject in the *Summa theologiae* (I-II, 109–14).[28] Toward the end of the book he appended material originally published in 1936 in *Revue Thomiste*.[29] Garrigou-

26. Karl Rahner, "Grace II: Theological," in *Encyclopedia of Theology: A Concise Sacramentum Mundi*, ed. Karl Rahner (London: Burns & Oates, 1975): 587–95 at 588.

27. Karl Rahner, *Foundations of Christian Faith: An Introduction to the Idea of Christianity*, trans. W. Dych (London: Darton, Longman & Todd, 1978), 116. For a brief overview of Rahner's teaching on grace, see S. J. Duffy, "Experience of grace," in *The Cambridge Companion to Karl Rahner*, ed. D. Marmion and M. E. Hines (Cambridge: Cambridge University Press, 2005), 43–62.

28. Réginald Garrigou-Lagrange, *Grace: Commentary on the* Summa theologica *of St. Thomas, Ia IIae, q. 109-14*, trans. the Dominican Nuns (St. Louis: Herder, 1952).

Lagrange begins by acknowledging the twofold scholastic distinction between uncreated and created grace. Grace refers first to the "love of benevolence on the part of God, conferring supernatural life. This love of God is uncreated grace." But then there is the "supernatural gift of grace itself, freely bestowed and ordained to eternal life; this is created grace. . . ."[30]

It may be interjected at this point that the distinction between uncreated and created grace is not well attested in Aquinas's own writings. A. N. Williams may be exaggerating somewhat when she speaks of Thomas's "extreme hesitation" in using the term *gratia create*.[31] Yet as she points out, in his reply to the claim in the first article of question 110 in the *prima secundae* that grace implies no created medium in the soul, Aquinas nowhere asserts the term "created grace" to the contrary. His use of terms is rather guided by his fundamental purpose, which is "to show that grace constitutes a genuine meeting of God and humanity: the divine agent who is the source of grace does not by gracious action obliterate the human person but respects her integrity and finite status, working within her according to the form proper to her."[32] If the supernatural light of grace is to be distinguished from God's own self, it is only because it includes some kind of adaptation to the limits of human receptivity. If we call it "created," it is because human beings "are created with reference to it, that is, are given a new being out of nothing."[33]

For Garrigou-Lagrange, the relation between so-called uncreated grace and created grace is something like infinite cause and finite effect. Yet putting it this way seems to keep the two too far apart, unless it is remembered that, in classic metaphysics, causes are always present in their effects. Thus the relation between them is not extrinsic but direct and causally intrinsic, "based upon the fact that God's love of benevolence . . . infuses and creates goodness in things."[34] Garrigou-Lagrange repeatedly insists on this point, distinguishing his doctrine from exclusively juridical theories that define grace in terms of an imputative act or external designation, without any real and necessary interior change or transformation.[35] Garrigou-Lagrange names Luther and Calvin as primary exponents of this extrinsicism, though it is worthwhile noting in passing that,

29. See ibid., chapter XII, "Recapitulation and Supplement," 399–503.

30. Garrigou-Lagrange, *Grace*, 3–4.

31. A. N. Williams, *The Ground of Union: Deification in Aquinas and Palamas* (New York: Oxford University Press, 1999), 87.

32. Ibid., 88.

33. *Summa theologiae* I-II, 110, 2 ad. 3.

34. Garrigou-Lagrange, *Grace*, 4.

35. Ibid., 110–11.

at least in the case of Luther and Lutheranism, such a wholesale characterization of their doctrine of grace and justification risks overemphasizing more idiosyncratic aspects of their teaching and neglecting more considered elaborations.[36] Moreover, aspects of a juridical or imputatory theory of justification have been credited, not least of all by Aquinas himself, with being demonstrably Pauline, making it a vital component of the Church's apostolic tradition.[37]

We saw in the previous chapter how Garrigou-Lagrange argues that the doctrine of the divine indwelling of the Holy Trinity embraces the truth that the Christian does not simply experience God's gifts and created effects, but in fact experiences God directly by means of his immediate, substantial, and deifying presence in the soul. At the same time, and as already pointed out above, it seems necessary to qualify this use of the word "immediate." The act by which the human being knows and loves God and, by means of such knowledge and love, comes to be really one with God, arises not from any natural, inborn human capacity, but from a new power "by which we are truly children of God, born of God, and participators in the divine nature."[38] The following two excerpts from Garrigou-Lagrange's 1947 classic *Three Ages of the Interior Life* typify his position in this connection:

> If a created intellect could by its natural powers alone see God immediately, it would have the same formal object as the divine intellect; it would then be of the same nature as God. This would be the pantheistic confusion of a created nature and a divine nature.[39]

> Sanctifying grace, which makes us begin to live in this higher, supra-angelic order of the intimate life of God, is like a divine graft received in the very essence of the soul to elevate its vitality and to

36. While I would wish to revise its account of Aquinas's thought, my essay on causality in the Lutheran doctrine of conversion briefly summarizes the Lutheran position as stated in the *Formula of Concord* of 1580, according to which justification necessarily entails a real change (*immutatio*) in the human subject. See Adam G. Cooper, "The Role of the Will in Conversion: Re-reading the Confessions with Thomas Aquinas," *Lutheran Theological Journal* 42, no. 1 (2008): 41–50.

37. See Bruce D. Marshall, "*Beatus vir:* Aquinas, Romans 4, and the Role of 'Reckoning' in Justification," in *Reading Romans with St. Thomas Aquinas*, ed. Matthew Levering and Michael Dauphinais (Washington, DC: Catholic University of America Press, 2012), 216–37.

38. Garrigou-Lagrange, *Grace*, 114.

39. Garrigou-Lagrange, *Three Ages of the Interior Life*, 1:33–34, quoted by Richard Peddicord, *The Sacred Monster of Thomism: An Introduction to the Life and Legacy of Réginald Garrigou-Lagrange, O.P.* (South Bend, IN: St. Augustine's, 2005), 195.

make it bear no longer merely natural fruits but supernatural ones, meritorious acts that merit eternal life for us. This divine graft of sanctifying grace is, therefore, in us an essentially supernatural life, immensely superior to a sensible miracle and above the natural life of our spiritual and immortal soul.[40]

What Garrigou is proposing here is a paradox with a long patrimony in Christian experience. A central biblical passage we have had reason to quote twice already, St. Paul's "It is no longer I who live, but Christ who lives in me" (Gal. 2:20), bears witness to the same mystery. On the one hand, Christ himself is the Christian's true life (Col. 3:4); yet this new life, while apparently not one's own, is in point of fact one's restored, renewed, and proper existence as originally planned and ordained in grace by the Father before the foundation of the world (Eph. 1:3–13).

Garrigou-Lagrange's thought is not so far removed from these primitive Christian expressions. This divine life to which the believer is raised is indeed his proper life. Despite Garrigou-Lagrange's use of the term "supra-angelic," it is not meant to be understood as some alien or nonhuman existence, but one that involves his whole being and brings it to its own true perfection. To describe this process, Garrigou-Lagrange speaks of a transformation—Aquinas's word is *transmutatio*—taking place in the very essence of the soul. We are essentially changed, or at least, our creaturely being is fundamentally qualified in some way and undergoes some kind of deep modal modification and elevation. We do not thereby cease to be human, but our humanity is imbued with a new, superhuman, divine character, utterly disproportionate to its natural capacities. By grace it is "even now" enabled to do what only God can do, that is, to know and love him as God knows and loves himself.

What kind of reality is this grace, that it brings about such momentous and paradoxical effects? What would Garrigou-Lagrange make of a doctrine of grace that understands it in terms of a divine quasi-formal actuation, as proposed by Mersch or Rahner?

For a start, Garrigou-Lagrange would deem it improper to think of grace as a "thing," a substance or reified entity in its own right. With St. Thomas he rather defines grace as a perfection, a principle, a quality, or a qualifying accident added to substance, which alone "renders God present in anything as the object known and loved," and which alone "constitutes a special mode of God's existence in things."[41] Drawing in the main on the same categories of

---

40. Garrigou-Lagrange, *Three Ages*, 1:50–51, quoted by Peddicord, *The Sacred Monster of Thomism*, 195 n. 52.

expression as we find in Aquinas, Garrigou-Lagrange posits sanctifying grace as a kind of participating intermediary between the soul and God. Yet it is not a third thing with a substantial reality of its own. On the contrary, while not in itself formally divine, it "assimilates us immediately to God as such in His intimate life; it is therefore a formal, analogical participation in the Deity as it is in itself."[42] For Garrigou-Lagrange this formal aspect of the life of grace is central; indeed, "it is always a question of formal participation in the intimate life of God," an "objective participation" by which the human person is "intrinsically specified" by the divine nature.[43] Moreover, since God is a trinity, this deifying assimilation to God's "intimate life" possesses a necessarily Trinitarian shape. Deification is adoption, an insertion into the transcendent filiality of the eternal Son of the Father in the Holy Spirit. This Father

> has loved us with a love that is not only creative and preserving, but vivifying, which causes us to participate in the very principle of His intimate life, in the principle of the immediate vision which He has of Himself and which He communicates to His Son and to the Holy Ghost. It is thus that He has predestined us to be conformable to the image of His only Son, that this Son might be the first-born of many brethren (Rom. 8:29). The just are accordingly of the family of God and enter into the cycle of the Holy Trinity.[44]

Grace, by this account, amounts to a dramatic, deifying inclusion in the eternal communion of the triune persons. Garrigou-Lagrange emphasizes that this participation is not merely metaphorical, virtual, nominal, or moral, that is, by external declaration, but formal, "real and intimate." The just person does not simply resemble God analogically as being (as a stone does), nor only as living (as a plant or animal does), nor even only as intelligent (as humans or angels do), but "resembles God precisely as He is God . . . his life is not merely intellectual but deiform, divine, theological."[45]

To speak of the "formal aspect" of the life of grace is to speak about what it actually is in its essential fullness. While materially speaking, grace is classified in a finite category of being, formally speaking, it is classified as a participation in the infinite divine nature.[46] Only when this fact is fully appreciated can we

---

41. *Summa theologiae* I, 8, 3. See also I, 12, 11; I, 43, 3; I, 88, 3; I, 84, 7; I, 85, 1.

42. Garrigou-Lagrange, *Grace*, 403.

43. Ibid., 407.

44. Ibid., 405.

45. Ibid., *Grace*, 406. See also 126–38.

qualify it by noting that, in us—that is, materially—grace is not a substance but an accident.[47]

Our present inquiry however requires us to go a step further, to ask how grace also brings this participation about. It is just here that the notion of formal causality can come into play. In contrast to God's transcendent, efficiently causal operations in the soul and the world, grace, says Thomas, "as a quality, is said to act upon the soul, not after the manner of an efficient cause, but after the manner of formal cause, as whiteness makes a thing white, and justice, just."[48] Just as the soul's vivifying activity in the body is immediate and formal, so grace renders God's vivifying activity, fundamentally extrinsic and efficiently causal, immediate and intrinsic.[49] Garrigou-Lagrange repeats Aquinas's teaching that, since grace belongs to a higher order than any created agent, God alone is its principal efficient cause.[50] The humanity of Christ and the sacraments of the church serve as instrumental causes, but the actual production of grace is always a miracle akin to resurrection, admittedly not on par in modality with *creatio ex nihilo*, yet far surpassing creation in terms of what it gives rise to.[51] Once present in the essence of the soul, however, grace acts with formal causality, informing the whole person and his acts by a process of interior renewal, like sap in a plant. As a foundational quality that proportions nature to final beatitude, it acts in the soul, affirms Garrigou-Lagrange, "not effectively but formally, justifying it or making it just as whiteness makes a thing white or justice renders one just."[52]

These comments allow us to attribute to Garrigou-Lagrange the view that grace does indeed operate in the human soul as a form, that is, by means of formal causality. But in saying this it must be understood that by sanctifying grace Garrigou means not *Deus ipse*, but a divinely assimilating power. The notion of a quasi-formal causality, understood as the pure formal actuation of the soul by God himself, has no place in Garrigou-Lagrange's theology. In fact he explicitly rejects any view that holds that God or the Holy Spirit is formally

46. Kevin F. O'Shea identifies this as "the cardinal distinction of the Thomist theory of divinization" in idem, "Divinization: A Study in Theological Analogy," *The Thomist* 29, no. 1 (1965): 1–45 at 2.

47. Garrigou-Lagrange, *Grace*, 409. Also: "Deity is substance in God, its participation is an accident in us." Ibid., 135.

48. *Summa theologiae* I-II, 110, 2.

49. *Summa theologiae* I-II, 110, 1. On the background of this notion in Albert the Great and Bonaventure, see Bernard Lonergan, *Grace and Freedom: Operative Grace in the Thought of St. Thomas Aquinas*, ed. J. Patout Burns (London: Darton, Longman & Todd, 1971), 26–33.

50. Garrigou-Lagrange, *Grace*, 305.

51. Ibid., 306–7; cf. *Summa theologiae* I-II, 113, 9.

52. Garrigou-Lagrange, *Grace*, 120.

our life: "[T]he divinity of the Holy Ghost intrinsically united to us or assisting and dwelling in us does not produce, by way of form, adoptive sonship. . . . God is our life not formally, but only effectively."[53] The foundation of this formally real deification is grace and "not indeed the Holy Ghost . . . since He assists us as an extrinsic cause, and is not the form by which anyone is regenerated as a child of God."[54]

This would seem to put Garrigou-Lagrange's theology of grace at odds with de la Taille, Mersch, Rahner, and others who, in order to emphasize the supernaturality of grace, have invoked the unique causality known as "quasi-formal causality." In so doing it perhaps raises questions concerning the accuracy of Garrigou-Lagrange's interpretation of Thomas, at least when compared to the account of A. N. Williams who, although acknowledging that Thomas "does not equate grace and God," nevertheless concludes by asserting, "What grace is, most truly and fundamentally, is *gratia increata*, the Holy Spirit, God *ipse*."[55] Be that as it may, Garrigou-Lagrange is not unmoved by those inspired scriptural intuitions that envisage sanctifying grace as more deeply homogeneous with the divine being. Grace, according to St. John, is "the seed of God" (1 John 3: 9). A seed is known to be what it is in its fullness by reference to its origin and to its eventually mature perfection, which, given the appropriate conditions, it reaches in conformity with its natural teleological constitution. Analogously, as *semen gloriae*, the grace present and operative in the soul of a believer is known for what it is by reference to its origin and end. Its origin lies in God: as his "seed" it seems somehow continuous with, or at least essentially inseparable from, his very being. What about its end? How does Garrigou-Lagrange characterize its mature realization? "When in heaven it has reached its full development, and can no longer be lost, it will be the source of operations which will have absolutely the same formal object as the eternal and uncreated operations of God's own inner life. . . ."[56] Is this anything else than to say that grace, in its perfect realization, is the formal cause of a constitutive activity of a finite being that is essentially the same as the constitutive activity of the infinite God? And does that not imply that this actuation can only arise on the basis of an ontological foundation according to which, without any loss of infinite divine transcendence or distinctness in creaturely being, God's own self—the one and holy Trinity of persons in communion—has become the

---

53. Ibid., 137–8.

54. Ibid., 142.

55. Williams, *The Ground of Union*, 89.

56. Réginald Garrigou-Lagrange, *The Three Conversions in the Spiritual Life* (Rockford, IL: Tan Books, 2002 [orig. 1933]), 11.

"innermost constitutive element," as Rahner puts it, of the human soul? In the first case, for Garrigou-Lagrange, the answer appears to be yes, but it is not quite so in the second case, inasmuch as for him it is only grace as materially finite, and not as infinite act, that constitutes "a real and formal participation in the divine nature."[57]

FREEDOM AND COOPERATION

I should like to conclude this chapter on Garrigou-Lagrange's doctrine of deification by making some final remarks about the kind of causality involved in human cooperation with divine grace. We can trace in Garrigou-Lagrange's expositions on grace as elaborated so far a kind of hierarchy or organic flow of causation. At the head belongs uncreated grace, understood as the effective and performatively operative love of God, essentially divine and therefore always creative, self-diffusive, and life-giving. From uncreated grace flows sanctifying grace, constituted in the very essence of the soul as a newly created, humanly adapted root principle of divine activity, and therefore as the actuating form of human participation in the divine nature. From here Garrigou-Lagrange goes on to describe the causal outflow from sanctifying grace of the infused virtues, of which the primary three are faith, hope, and love. And it is especially at this third level that willing human cooperation with divine grace becomes behaviorally manifest.

For the Fathers of the ancient Church, especially for those who in the course of the monothelete christological controversy were pressed to defend the integrity of Christ's human will, there was always a concern, in articulating the dynamics of deification, to maintain the free and cooperative character of human action. Deification is at once divinely wrought and humanly willed. Maximus the Confessor classically expresses the first of these two aspects:

> For nothing created is by nature capable of deification, since it is incapable of grasping God. For it is intrinsic and peculiar to divine grace alone to bestow deification proportionately on beings, for only divine grace illuminates nature with supernatural light and elevates nature beyond its proper limits in excess of glory.[58]

---

57. See Garrigou-Lagrange, *Grace*, 172–73.

58. Maximus Confessor, *Quaestiones ad Thalassium* 22, 93–98 (CCSG 7, 141). We shall see this quote appear significantly in our discussion in chapter 11 of de Lubac's *Surnaturel.*

For the Thomistic tradition, the freedom of movement that necessarily constitutes voluntary human acts depends upon the proximate interiority of the principle from which they arise. "It is impossible for the will to be moved by an extrinsic principle as by an agent; rather, every movement of the will must proceed from within."[59] Even if the intrinsic principle itself has some prior, exterior cause, "it is essential to the voluntary act that its principle be within the agent."[60] These statements are another way of saying that nothing operates on the will by means of efficient causality, which always implies exteriority. Not even God can move the human will in this way, not even by the action of grace, for to do so would run against the very fabric of created human freedom.[61] Any act arising from this mode of causality would be neither free nor human, and so unworthy of the name of "synergy" or "cooperation." Rather it would amount to *coactio* or violent coercion.[62]

How then are our wills converted, moved to respond to the voice of the Holy Spirit, moved to the assent of faith, moved to that love for God without which beatitude is impossible? Anyone who has studied Aquinas's questions concerning the divisions, causes, and effects of grace in the *Summa theologiae* I-II, 111–13 will know that the causal chains and orders of operation are complex and in many cases reciprocally determined. Still more complex is the mutually causal interaction between the intellect and will. In *De veritate* Aquinas simplifies matters by specifying only two ways in which God changes the human will. The first is "merely by moving it," a modality left unexplained in this context except to exclude any sense of an efficient causation, "for even God could not do this." The second way is "by introducing some form into the will itself." Thus "by something additional, such as grace or a virtue, the soul is inclined to will something to which it was not previously determined by a natural inclination."[63]

Once again we see the notion of formal causality, in this case applied to the action of grace with respect to the will. Since the human will is more an appetite than an instrument, it is not liable to being "steered" by some external

59. Thomas Aquinas, *Summa contra gentiles* III, 88, 5.

60. Thomas Aquinas, *Summa theologiae* I-II, 6, 1.

61. Thomas Aquinas, *Summa contra gentiles* III, 148, 2.

62. See *Summa contra gentiles* III, 148, 1. In Thomas's writings *coactio* is a synonym of *violentia*, the very opposite of *libertas*. See R. J. Deferrari, *A Lexicon of Saint Thomas Aquinas* (Boonville, NY: Loreto, 2004), 160. For an elucidating discussion of the complexities involved in Thomas's theory of the will, see Eleonore Stump, "Freedom: action, intellect and will," and "Grace and free will," in idem, *Aquinas* (London: Routledge, 2003): 277–306, 389–404.

63. Thomas Aquinas, *De veritate* 22, 8–9.

power but must be as it were wooed or attracted by some desirable object or choice-worthy good. In this connection theological tradition has often spoken of the "drawing" action of God upon it, at the same time acknowledging the power of the will to resist and impede the reception of grace. But the emphasis is always upon an interior motion, one native to the integral nature of human freedom—freedom being understood not as deliberative autonomy but as a cooperative venture or project to be actualized in harmony with our most fundamental trajectory. In the words of St. Augustine, "God acts within, takes hold of hearts, moves hearts, and draws men by their wills which He Himself operates within them. . . ."[64]

The question of how God moves the will is treated by Garrigou-Lagrange in his 1951 *De Beatitudine*, a commentary on the first fifty-four questions of Aquinas's *prima secundae*.[65] Garrigou-Lagrange points out that, while the will normally moves only in response to the good as presented to it by the intellect, in the case of Christian faith and experimental knowledge, in which the object is not clearly grasped by the intellect, the will itself plays a more direct and determinative role.[66] In keeping with the Thomistic axiom that the will is not liable to coercion by some external force, even a divine one, Garrigou-Lagrange asserts that when it comes to the movement of the will necessary for justifying faith or the quasi-experimental knowledge of God, "God moves our will by an action formally immanent."[67] This interpretation has a twofold implication: it preserves the integrity of human freedom and the contingent character of self-determination, but at the same time excludes any Pelagian understanding of human cooperation. Indeed, Garrigou-Lagrange expressly rejects any presumptuous attribution of deification to natural powers. "God is the cause of all virtue, and of all acts which are in any way good. . . . God is the author of all that is good, even of merely natural good. . . . How much more is God the source of supernatural good! Without me you can do nothing."[68] In the movement from unbelief to faith, therefore, God moves the will "in a special manner, so suddenly that the will does not move itself." In this situation the supernatural act of faith is "due solely to operating grace."[69]

---

64. Augustine, *De correptione et gratia* 14 (NPNF 5, 490). Quoted by Garrigou-Lagrange, *Grace*, 243.

65. ET: Réginald Garrigou-Lagrange, *Beatitude: A Commentary on St. Thomas's Theological Summa, Ia IIae, qq. 1–54*, trans. P. Cummins (St. Louis: Herder, 1956).

66. Ibid., 183.

67. Ibid., 184.

68. Ibid., 190–91.

69. Ibid., 191–92.

This leaves open the question of where and how human cooperation enters in. On the one hand, the Scriptures speak of God "willing and working" in us what is good (Phil. 2:13). On the other hand, human beings are responsible for working out their own salvation (Phil. 2:12). Having cited the passage above from Augustine, which refers to God's "drawing" action upon the human will, Garrigou-Lagrange proffers the following description of the divine-human synergy:

> Divine motion is not a mechanical action, like the action of a man rowing a boat; it is of a higher order, to be compared rather to the influx of life-giving sap by which a plant nourishes and renders itself fruitful. In fact, this infusion is proper to the eternal cause, existing beyond time, which is much closer to our will than our will is to itself; and the divine cause, moving our will from within, inclines it to self-determination through deliberation towards this particular salutary, meritorious act rather than to its contrary. Thus God actualizes our liberty, causing together with us the free mode of our choice.[70]

Garrigou-Lagrange finds the paradigmatic exemplar of this actualized liberty in the Theotokos. True human freedom is enacted in the form of consent—verbalized in Mary's *fiat*—to the prior movement of God. In this way,

> God touches our created liberty with a virginal contact, which contains no violence. Just as, by the operation of the Holy Spirit, the Blessed Virgin conceived and brought forth without damage to her virginity, so under the grace of the Holy Spirit our liberty remains unharmed. God does not violate liberty, but preserves, elevates, vivifies, sanctifies, and strengthens liberty. To depreciate the strength of efficacious grace would be to reduce its sweetness, because the two, strength and sweetness, are intimately connected in the most profound harmony.[71]

This delicate statement serves well to close this chapter and to confirm our basic judgment, that for all his often long-winded technical elaborations and penchant for philosophical rigor, Garrigou-Lagrange ultimately would have us envision deification in the nuptial and mystical-experiential terms of the

---

70. Garrigou-Lagrange, *Grace*, 258.

71. Garrigou-Lagrange, *Beatitude*, 230.

great Fathers and saints of the church. Accordingly, the life of grace is not a mechanical process involving a determined causal series of impersonal interactions, but involves God's loving and dramatic inclusion of the consenting human person within the intimacy of his blessed interior life. Which is perhaps the reason why, when articulating his final vision of the beatified state, Garrigou-Lagrange could do no better than to draw upon certain expressions by such contemplatives as St. John of the Cross according to which, in the deified state, human action eventually seems to play no part, or is at least indistinguishable from the action of God, since the soul, completely overwhelmed like a vanquished lover, has become thoroughly wounded and liquefied by divine love. In this state of sublime pathos, says the Carmelite, "the soul can perform no acts, but it is the Holy Spirit that moves it to perform them."[72] All the powers of the soul, including the will, "are then as though melted" in the splendor of infinite glory. Like a burning bush, fully aflame yet unconsumed, the graced soul is at last "penetrated by God" like the union of air and fire in a flame, "which is nothing else but air on fire."[73]

72. Quoted by Garrigou-Lagrange, *The Three Conversions*, 99.
73. Garrigou-Lagrange, *The Three Conversions*, 100–101.

PART II

Karl Rahner

6

Deification and Transcendental Experience

It is no exaggeration to say that the motif of deification stands right at the very heart of Karl Rahner's entire theological project. Rahner's representative article in the multivolume *Lexikon für Theologie und Kirche* on the central scholastic category of sanctifying grace amounts essentially to an attempted recovery, under that term, of the biblical and patristic understanding of uncreated grace as "Vergöttlichung" (deification), or "die Selbstmitteilung Gottes" (the self-communication of God), or "die vergöttlichenden Teilnahme an der göttliche Natur" (deifying participation in the divine nature).[1] According to Francis J. Caponi, far from it being a peripheral element in Rahner's theological oeuvre, this process of human *theopoiesis* "is the center of gravity around which move Rahner's understanding of creation, anthropology, Christology, ecclesiology, liturgy, and eschatology."[2]

In the previous chapter, within the context of situating and examining Garrigou-Lagrange's theology of deifying grace, I had occasion briefly to expound an aspect of Karl Rahner's notion of quasi-formal causality. In so doing I anticipated a fuller and more rigorous analysis of the notion with respect to Rahner's theology of deification that would allow us to compare it with the theology of Garrigou-Lagrange and at the same time lay the ground for my argument that the doctrine of Henri de Lubac offers a more accessible, reliable, and well-trod path. At the start of this second part of the book, then, we

1. Karl Rahner, "Heiligmachende Gnade," in *Lexikon für Theologie und Kirche*, vol. 5, ed. J. Höfer and K. Rahner (Freiburg im Breisgau: Herder, 1960): 138–42. Although the article is brief, it should be noted how heavily weighted the bibliography is with numerous works from the 1920s that explicitly treat the topic of deification.

2. Francis J. Caponi, "Karl Rahner: Divinization in Roman Catholicism," in *Partakers of the Divine Nature: The History and Development of Deification in the Christian Traditions*, ed. M. J. Christensen and J. A. Wittung (Grand Rapids: Baker, 2007), 259–80 at 259.

shall begin our treatment of Karl Rahner's theology of deification by focusing our attention on his concept of transcendental experience and analyzing its connection to his doctrine of grace understood as divine self-communication. This approach will serve two purposes. First, it will help to introduce structural features inherent in the broader horizon of Rahner's theology and provide some interpretative tools for exploration of more particular themes central to our book in subsequent chapters. Second, it will further develop the already-anticipated theme of quasi-formal causality and demonstrate its function within Rahner's understanding of God's gracious, forgiving, and deifying self-communication to the human creature. This in turn will give rise to critical questions about Rahner's account of the purpose and scope of the Christ event and the vocation of the church as the locus of deification, questions that we shall deal with at greater length in chapters 7 and 8 respectively.

In the meantime we begin by turning to study Rahner's deployment of the key term "transcendental experience," an appreciation for which will be helped by a brief consideration of the general category "experience."

THE CATEGORY OF EXPERIENCE

From the time when Friedrich Schleiermacher (1768–1834) made it central to his anthropocentric theological system, the category of "experience" has undergone a noticeable ascendancy to central prominence in contemporary theological reflection.[3] Of course, even if it is an ambiguous and complex concept, it is not one that is entirely new. We have seen in a previous chapter how the Fathers conceived of the highest kind of learning or knowing as a form of "suffering" or "experience" of divine things. Maximus the Confessor regards this experience alone as "truly authentic knowledge" and equates it with deification inasmuch as "it provides a total perception of the known object through a participation (μέθεξις) by grace."[4] Inseparable from patristic intellectualism, expressed in the formula "I believe in order that I may understand," one finds an equally important role granted to experience: *credo*

---

3. See the constitutive role of *das Gefühl* or "the feeling of absolute dependence" in Friedrich Schleiermacher, *The Christian Faith*, trans. H. R. Mackintosh and J. S. Stewart (Edinburgh: T. & T. Clark, 1928 [orig. 1821]). On the category of experience more generally, see the collection of essays devoted to the topic in the Summer 2010 edition of the international journal *Communio* (vol. 37, no. 2); also Alister E. McGrath, "Theology and Experience: Reflections on Cognitive and Experiential Approaches to Theology," *European Journal of Theology* 2 (1993): 65–74; Donald L. Gelpi, *The Turn to Experience in Contemporary Theology* (New York: Paulist, 1984).

4. Maximus Confessor, *Quaestiones ad Thalassium* 60, 67–69 (CCSG 22, 77).

ut experiar.[5] In the writings of Aquinas also the words *experientia* and *experior*, meaning acquaintance, feeling, and learning by personal experience, are also not without importance, and we have already seen how Garrigou-Lagrange, following Aquinas, made much in his theology of deification of the idea of "quasi-experimental" or experiential knowledge of God.

With the subjective turn in modern thought, however, the category of experience has come to demand even more heightened reflection, and while in the theology of Henri de Lubac the word is largely inconspicuous, in the *Communio* tradition of theology inspired in good part by the Lubacian vision, experience features as a crucial term. One of the key concepts in the *Communio* tradition of nuptial theology in particular, especially as it has been developed by Angelo Scola, is that of "elementary experience." In 2003, it formed the title of a book Scola wrote on John Paul II's theological anthropology to honor the twenty-fifth year of his pontificate: *L'esperienza elementare: La vena profonda del magistero di Giovanni Paolo II.* Scola's interest in "elementary experience" seems to have its roots in his involvement in the *Comunione e Liberazione* movement, founded by Monsignor Luigi Giussani in 1969. One of the early texts passed around at meetings was Jean Guitton's *Nouvel Art de Penser* in which Guitton states that "a reasonable person is one who submits reason to experience." Giussani's own educational methodology followed this basic plan. The category "experience" appeared in numerous book titles of his: *Reflections on an Experience* (1959), *Traces of the Christian Experience* (1960), two works that were reissued in English in 1995 with the title *The Journey to Truth Is an Experience.* The common aim of these works is to help people return to and dwell in experience. In his two-page foreword to the English translation of this work, in which the word "experience" appears some twelve times, Marc Ouellet summarizes Giussani's overall pedagogy as one that "begins from human experience and leads to a deeper level of this same experience."[6]

But in Christian theology, experience *per se* cannot be an end in itself. With every claim to have had a profound or definitive experience, we must ask: experience of what? At the opening address at youth gatherings Giussani would say, "Let us aim above all at announcing Christ, the all-embracing event in man's life and the centre of history."[7] Experience is simply the concrete

---

5. See Killian McDonnell, "Spirit and Experience in Bernard of Clairvaux," *Theological Studies* 58 (1997): 3–18.

6. In L. Giussani, *The Journey to Truth Is an Experience*, trans. J. Zucchi (Montreal: McGill-Queen's University Press, 2006), viii.

7. Giussani, *The Journey to Truth Is an Experience*, 6.

mode by which we encounter the personal and objective reality who is Jesus Christ. The possibility of this encounter, however, depends on first being open to one's own experience, of facing one's own reality. "In other words, we must be acutely aware of our experiences and look on the humanity within us with sympathy; we must take into consideration who we really are. To take into consideration means to take seriously what we experience, *everything* we experience, to discover every aspect, to seek the complete meaning."[8] For Giussani, openness to experience is openness to reality, and openness to reality is the precondition for encountering Christ.

For Scola too, "experience" functions as a fundamental philosophical, theological, and educational category. In his writings he speaks of "affective experience," "nuptial experience," "original experience," the "experience of creaturely contingency," the "experience of otherness," the "experience of freedom," the "experience of love," and finally, "fundamental human experience." When in 1996 Scola argued for the "ontological" primacy of the experience of faith over the systematic and scientific elaboration of theology, he claimed to be echoing a sentiment typical of the personalist theological tradition exemplified for example by Jean Mouroux, but which we may further trace back to such seminal proposals as those of M.-D. Chenu and Pierre Rousselot which, each in their own circumstances, were regarded by no few contemporaries as expressions of the dubious modernist spirit.[9] Mouroux's burden was to show that faith is essentially an experience of a(nother) person, the "orientation of a person towards a good which can only be another person." It involves "a sort of *contact* and *coincidence* with the being discovered," the sort of contact that calls for and results in "an act of communion."[10] Defined in this way, deifying faith and the infinite realities that it embraces cannot be conceived apart from the concrete conditions of human experience. This is not to make one's experience the object of faith. Rather, experience is the necessary mode or "place" within which faith, as self-entrustment to Christ and act of communion, unfolds and takes shape.

Earlier still Chenu had similarly argued that faith begins with "that which is given (*le donné*)," or more precisely, given to experience. Reason, in its attempts to unpack this perceived and experienced given, and from it construct a systematic body of coherent propositions (*le construit*), can never fully contain or exhaust it. It is the law of all sciences, said Chenu, citing the great

8. Ibid., 54.

9. See Angelo Scola, "Christian Experience and Theology," *Communio* 23 (1996): 203–6.

10. See Jean Mouroux, *I Believe: The Personal Structure of Faith* (London: Geoffrey Chapman, 1959), 59, 51, 61.

mathematician and philosopher of science Henri Poincaré (1854–1912), that genuine discoveries come not from studying a system, "but from a return to the primitive 'given,' viz. the direct experience of things." In a similar way, it is only by returning to "the Christian experience" that theology finds its "given."[11] Scola's agenda is strikingly similar: "[T]heology is born of Christian experience and must ceaselessly refer to the horizon that this experience sets for it."[12]

In Rahner's theological worldview the category of experience likewise plays a pivotal role. The experience of God above all lies at the very heart of what Rahner believes it means to be human. But what calls for special attention in connection with our study is Rahner's particular understanding of why this is the case. According to Rahner, the human being is constituted in such a way that not only is he related to God as creature to creator or as effect to efficient cause, but that God himself, in all his absolute and infinite transcendence, is somehow also coessential and formally intrinsic to the human structure. Humanity, when fulfilled, is "the event of God's self-communication," which is to say "that God in his own most proper reality makes himself the innermost constitutive element in man."[13] A consequence of this is that all human experience, even the most elementary and ordinary, is shot through with mystery and what one might call an intrinsic openness, even a positive orientation, to the absolute. It is characteristic of all our many experiences in the world—of other people and things, of our bodies, of our own self-consciousness—that within them we experience ourselves as something "more" than the sum of these various experiences. We experience ourselves in the midst of these finite components as a transcendent person and subject, for "[a] finite system cannot confront itself in its totality."[14] Rahner applies the term "transcendental experience" to this mysterious self-awareness. It is transcendental in that "the object of such a transcendental experience does not appear in its own reality when man is dealing with something individual and definable in an objective way," as he does in all the experiences that comprise the "finite system" of his life in the world, "but when in such a process he is *being* subject and not dealing with a 'subject' in an objective way."[15]

11. M.-D. Chenu, "What Is Theology?," in idem, *Faith and Theology*, trans. D. Hickey (Dublin: Gill & Son, 1968), 15–35.

12. Scola, "Christian Experience and Theology," 204.

13. Karl Rahner, *Foundations of Christian Faith: An Introduction to the Idea of Christianity*, trans. W. V. Dych (London: Darton, Longman & Todd, 1978), 116.

14. Ibid., 30.

15. Ibid., 31.

Let us attempt to unpack these dense thoughts a little further. Human life is made up of countless experiences within the finite horizon conditioned by space and time. To these finite experiences Rahner gives the name "categorical experience." Hidden and enclosed within all such categorical experiences, however, lies "transcendental experience," the subtle sense or awareness on the part of the personal subject that she is not simply the product of all these finite experiences, but somehow precedes and transcends them. In this sense of her transcendental subjectivity and origin, the human person possesses an implicit experience of infinite being.[16]

Now although Rahner employs the word *Vorgriff*—often translated as "awareness" or "pre-apprehension"—to indicate this transcendental sense, and commonly draws on an epistemological model to explain it, what he is proposing is not limited to the order of knowing. It is rather ontological.[17] Although this ontological ordination to infinite being can easily be overlooked or suppressed, it is as it were built into our nature as an "unthematic," unspecified dynamism, whether we are conscious of it or not.[18]

Thus *Vorgriff* may better be understood as "anticipation" or "dynamic openness" than "awareness." It betokens an underlying relatedness, "a mode of being," that is inescapably bound up with the human being's simultaneously contingent and transcendent structure, with his being a finite event of God's self-communication. So deeply is it part of our being that Rahner calls it "an irreducible datum of existence, copresent in every individual experience as its a priori condition."[19] This means that the very possibility of a person's experiencing finite things, and of knowing and willing them, is conditional upon the even more fundamental dimension of "transcendental experience," the dynamic, ontological interiority of transcendence in the human constitution. It is this dimension especially that in fact characterizes the human spirit, which is radically *capax infiniti*, that is, "fundamentally and by its very nature pure openness for absolutely everything, for being as such."[20] In this way every human experience at the level of categorical and contingent being, when

---

16. The distinction between categorical and transcendental experience in Rahner's theology is lucidly explained by Karen Kilby, *Karl Rahner: A Brief Introduction* (New York: Crossroad, 2007), 1–14.

17. "[A]s opposed to Kant, there is always question of a noetic hylomorphism, to which there corresponds an *ontological* hylomorphism in the objects, in the sense of a thoroughgoing determination of knowing by being." Karl Rahner, *Spirit in the World*, trans. W. V. Dych (New York: Continuum, 1994 [orig. 1957], 2nd ed.), liii–liv.

18. Rahner, *Foundations of Christian Faith*, 32–35.

19. Ibid., 31.

20. Ibid., 20.

attended to, presents a transcendent "horizon"—a real point of contact with and mute call to enter into the "silent and uncontrollable" sphere of transcendent and absolute being, which is another name for what the Christian knows as God.

THE EXPERIENCE OF GRACE

Rahner's development of the concept of transcendental experience forms a crucial metaphysical prolegomenon to his exposition of the impact of justifying and deifying grace upon the human reality. Its prior articulation belongs to "the presupposition without which the Christian message about man would not be possible."[21] Notice how Rahner here says "possible" and not just "intelligible." This raises the critical methodological question whether Rahner, in a foundationalist manner, tends too much to manipulate the data of revelation to fit an already-worked-out philosophical and anthropological framework. This at least is a common criticism that has been leveled at Rahner from all kinds of angles. It is not my intention to adjudicate on it here, except perhaps to mention that Rahner himself insists that when he reflects upon the necessary conditions of possibility for a reality, he does so only from the perspective of one who has already encountered that reality.[22] However, as we delve further into Rahner's understanding of the deifying experience of grace, it is important to keep this query in mind precisely because the ontological structure that he has outlined in his exposition of the notion of transcendental experience already contains within itself the fundamental structure of deification by which God himself constitutes an interior ontological constituent in the human being's concrete quiddity. The question that will hover in the background of our discussion therefore will always be whether God's self-communication in Christ *fits* or *governs* the shape of human transcendence.[23] This form of the question was posed by R. R. Reno, who, while drawing attention to this ambiguity especially in Rahner's later work *Foundations of Christian Faith* (*Grundkurs des Glaubens,*

---

21. Ibid., 116.

22. Ibid., 177. In any case, a number of scholars have called for due attention to the nonsystematic character of Rahner's writings, warning against any generalizing, ahistorical treatment of them as some kind of monolithic "foundationalist" project. See Karen Kilby, *Karl Rahner: Theology and Philosophy* (London: Routledge, 2004); also Nicholas Healy, "Indirect Methods in Theology: Karl Rahner as an ad hoc Apologist," *The Thomist* 56 (1992): 613–34; J. A. Colombo, "Rahner and His Critics: Lindbeck and Metz," *The Thomist* 56, no. 1 (1992): 71–96.

23. R. R. Reno, *The Ordinary Transformed: Karl Rahner and the Christian Vision of Transcendence* (Grand Rapids: Eerdmans, 1995), 127 n. 62.

1976), nevertheless in other comments seemed to suggest that a simple either/or division between the two is untenable:

> Rahner does not begin with human experience in anything like a foundational sense. Rather, he turns to our condition in order to explore the conceptual shock waves which result from the discovery that in Christ we are blessed by a God who is love. These shock waves shape every aspect of the created order, especially the human dimension.[24]

These words indicate how far-reachingly *theological* Rahner's anthropology is meant to be. So that when he says "Mensch," he is referring to a reality that can be known in truth only in terms of its ultimate ordination and absolute fulfillment, in terms of what it is intended to be by irreversible divine decree.

Yet immediately we must qualify our remarks by recalling Rahner's own point of departure from the thesis of Henri de Lubac and representatives of the so-called *nouvelle théologie*. With them, Rahner stood shoulder to shoulder in opposition to the extrinsicism staunchly defended by such figures as Garrigou-Lagrange and Charles Boyer, according to which there is posited an integral *natura pura* without reference to that nature's interior ordination to beatitude.[25] Rahner entered the debate on this specific issue in 1950—already after no few exchanges between the *nouvelle théologie* theologians and their critics—with the following critical remarks:

> [I]f man, just so far as he experiences himself existentially by himself, is really nothing but pure nature, he is always in danger of understanding himself merely as a nature and of behaving accordingly. And then he will find God's call to him out of this human plane merely a disturbance, which is trying to force something upon him (however elevated this may be in itself) for which he is not made (on this view he is only made and destined for it *after* he has received grace, and then only in a way entirely abstracted from experience). This is particularly true since this offer

---

24. Ibid., 7.

25. See Réginald Garrigou-Lagrange, "Le désir naturel de bonheur: Prouve-t-il l'existence de Dieu?," *Angelicum* 8 (1931): 129–48; "La nouvelle théologie: Où va-t-elle?," *Angelicum* 23 (1946): 126–45; C. Boyer, "Nature pure et surnaturel dans le 'Surnaturel' du Père de Lubac," *Gregorianum* 28 (1947): 379–96. For a more recent defense of the pure nature theory, see Steven A. Long, *Natura Pura: On the Recovery of Nature in the Doctrine of Grace* (New York: Fordham University Press, 2010).

of inwardly elevating grace remains *ex supposito* outside or above his real experience, and only becomes known in a faith which knows of its object *ex auditu* alone.[26]

But having said as much, Rahner went on to register concern for the way in which, in his judgment, de Lubac's theoretical reconfiguration of the nature and grace relation failed adequately to guard the absolutely "unexacted" (*Ungeschuldet*) character of grace.[27] No intrinsic desire for beatitude or openness to grace on the part of human nature can be invoked to account for the actual eventual bestowal of grace by God. If the ordination to grace and the beatific vision cannot be detached somehow from nature, then the fulfillment of the ordination, "from *God's* point of view precisely, is exacted."[28] Rahner's preferred solution, which was not occasioned by the nature and grace debate but had already been developed in his 1937 lectures published as *Hörer des Wortes* (1941), is to restate the matter in very different terms:

> God wishes to communicate himself, to pour forth the love which he himself is. That is the first and the last of his real plans and hence of his real world too. Everything else exists so that this one thing might be: the eternal miracle of infinite Love. And so God makes a creature whom he can love: he creates man. He creates him in such a way that he *can* receive this Love which is God himself, and that he can and must at the same time accept it for what it is: the ever astounding wonder, the unexpected, unexacted gift.[29]

From this "kerygmatic" way of viewing the situation, Rahner offers four important theological transpositions. First, this vision implies that man must have an existential "congeniality" for this divine love and self-communication, a real scope or "obediential potency" for it. "To this extent this 'potency' is

26. Karl Rahner, "Concerning the Relationship between Nature and Grace," in TI, vol. 1, 297–318, at 300.

27. It seems that Rahner's acquaintance with de Lubac's *Surnaturel* thesis depended in the main upon an exposition published anonymously under the authorship of "D" [=Emile Delaye?]: "Ein Weg zur Bestimmung des Verhältnisses von Natur und Gnade," *Orientierung* 14 (1950): 138–41. De Lubac responded to Rahner by pointing out that, by relying on a secondary commentator, he had misrepresented his (de Lubac's) thesis. See further Noel O'Sullivan, *Christ and Creation: Christology as the Key to Interpreting the Theology of Creation in the Works of Henri de Lubac* (Bern: Peter Lang, 2009), 265–74.

28. Rahner, "Concerning the Relationship between Nature and Grace," 306.

29. Ibid., 310.

what is inmost and most authentic in him, the centre and root of what he is absolutely." So innate is this existential congeniality that it exists even in the damned, in whom it is experienced as a painful, gnawing evil. Second, this congeniality for unexacted grace is itself unexacted, and indeed "only allows grace to be unexacted grace when it is itself unexacted, and at the moment when, fulfilled by grace, it becomes conscious of itself *as* supernatural. . . ." Third, it is impossible to conceive, except perhaps by way of an abstract "remainder concept" (*Restbegriff*), what human "nature" and experience would be like apart from this existential congeniality for grace. Life as we know it is essentially inseparable from this supernatural condition of our being, whether or not we are conscious of it, and "man can experiment with himself only in the region of God's supernatural loving will. . . ." Accordingly nature always already exists within the conditions of this dynamism of unexacted grace. Fourth and finally, one must guard against identifying the various components that go toward making up our concrete spiritual experience with this more interior, antecedent dynamism, for it is this latter which constitutes "the indispensable transcendental condition of the possibility of a spiritual life at all."[30]

For all their merits, these conclusions—which admittedly were not intended by Rahner to be definitive or in any way exhaustive—have the effect of solving the impasse between extrinsicism and intrinsicism only by virtually doing away with the controverted concept of "nature" altogether, at least in any sense of the term as hitherto understood in catholic theological or philosophical tradition. This in fact would become the nub of de Lubac's own criticism of Rahner's solution to the nature and grace problematic.[31] It wasn't so much Rahner's adoption of the term "obediential potency" (*potentia obedientalis*), for it had an established background in late scholasticism. It is true that de Lubac considered it infelicitous to apply the term to human beings *qua* intelligent spirits, since in its original usage it denoted a passive receptivity or nonresistance, characteristic of material, nonintelligent creation, to receiving the miraculous action of God. By contrast, what takes place in the action of grace and justification in a human being is not an alteration or miraculous intervention within the sphere of laws governing passive matter but a gratuitous divine offer and free personal acceptance of a supernatural vocation. If the concept continues to be used, at the very least it calls for careful qualification.[32]

---

30. Ibid., 311–15.

31. See Henri de Lubac, *The Mystery of the Supernatural*, trans. R. Sheed (New York: Crossroad, 1998), 101–2 n. 2.

Rather de Lubac's concerns lay deeper. Finding in the category "nature" little more than the *Restbegriff*, Rahner posits instead a "supernatural existential," an ambiguous and eventually much-controverted term. De Lubac found it overly Heideggerian, but clearly Rahner is trying to say something explicitly theological.[33] Although he never really defines the term, from the way he uses it in this early period, Rahner seems to want to indicate an inner orientation to God that influences human nature but is not actually part of human nature. It is that which answers to the question: What is the condition for human nature to receive the self-communication of God in a way that deifies it? It is that which is implied or presupposed in the actual experience of deifying grace.[34]

Given this ambiguity, it seems impossible to avoid the conclusion that by virtue of this supernatural existential, Rahner wants to say that the extrinsic divine "offer" *is* the element that most intrinsically defines, and, given its gratuitous acceptance, ultimately completes, the human creature. Deifying grace, understood as God's gratuitous self-communication, is then seen not as a therapeutic or redeeming intervention on God's part but the primary, all-encompassing intention standing behind the whole of created history and therefore intrinsic to its quiddity or "whatness," and especially to that part of created history which is the human species. So that,

> [f]or an ontology which grasps the truth that man's concrete quiddity depends utterly on God, is not his binding disposition *eo ipso* not just a juridical decree of God but precisely what man *is*, hence not just an imperative proceeding from God but man's most inward depths?[35]

Ironically, as it therefore seems in retrospect, Rahner's ostensible stepping back from what he perceived to be an overly radical unification of nature and the supernatural turns out even more deeply to radicalize the structural anticipation

---

32. See Henri de Lubac, *Augustinianism and Modern Theology*, trans. L. Sheppard (New York: Herder, 1969), 224–33; idem, *The Mystery of the Supernatural*, 107 n. 36, 140–45. In defense of the applicability of the term to the natural desire for God in human beings, see Steven A. Long, "Obediential Potency, Human Knowledge, and the Natural Desire to See God," *International Philosophical Quarterly* 37 (1997): 47–63; Ralph M. McInerny, *Praeambula fidei: Thomism and the God of the Philosophers* (Washington, DC: Catholic University of America Press, 2006), 69–90.

33. See Henri de Lubac, *At the Service of the Church: Henri de Lubac Reflects on the Circumstances That Occasioned His Writings*, trans. A. E. Englund (San Francisco: Ignatius, 1993), 62 n. 5.

34. See David Coffey, "The Whole Rahner on the Supernatural Existential," *Theological Studies* 65 (2004): 95–118.

35. Rahner, "Concerning the Relationship between Nature and Grace," TI, vol. 1, 302.

or presence of the supernatural within the creaturely order, and that not simply in the mode of transcendent efficient cause. As we move on to consider these perspectives alongside Rahner's understanding of formal causality, we shall see more clearly how the defining characteristic of Rahner's theological anthropology lies in the way he understands the human being as ultimately established and completed by a single ontological continuum that unfolds in two modes or degrees of existence. The ontological structure is defined as God's self-communication. The two degrees of existence consist in efficiently caused existence, by which persons are initially established in being, and formally caused existence, by which they are perfected and deified.

FORMAL CAUSALITY

We have already dedicated some discussion to Rahner's notion of (quasi-)formal causality in an earlier chapter. At that point we considered it without the benefit of reflection on its relation to the notion of transcendental experience. In Rahner's theology, however, the notion of transcendental experience comprises the conceptual and ontological justification for the formally causal relation that he posits between God and the deified human being. For this reason it will be beneficial to revisit Rahner's understanding of grace and formal causality equipped with the conceptual vision we have built up in the last two sections. We shall follow this exposition with a critical analysis of the concept of formal causality as applied to uncreated grace and a consideration of the problem in relation to transcendental experience and deification.

It will be recalled that Rahner was one of a number of theologians in the pre-war period—I specifically made mention of Maurice de la Taille and Emil Mersch—who found the notion of efficient causality inadequate to account for the revealed and experienced dynamism of divine indwelling and deifying grace operative within the human creature re-created in Christ. Within the context of accounting for the supernatural transformation of the human person through Christ, the notion of efficient causality does not call for or imply any intrinsic community between God and the believer, nor does it sufficiently account for the kind of intimate, personal self-communication by which the New Testament would appear to indicate the operative, deifying presence of the Holy Spirit in the life of the believer. Sensing this inadequacy, Rahner adopted the alternative scholastic notion of formal causality, which in his earlier works he qualified with the prefix "quasi" in an effort to avoid too close an ontological identification between the uncreated divine agent and the actuated creature.[36] When we turn to Rahner's more mature work *Foundations of*

Christian Faith, however, we find that the prefix "quasi" has dropped away altogether and Rahner is content to run with the word "formal" simply.

Rahner's effort to distinguish between efficient and formal causality in this work forms part of his more basic assertion that in God's deifying self-communication to human beings, the giver himself *is* the gift. "It is decisive for an understanding of God's self-communication to man to grasp that the giver in his own being is the gift. . . ."[37] This assertion places Rahner squarely within the tradition of interpretation that understands grace as primarily uncreated, indeed, as equivalent to God's own Spirit. He proceeds then to account for this claim in the following way. Philosophy tells us that in efficient causality "the effect is always different from the cause." In formal causality, by contrast, a principle of being becomes "a constitutive element in another subject by the fact that it communicates itself to this subject, and does not just cause something different from itself. . . ." In this way, the cause becomes "an intrinsic, constitutive principle" of the being it informs.[38]

These two kinds of causality are manifestly operative in the two dimensions of creation and grace. In creation, God "establishes" a reality that is ontologically different from himself. In grace, God communicates his own being so as to become an intrinsically defining, constitutively formal element of the creature's ontological makeup with real "divinizing effects." Yet God does so in such a way that he in no respect loses divinity or limits his transcendence in this communication.[39] This latter qualification should be carefully noted, for it is one that Rahner often reiterates. Indeed it was the original function of the prefix "quasi" to emphasize just this point. Rahner presupposes and everywhere seeks to maintain the fundamental and ineradicable difference between God and creation. Unlike the notion of pure divine self-extension, divine self-communication presupposes the real and ongoing otherness between communicated and communicatee. He explains:

> Divine self-communication means . . . that God can communicate himself in his own reality to what is not divine without ceasing to be infinite reality and absolute mystery, and without man ceasing to be a finite existent different from God. . . . Even in grace and in the

---

36. Karl Rahner, "Zur scholastischen Begrifflichkeit der ungeschaffenen Gnade," *Zeitschrift für katholische Theologie* 63 (1939): 137–71, reprinted in idem, *Schriften zur Theologie* 1 (1954): 347–75. ET: "Some Implications of the Scholastic Concept of Uncreated Grace," in TI, vol. 1, 319–46.

37. Rahner, *Foundations of Christian Faith*, 120.

38. Ibid., 121.

39. Ibid., 121.

immediate vision of God, God remains God, that is, the first and the ultimate measure which can be measured by nothing else.[40]

And again, a little further on:

> Of course this divine self-communication, in which God makes himself a constitutive principle of the created existent without thereby losing his absolute, ontological independence, has "divinizing" effects in the finite existent in whom this self-communication takes place.[41]

Rahner adds still another qualification, which is important not to overlook. The adoption of the concept of formal causality to describe God's gracious self-communication to the human spiritual subject is precisely an analogous modification of a concept which, familiar to us from the world of categorical experience, goes some way toward accounting for a transcendent reality that ultimately escapes finite description or conceptual classification. Formal causality is not an exhaustive nor dogmatically definitive category. It provides Rahner with a "mode of conceptualization" that approximates the ontological essence of this self-communication "only by a dialectical and analogous modification."[42] The justification for adopting this analogous concept lies in the more fundamental concept of "transcendental experience" according to which every finite existent is essentially oriented "to the absolute being and mystery of God."[43] Thus Rahner distinguishes between two levels or modes by which God constitutes an interior element of creaturely existence, one of which comprises the necessary ontological foundation, the other its concrete and personal appropriation. The second, which "consists in the fact that God becomes immediate to the subject as spiritual, that is, in the fundamental unity of knowledge and love," can only arise within the context of the first, its essential ontological condition. But this formally caused immediacy is not to be understood as some new or alien phenomenon "added to another reality," as it had been in the *duplex ordo* tradition of Baroque scholasticism, but as the proper perfection and completion of the efficiently caused constitution. Its unfolding takes place as a second and more perfect mode of one and the same ontic reality. This of course is to say that creation is in a certain sense imperfect, or at best

---

40. Ibid., 119.
41. Ibid., 120.
42. Ibid., 121.
43. Ibid., 121.

on the way toward a perfection that it initially lacks. Here we find echoes of the distinction made by Irenaeus—and which as we shall see is so important for Henri de Lubac—between image and likeness, according to which human beings are created in a state of immaturity and latent potential with a view to a vocation involving increasing maturation and christo-form assimilation to God. Rahner likewise views creation not as an original pristine perfection to which now fallen humanity must return but as a partial and inchoate anticipation of a perfect reality only realized in Christ. As the establishment by God of what is not God by efficient causality, creation is the "deficient mode of that absolute and enormous possibility of God which consists in the fact that he who is *agape* in person . . . can precisely for this reason communicate himself to another."[44]

There is certainly something novel, perhaps even unsettling, in the way Rahner poses the nature and grace, creation and redemption relation in such terms. Francis Caponi has argued however that in this way Rahner is simply trying to transpose into a contemporary conceptual and terminological framework the substance of a distinction long ago already made by Aquinas between two modes of God's ontologically identical self-presence: "God is in all things by his activity, inasmuch as he joins himself to them as giving *esse* and conserving it; but [he is] in the saints by their very activity, by which they attain to God and in a way comprehend him, which is to know and to love him."[45] God's gracious and deifying self-bestowal is viewed by Rahner in what we might call evolutionary terms, that is, as a continuous dynamic trajectory that unfolds in two distinct modes or degrees of existence. This trajectory begins in the act of creation—understood not just in terms of an isolated *fiat ex nihilo* but also in terms of the ongoing establishment and conservation of beings in existence by participation in the divine *esse*—and attains its always divinely intended yet nonetheless absolutely gratuitous and unexacted completion in the freely accepted and personal appropriation of God by spiritual beings as what he

---

44. Ibid., 122.

45. Thomas Aquinas, *In II Cor* 6.3; see the numerous references aimed at highlighting substantial continuities between Rahner and Aquinas in F. J. Caponi, "Karl Rahner: Divinization in Roman Catholicism," 259–80. In another essay Caponi offers this illuminating remark: "His [Rahner's] project hinges upon the transposition of Thomistic ontology into the idiom of human knowing." F. J. Caponi, "Karl Rahner and the Metaphysics of Participation," *The Thomist* 67 (2003): 375–408, at 388. This comment seems to suggest a shift beyond Thomas to something more like the psychologism of Ockham who, in the judgment of Gilson, "was convinced that to give a psychological analysis of human knowledge was to give a philosophical analysis of reality," an error that always occurs "whenever a philosopher mistakes the empirical description of our ways of knowing for a correct description of reality itself." E. Gilson, *The Unity of Philosophical Experience* (San Francisco: Ignatius, 1964 [orig. 1937]), 69, 71.

already is at the level of self-communicating "offer": their transcendental origin and the intrinsic, formal principle of their final, supernatural actualization.

It is time now to make some summary remarks. We saw in the previous chapter on Garrigou-Lagrange's doctrine of causality how Rahner's conceptualization of formal causality went beyond anything envisaged by the Dominican, who was himself no stranger to the concept. Indeed, while other theologians such as de la Taille and Mersch also employed the concept and adapted it to the dynamism of human deification by grace, Rahner's more mature expressions on the topic suggest he is willing to go further, a willingness possibly indicated by his dropping of the prefix "quasi." In this chapter we have shown how Rahner envisages creation and deification as two modes of existence along a single continuum whose ontological *logos* or form is defined by a progressive divine self-communication. But as we have noted along the way, and as various other critics have argued, Rahner's particular way of expressing this continuum tends to leave him open to the charge that, whether in his doctrine of creation, or in his christology, or in his doctrine of grace, he insufficiently distinguishes between the divine and human forms.[46] In Rahner's defense, it is possible to cite passages in which he insists that there is and forever remains an ontological difference between creature and creator. "[W]e ourselves never cease being creatures even when we become partakers of the Godhead."[47] Yet the question that cannot be ignored concerns the degree to which such assertions are consistent with Rahner's wider insistence upon the crucial intersection between formal causality, transcendental experience, and deification. For Rahner the very act of human knowing is already "a participation in the light of Absolute Spirit."[48] This may be just another way of saying that in every use of the verb "to be" there is an implicit affirmation of God who is being itself, a point advanced well before Rahner by both Maurice Blondel and Henri de Lubac. What Rahner seems to mean, however, and this may be related to his Kantian, Heideggerian, and Maréchalian method,[49] is that in the unspecific, transcendental character of human consciousness we discover an indication of an already-incipient, formally caused supernatural existence, an existence whose final defining form is the absolute divine being.

---

46. See, for example, Guy Mansini, "Quasi-formal Causality and 'Change in the Other': A Note on Karl Rahner's Christology," *The Thomist* 52 (1988): 293–306.

47. Karl Rahner, "The Eternal Significance of the Humanity of Jesus for Our Relationship with God," in TI, vol. 3, 35–46, at 46.

48. Rahner, *Spirit in the World*, 226.

49. Caponi, "Karl Rahner and the Metaphysics of Participation," 387.

In this regard one senses the relevance to this discussion of the thesis of contemporary French philosopher Jean Borella. In his book *Le Sens du Surnaturel* (1996), in which he explicitly cites the seminal inspiration of de Lubac, Borella upbraids those who, overly anxious to maintain the distance between God and the creature, would reject the possibility of any "entitative" contact or participation of the creature in the uncreated act.[50] He admits that this may be a legitimate concern on the part of the rational philosopher—in this case the concern is expressed by none other than Jacques Maritain. But according to Borella, this rejection runs counter to the lived experience of many a mystic who knows "that there are possibilities of being other than those customarily imagined by a conventional philosopher." The mode of being that Christianity calls deification presupposes a certain kind of creaturely structure in which, "at its very core, in its most intimate heart," there lies "something uncreated and divine. . . ." Theology affirms that human beings are made for union with God, for real communion in his nature and intimate Trinitarian life. Hence, argues Borella, "[i]t is quite necessary that this ordination to deification possess an ontological root in created being if we are not to lapse into unintelligible supernaturalism."[51]

So are not Borella and Rahner basically saying the same thing? I think not. For one gets the continual impression that the deifying experience of grace outlined by Rahner takes place in the individual primarily in the form of a heightened consciousness of what is universally already the case. The concrete bodily and communal events of ecclesial incorporation and sacramental participation seem not so much to be constitutively causative of a new reality as occasions for the conscious experience of an already-existing one. Basically they have as their aim the stimulation of a psychological state of awareness, the elicitation of a primarily *gnoseological* orientation. Or, put another way, they have as their aim the making explicit of what hitherto was already present, given, and real at the level of the "unthematic." For every categorical, thematic "yes" or "no" to God in Christ corresponds to an already-existing transcendental, unthematic "yes" or "no" to the absolute. "In this sense," Rahner explains,

> we encounter God in a radical way everywhere as a question to our freedom, we encounter him unexpressed, unthematic, unobjectified and unspoken in all of the things of the world. . . . This does

50. Jean Borella, *The Sense of the Supernatural*, trans. G. J. Champoux (Edinburgh: T. & T. Clark, 1998), 127–28.
51. Ibid., 133–34.

not preclude the necessity of making this thematic. But this latter does not give us our original relationship to God in our freedom, but rather it makes thematic and objectifies the relationship of our freedom to God which is given with and in the original and essential being of the subject as such.[52]

To which one might well reply: What need then is there of Christ? Only to make the unthematic thematic? The absolute categorical? The implied explicit? These difficult and provocative questions cannot adequately be answered here, but they do open the way to the important christological inquiries of the next chapter.

---

52. Rahner, *Foundations of Christian Faith*, 98–99.

7

Deification and Cosmic Christology

It has become increasingly common for theologians from across a broad range of Christian traditions to acknowledge the truly cosmic character and profoundly universal scope of the new creation established in Jesus Christ the eternal Son of God become human. In a recent work by Australian theologian Denis Edwards, a number of contemporary voices are gathered together to bear witness to the cosmic and ecological implications of the incarnation.[1]

> An evolutionary theology, I would suggest, may picture God's descent as entering into the deepest layers of the evolutionary process, embracing and suffering with the *entire* cosmic story, not just the recent human chapters. Through the liberating power of the Spirit, God's compassion extends across the totality of time and space, enfolding and finally healing not only human suffering, but also all the epochs of evolutionary travail that preceded, and were indispensable to, our own emergence.[2]

Besides claiming inspiration from the early patristic tradition from such Fathers as Athanasius of Alexandria and Maximus the Confessor, Edwards also invokes

---

1. Denis Edwards, *How God Acts: Creation, Redemption, and Special Divine Action* (Minneapolis: Fortress Press, 2010). The book argues that the deifying transformation of matter that takes place in Christ bespeaks a thoroughgoing solidarity of God in the cosmic evolutionary process, whose deepest meaning and ultimate destiny, radically shrouded in mystery, do not necessarily include an anthropological dimension. Here the incarnation is understood as more God's way into the universe and less God's way to human beings. And so for instance the Danish theologian Niels Gregersen speaks of God's "deep incarnation" into "the very tissue of biological existence." Neil Darragh speaks of God's becoming "a complex Earth unit of minerals and fluids . . . an item in the carbon and nitrogen cycles." John Haught outlines the basic but important lineaments of this emerging cosmic theology:

2. Quoted by Edwards, *How God Acts*, 123–25.

insights from none other than Karl Rahner, and specifically in his proposal of a cosmic christology and a concomitant cosmic deification.

Our task therefore in this chapter is to ask of Rahner what this understanding of Christ as the apex of a cosmic evolutionary process through which matter finally arrives at the pinnacle of its own spiritual self-consciousness means for the interpersonal and communional aspects of deification characteristic of what we might call a more soteriocentric and anthropocentric christology. This is a question of peculiar topical interest at present in the light of global environmental and socio-ecological concerns, in which personal human interests are often viewed as a detrimental cause of global destruction. For the purposes of this book, we shall be limiting ourselves to an examination of Rahner's contribution to this cosmic and evolutionary christology, both in his initial foray into the field in his 1966 essay "Christology within an Evolutionary View of the World"[3] and in his mature and definitive work *Foundations of Christian Faith.*[4] This will also entail some analysis of the question of the purpose of the incarnation within the broader context of cosmic history, and the status of the human species within God's overall *ad extra* activity. Finally, we shall apply our findings to the question of special divine action, asking from Rahner whether the deification of the cosmos can adequately be accounted for by its own ontological structure, or whether it requires some "special" intervention that answers to the unpredictable spontaneity of divine love and that might also serve to justify the New Testament appellation "new creation."

Cur Deus Homo?

It is well known that in the history of Christian thought in the west, there have been basically two ways of answering the question *cur Deus homo factus est,* that is, the question why God became a human being. The first way, popularly associated with Anselm of Canterbury (1033–1109), is to find the motivating reason for the incarnation in the need to satisfy the demands of divine justice and pay for the human debt of sin. The second way, popularly associated with Duns Scotus (1266–1308), is to find the motivating reason for the incarnation

---

3. In Rahner, TI, vol. 5, 157–92.

4. Originally published as *Grundkurs des Glaubens: Einführung in den Begriff des Christentums* (Freiburg im Breisgau: Herder, 1976). In an interview conducted in the 1980s Rahner stated that this book contains "a summary of my theology." Karl Rahner, *I Remember: An Autobiographical Interview with Meinold Krauss* (London: SCM, 1985), 59.

not in sin but in God's eternal will to communicate his goodness to beings other than himself.

It would take us too far beyond the scope of our purposes here to fill out this very general and simplistic sketch of the question by way of a more thorough and subtle investigation of the biblical, patristic, and medieval contributions to the subject.[5] It is enough here simply to point out that it is possible to find both positions substantiated in the New Testament writings themselves. On the one hand Christ is "the Lamb of God who takes away the world's sin" (John 1:29), the "atoning sacrifice for our sins" and "the sins of the whole world" (1 John 2:2), the suffering servant who came to give his life "as a ransom for many" (Mark 10:45; cf. Isa. 53:4-6), and the sinless one who became "sin for us" to reconcile sinners to God (2 Cor. 5:21; cf. Rom. 5:6-10). In these and many similar expressions, the incarnation and especially the death of Christ are understood as the definitively atoning and redeeming divine intervention into world history on behalf of fallen humanity. On the other hand the grace that has been manifested in Christ "was given us in Christ Jesus before the beginning of time" (2 Tim. 1:9-10). He is the spotless lamb "foreknown before the foundation of the world" (1 Pet. 1:20). All creation exists "by him and for him" (Col. 1:16); indeed, he is the "firstborn of all creation" (Col. 1:15). From eternity it has been the Father's will to "bring all things in heaven and earth together under one head, even Christ" (Eph. 1:10). Such expressions subordinate creation to the incarnation in such a way that the latter constitutes the original and supreme goal of the former.

Later theologians were not insensitive to these two possible paths of interpretation, and gave voice to both. "Had man not sinned, the Son of Man would not have come," says Augustine (*Serm* 174, 2). "O happy fault, which merited so great and beautiful a Redeemer," proclaims the church in the Easter *Exultet*. Yet the Fathers were also well aware of the old Aristotelian principle of final causality, which determines that that which is last in execution can

---

5. See further Gerald O'Collins, *Jesus Our Redeemer: A Christian Approach to Salvation* (Oxford: Oxford University Press, 2007), 19–42, 133–60; D. P. Horan, "How Original Was Scotus on the Incarnation? Reconsidering the History of the Absolute Predestination of Christ in the Light of Robert Grosseteste," *Heythrop Journal* 48 (2010): 1–18; P. Gilbert, H. Kohlenberger, and E. Salmann, eds., *Cur Deus Homo*, Studia Anselmiana 128 (Rome: S. Anselmo, 1999); Joseph Ratzinger, *In the Beginning: A Catholic Understanding of the Story of Creation and the Fall* (Grand Rapids: Eerdmans, 1995), 19–39; Vladimir Lossky, "Redemption and Deification," in idem, *In the Image and Likeness of God* (London and Oxford: Mowbray, 1974), 97–110; Georges Florovsky, "Cur Deus Homo? The Motive of the Incarnation," in *Evharisterion*, ed. H. S. Alivisatos (Athens, 1957), 70–79, reprinted online at http://www.holytrinitymission.org/books/english/ theology_redemption_florovsky_e.htm#_Toc104243114, accessed October 2010.

often be first in intention. Maximus the Confessor, drawing into his elaboration several of the scriptural passages cited above, and inspired by obviously Irenaean themes, refers to the incarnation as "the blessed goal for which all things are ordained," and "the divine purpose conceived before the beginning of created beings." He goes on:

> With a clear view to this end, God created the essences of created beings. . . . Inasmuch as it leads to God, it is the recapitulation of the things he has created. It is the mystery which circumscribes all the ages, and which reveals the grand plan of God, a super-infinite plan infinitely preexisting the ages. The Logos, by essence God, became a messenger of this plan [Isa. 9:5, **LXX**] when he became a man and, if I may rightly say so, established himself as the innermost depth of the Father's goodness while also displaying in himself the very goal for which his creatures manifestly received the beginning of their existence.[6]

If we take this proposal seriously, it challenges us to reverse our usual way of thinking that the incarnation presupposes creation, let alone sin. It suggests rather that creation presupposes the incarnation, and can only be understood in its light.

All three of our theologians were inspired by this biblical and patristic stream in tradition that interpreted creation intrinsically ordered to divine incarnation—and by extension, to deification. In his book *Reality: A Synthesis of Thomistic Thought*, after briefly reviewing the history of the question, Garrigou-Lagrange ends up affirming a twofold distinction. In the order of material causality, the incarnation of the Word has a strictly redemptive purpose, and so depends on the human fall into sin. In the order of final causality, however, that is, from the perspective of what God ultimately had in mind in creating the world and human beings to begin with, the incarnation is not "subordinated" to redemption, but to the higher and transcendent revelation of God's infinite goodness.[7]

Henri de Lubac is even more explicit in proposing not just the incarnation but deification as the primary goal, one might even say the final cause, of creation. In a striking comment recorded in an as-yet unpublished archival manuscript, de Lubac refers to deification or, more specifically, to "divine

---

6. Maximus Confessor, *Quaestiones ad Thalassium* 60, 32–48 (CCSG 22, 75).

7. Réginald Garrigou-Lagrange, *Reality: A Synthesis of Thomistic Thought*, trans. Patrick Cummins (New York: Herder, 1950 [reprinted by Ex Fontibus 2007]), 171–75.

filiation," as "le but obligé de l'Univers," that is, "the necessary purpose of the universe."[8] O'Sullivan has commented on this assertion and interprets it as follows: "This means that the Incarnation is not a contingent event required by, for example, sin; it is not an after-thought. It is, rather, the supreme act of God, which is envisaged from all eternity." For de Lubac, says O'Sullivan, this means that "the Incarnation is in continuity with the creative act of God in creation," not in the sense of a mere quantitative extension, but in the sense that "it surpasses and completes it."[9]

But it is important not to misunderstand de Lubac on this point, or make him say too much. On the one hand, he affirms the view taught by Augustine and Scotus that "it is because he wills us to be one day with him that God has willed for us 'to be.' . . ." But this does not allow us to conclude "that created nature has, in the order of execution, any kind of continuity with the supernatural."[10] This qualification will become all the more important when we come to examine de Lubac's theology of nature, grace, and the supernatural.

Karl Rahner also held explicitly and clearly to this same idea, and to some extent goes even beyond de Lubac. For Rahner, deification designates an exalted degree of cosmic existence comprised by God's ontological self-communication to the spiritual creature and the gratuitously enabled, free acceptance of that communication by the spiritual subject. In his famous 1954 article "Chalkedon: Ende oder Anfang"—better known in the English-speaking world by its title "Current Problems in Christology"—Rahner posed the incarnation as the "*ontologically* (not merely 'morally', an afterthought) unambiguous goal of the movement of creation as a whole, in relation to which everything prior is merely a preparation of the scene."[11]

In later works Rahner deepens and strengthens this point. In 1966 he asserted that it was entirely permissible "to see the Incarnation first of all, in God's primary intention, as the summit and height of the divine plan of creation. . . ."[12] Both in terms of stuff and event, creation is as it were a means to an end, or as Rahner concludes in his definitive theological *summa*, "a passing moment in the process in which God becomes world. . . ." And hence,

8. "Sur la liberté du Christ," unpublished manuscript (Archives Chantraine No. 23403), quoted by Noel O'Sullivan, *Christ and Creation: Christology as the key to interpreting the theology of creation in the works of Henri de Lubac* (Bern: Peter Lang, 2009), 355.

9. O'Sullivan, *Christ and Creation*, 355.

10. Henri de Lubac, *The Mystery of the Supernatural* (New York: Crossroads, 1998), 96–97.

11. Karl Rahner, "Current Problems in Christology," TI, vol. 1, 149–200 at 165.

12. Karl Rahner, "Christology within an Evolutionary View of the World," TI, vol. 5, 185.

Rahner

> We are entirely justified in understanding creation and Incarnation not as two disparate and juxtaposed acts of God "outwards" which have their origins in two separate initiatives of God. Rather in the world as it actually is we can understand creation and Incarnation as two moments and two phases of the *one* process of God's self-giving and self-expression, although it is an intrinsically differentiated process.[13]

At first glance this might appear to be the same view as de Lubac's. The differences become more patent however when we dig a little deeper. In harmony with its dominical and apostolic foundation, the church in its creedal tradition has always been explicit in affirming the salvific, "*pro nobis*" character of the incarnation and especially of the paschal mission of Christ. Yet the question what all this means in the light of a fifteen-billion-year process of cosmic evolution in which human life seems to represent an infinitesimally minute and chance moment is surely not unimportant. It was Teilhard de Chardin who already in 1933 provocatively insisted that "[a] Christ whose features do not adapt themselves to the requirements of a world that is evolutive in structure will tend more and more to be eliminated out of hand. . . ."[14] Rahner's basic approach to christology was to ask whether and to what extent the event of the incarnation "fits" into this evolutionary framework. He tried to demonstrate that not only does the doctrine of evolution—properly understood—pose no contradiction to the Christian doctrine of the incarnation, but that there in fact lies a deep and "inner affinity" between them, a mutual relation characterized not by necessity but by a "similarity of style."[15] For to say "The Logos became flesh" is to refer "to that dimension with which the man of today is most familiar on the scientific, existential and affective plane, i.e. the dimension of our material world and of tangible history."[16]

CHRIST AND EVOLUTION

In Rahner's exposition of this relation of affinity, it is possible to note some recurring themes and emphases. First, all finite reality is marked by an inner

13. Karl Rahner, *Foundations of Christian Faith: An Introduction to the Idea of Christianity*, trans. W. V. Dych (London: Darton, Longman & Todd, 1978), 197.

14. Pierre Teilhard de Chardin, "Christology and Evolution," in idem, *Christianity and Evolution*, trans. R. Hague (London: Collins, 1971), 76–95 at 78.

15. Rahner, "Christology within an Evolutionary View," 157–58.

16. Ibid., 159.

dynamism, an impulse toward a consummating goal. This is true of beings in and of themselves, just as it is true of all beings together. The cosmos has a history, and that history is heading somewhere. Evolutionary theory supports this conception inasmuch as it proposes a line of development moving from matter through life to (human) spirit. The sphere of spirit, freedom, and culture does not leave matter behind, even if it transcends it. Human freedom "is always still supported . . . by the structures and necessities of this material world."[17] Matter itself does not contain the principle of its own transcendence, even if the dynamic orientation toward spirit is not extrinsically imposed but arises out of the very "inner being" of matter.[18] The "becoming" which is essential to cosmic evolution and human history involves not a becoming *other* but a becoming *more*. It is "the coming into being of more reality, as an effective attainment of a greater fullness of being."[19]

Second, within this inherent dynamism of the cosmos oriented toward its absolute goal, human beings hold a special and unique place. The human is "the being in whom the basic tendency of matter to find itself in the spirit by self-transcendence arrives at the point where it definitively breaks through."[20] Bound up with matter, the human is nevertheless "the self-transcendence of living matter,"[21] the concrete physical realization of cosmic self-consciousness. In their corporeality and not apart from it, each and every human being contains and expresses the whole universe, communicating with it in such a way that "through this corporeality of man taken as the other element of belonging to the spirit, the cosmos really presses forward to this self-presence in the spirit."[22]

Here Rahner brings to light a contradiction often present in the approach of the natural sciences and in their subsequent assessment of man's place in the universe. On the one hand, the human species is commonly regarded as a weak and by and large inconsequential being "exposed to a Nature quite indifferent to it and passing its existence in this world as a kind of day-fly until it is swallowed up again by 'blind' Nature which has produced it quite by accident. . . ." On the other hand, the very discipline of the empirical sciences cannot but presume, in their study of cosmic and human evolution, a certain finalistic and teleological framework according to which the scientist "concludes from

17. Ibid., 168.
18. Ibid., 164.
19. Ibid., 164.
20. Ibid., 160.
21. Ibid., 168.
22. Ibid., 170.

the result to a movement oriented towards it." To deny this implicit teleology is either to render the scientific endeavor meaningless, or else, as Rahner rightly observes, it is to fall into a version of dualism whereby the human person is regarded as an inexplicable stranger and alien in the world, an opponent of nature and a being "who exists quite apart from it."[23]

A third emphasis concerns the infinite and absolute nature of the goal toward which the cosmos is dynamically projected. If the human species constitutes a culminating point in the natural evolution of the material universe toward spirit, it must be the case that only in the human being and in the shape of human history does the cosmos press toward and arrive at its proper goal. Yet because this universe is divinely created, its ultimate goal, being in God, "remains hidden and unattainable for the natural powers of man." Herein lies the classic paradox. How can the history of human freedom and spirit, whose roots remain inseparably bound to the "pre-determined structures of the living world" arrive at a goal that utterly exceeds it, and does so not just as *more* but infinitely *other*? The self-transcendence of the cosmos must arise from the interior of its being, as an active achievement in a process of becoming. At the same time, this becoming is only consummated in the free and radical reception of absolute being itself. Referring to this paradox as an experiential "dialectic," Rahner argues that the history of cosmic self-transcendence only reaches its goal when it receives God as its innermost being and life, that is,

> when the cosmos in the spiritual creature, its goal and its height, is not merely something set apart from its [material] foundation—something created—but something which receives the ultimate self-communication of its ultimate ground itself, in that moment when this direct self-communication of God is given to the spiritual creature in what we—looking at the historical pattern of this self-communication—call grace and glory (in its consummation).[24]

In creating the world, God willed to communicate himself to it in such a way that he would become directly interior to it. But for this to take place without rendering creation incapable of *becoming*, that is, for this to take place without absolute being constituting the very nature of finite being, it is necessary that this self-communication of God be accepted by creation within the dynamism of free event. The history of the cosmos unfolds as the dialectic of God's ever more complete self-communication and creation's ever more complete

23. Ibid., 169.
24. Ibid., 168–71.

acceptance of it, climaxing definitively and irrevocably in the double-sided event of Christ. "The whole movement of this history lives only for the moment of arrival at its goal and climax—it lives only for its entry into the event which makes it irreversible—in short, it lives for the one whom we call Saviour."[25]

From this summary analysis of Rahner's argument for the congruence between christological dogma and cosmic evolution, we may come back to the concerns raised earlier as to whether Rahner too baldly posits the deification of the cosmos—its interior penetration by God—as resulting in some way from natural evolutionary processes. For Rahner, human beings are the spiritual summit of cosmic self-transcendence, and Jesus is the supreme point of human openness to God. What Christianity calls the incarnation is therefore essentially "the way in which the divinization of a spiritual creature is and must be accomplished. . . ."[26] But if this is the case, then it seems legitimate to question in what way Jesus is really and qualitatively unique, to question in what way he in fact is Savior.[27]

Rahner's insistence on the compatibility and inner affinity between christology and evolution follows from his conviction that the rationale for the incarnation is not alien to creation but already inherent in the being and becoming of the cosmos, for God created the world precisely with the incarnation in mind. The incarnation is not simply the absolutely unexpected entry of God into the world of history from outside in order to bring it to a fulfillment utterly unrelated to its own dynamic process of becoming, its own goal-directed evolution. Constantly Rahner is anxious to steer away from what he considers to be a monophysite and therefore "mythological" interpretation of the incarnation, according to which "[t]he humanity of Jesus is thought unreflexively to be the livery which God donned and in which he discloses himself and at the same time hides himself. . . ."[28] For Rahner, traditional christology is stuck between two problematic extremes. On the one hand there is the two-nature christology of Chalcedon and the Tome of Leo, which seems impossible to untangle from conceptions that envisage in Christ two centers of consciousness. On the other hand there is the more Cyrilline emphasis upon the one divine incarnate person. But this maintenance of a single, divine center of unity comes at the effective cost of Jesus' real humanity.[29] Of these two

25. Ibid., 175–76.

26. Rahner, *Foundations of Christian Faith*, 199.

27. This is in fact precisely the nub of von Balthasar's concern with Rahner's evolutionary christology. See Hans Urs von Balthasar, *The Moment of Christian Witness* (San Francisco: Ignatius, 1994), 100–109.

28. Rahner, *Foundations of Christian Faith*, 290.

29. Rahner, *Foundations of Christian Faith*, 290–92.

polarities, Rahner would rather err on the side of the former, for it is less mythological and more rationally coherent. "Perhaps it is possible to be an orthodox Nestorian or an orthodox Monophysite. If this were the case, then I would prefer to be an orthodox Nestorian."[30] By contrast, Rahner judges that the more Cyrilline emphasis on the divine personhood of Christ, which as we saw in the previous chapter so centrally controlled the christology of Garrigou-Lagrange, tends to

> overlook the fact that the man Jesus *in* his human reality exists with a created, active and "existentiell" center of activity vis-à-vis God and in an absolute difference from him. He prays, he is obedient, he comes to be historically, he makes free decisions, and in a process of genuine historical development he also has new experiences which surprise him, and these are clearly in evidence in the New Testament. But to overlook this is basically to have a mythological understanding of the Incarnation. . . .[31]

Moving beyond both of these traditional approaches, a christology from an evolutionary perspective affirms that Jesus, like all human beings, is a being with a history, an evolutionary history in which matter, life, and the cosmos are bound together in a dynamic yet homogeneous solidarity. His uniqueness consists in the fact that he is at once both the most fully evolved human being and the climactic summit of God's radical self-communication to what is not Godself. Jesus is both a part of cosmic history and the definitive self-expression of God. Rahner states it this way:

> This is a fact stated in the Christian dogma: Jesus is a true man; he is truly a part of the earth, truly a moment in the biological evolution of this world, a moment of natural history, for he is born of woman; he is a man who in his spiritual, human and finite subjectivity is just like us, a receiver of that self-communication of God by grace which we affirm of all men—and hence of the cosmos—as the climax of development in which the world comes absolutely into its own presence and into the direct presence of God.[32]

---

30. Karl Rahner, *Karl Rahner in Dialogue*, ed. P. Imhof and H. Biallowons, trans. H. Egan (New York: Crossroad, 1986), 126–27.

31. Rahner, *Foundations of Christian Faith*, 292.

32. Rahner, "Christology within an Evolutionary View," 176.

The Jesuit hereby may be understood as trying to naturalize Jesus and profoundly humanize the Christ of traditional christology, in a way that remains in keeping with that tradition's basic intuitions and trajectory. Rahner recognizes in the gnostic aversion to the real fact of God's becoming material not only "the most dangerous heresy against which primitive Christianity had to fight," but a perennial spirit against which the theologian must constantly do battle.[33] In Jesus, God who is infinite being appropriates finite human nature as his own, making of himself, in that nature, a being that becomes and (thus) evolves. The Logos "bears the matter just as much as the soul, and this matter is a part of the reality and the history of the cosmos." And again,

> The divine Logos himself both really creates and accepts this corporeality—which is a part of the world—*as his* own reality; he brings it into existence as something other than himself in such a way, therefore, that this very materiality expresses *him*, the Logos himself, and lets him be present in his world.[34]

THE UNIQUENESS OF JESUS

In order to bring this chapter to a close, it will be helpful to consider a number of questions that more precisely attempt to relate the discussion so far to the question of human and cosmic deification. Is Christ truly God, or is he simply a deified human being, and is there a difference? How is his "deification" to be understood? How is it communicated to other beings, and in what sense does the incarnation mediate deification to the whole creation?

According to Rahner, there are a number of necessary conditions for humanity to be deified, understood as the self-transcendence of the cosmos into God by means of God's absolute self-communication. For human beings to attain their consummation, three conditions stand out in particular. First, this deification must take place as a tangible, concrete phenomenon in cosmic history; it cannot be an a-cosmic event. Second, as a corollary of the first, it must come into existence precisely within, and not despite of or apart from, human sociality and interrelationality. Third, it must be irrevocable, definitively constituted for all time, and not just a temporary offer or passing phase.[35]

33. Ibid., 177.
34. Ibid., 177.
35. Ibid., 181–82.

And this, argues Rahner, is just what we have in the hypostatic union. There is only one hypostatic union, which alone justifies the *communicatio idiomatum*—the reciprocal predication of divine and human properties of the one subject, Jesus Christ. In him, the world encounters a finite medium which is not other than God, not just "posited by God," but is God himself. It is this factor that makes the divine self-manifestation and self-communication in Jesus irrevocable, definitive, and unsurpassable. Prior to Christ, God's self-manifestations take place via finite media, but always in such a way that those media remain transitory and distinct from God, and thereby able to be revoked or surpassed. For the revelation to be definitive and absolute, the finite media must belong absolutely to God himself; they must not just be "his," but "him." There must be a hypostatic union.

It is in this sense that the incarnation may rightly be regarded as "an absolutely proper and new rung in the hierarchy of world-realities which quite simply surpasses all the world-realities given so far or to be given in the future."[36] But Rahner is also deeply concerned to understand how this unique world-reality relates to the rest of world reality. Does Jesus represent

> a *proper*, still higher stage of an essentially newer and higher kind of divine self-communication to the creature, which this time is given only in one single "case"? Or is it possible to conceive that, even though this Hypostatic Union is given only once in its essential characteristics, it is nevertheless precisely the way in which the divinization of the spiritual creature is and *must* be carried out if it is to happen at all?[37]

What then distinguishes the case of Jesus from the way deification unfolds in other human beings? For Rahner, "the Hypostatic Union does not differ from our grace by what is pledged in it, for this is grace in both cases (even in the case of Jesus). But it differs from our grace by the fact that Jesus is our pledge, and we ourselves are not the pledge but the recipients of God's pledge to us." In the bodily human reality who is Jesus, the world possesses within the living drama of its own history and structure the whole of God, and with him, his absolute saving purpose, "absolutely and irrevocably present."[38] It is from this perspective that we can better appreciate the meaning of Rahner's assertion that in the incarnation, "the world becomes the history of God himself."[39]

---

36. Ibid., 180.
37. Ibid., 179.
38. Ibid., 183.

As for how this unique event relates definitively to the rest of human and cosmic history, part of the difficulty lies in our limited and myopic vision of the spatio-temporal horizon. Whereas it has often been the case that the incarnation of the Word has been understood as taking place at a point fairly late in world history, at "the eleventh hour" as it were, it is also possible to envision the incarnation as an event that has taken place right near the very beginning of human history,

> as the beginning of a new epoch, as the new foundation of a Church which is to expand only slowly in an unforeseeably long history, and as the beginning of a leavening process within the very matter of world-history, a raw material which only this divinization of the world—which seems to begin with Christ—can change from an unformed material into the form God really intends it to have.[40]

Rahner, acknowledging this perspective as traditional, seeks to clarify and extend it in a number of aspects. Initially, his proposal appears naïve. He believes that, without falling into utopianism, the cosmocentricity characterizing the mythological worldview of times past should properly give way to an anthropocentric period characterized by man's technological manipulation of the material world in aid of his developing self-transcendence. In view of the post-Cartesian mechanization of the world and the subsequent abolition of humanity and nature at the hands of technology and industrial domination, such an expression can only appear to us now as curiously shortsighted and optimistic. On the other hand, Rahner affirms that Christ is indeed the beginning of the end. In him is present the *telos* of all ages past and future. Humanity's ultimate consummation lies not in its intramundane achievements, but in a form of life received from God in Christ and realized concretely in communion with him. Yet this does not render world history expendable or obsolete. While christology does not specify any definite course for human history, nor the gospel plot the chart for a political or social program,

> man can realize his transcendental future, his attainment of God in himself, only by means of the material of this world and its history, i.e. also by exposing himself to, and either holding his own or failing in, this intramundane future with both the happiness and death necessarily attendant on it. To this extent, the promise of a

39. Ibid., 186.
40. Ibid., 188–89.

supra-historical consummation in the absoluteness of God himself—a promise given together with Christology—does not diminish man's task in this world but provides it with its ultimate dignity, urgency and danger.[41]

For all the real continuity between many of these assertions and the definitive christological expressions of the Christian church, the question that lingers is whether Rahner tends too much to "anthropologize" christology, as von Balthasar has put it.[42] It is not an evolutionary christology itself which presents the problem (just as an evolutionary creation theology may have its own relative legitimacy), but one in which the difference *in kind* between Christ and the rest of us is finally reduced to a difference *of degree*. In this respect, the critical observation of de Lubac with positive reference to the evolutionary christology of Teilhard de Chardin is especially apposite:

> Only by holding fast to the dogma of Chalcedon—Christ's divine humanity in its qualitative difference from the grace given to all other men—do Christians have the opportunity, but also the responsibility, of recognizing and showing humanity the way out of the dead-ends of evolution.[43]

This judgment is not adduced here in order to render all that Rahner has proposed in this chapter null and void. It is meant rather to indicate the potential shortcomings in any approach to the givens of salvation history that seeks to ameliorate or even domesticate those elements in it that come across as alien and ill-fitted to the contemporary scientific or philosophical worldview, which is anyway always liable itself of proving to be a passing fad. Any such approach, if sustained, will finally reduce the supernatural to a function of the natural.[44]

I have shown how Rahner attempts to provide a somewhat sophisticated but nonetheless engaging account of the way christology both "fits into" an evolutionary view of the cosmos and makes sense within the context of the

41. Ibid., 191.

42. Von Balthasar, *The Moment of Christian Witness*, 86.

43. As paraphrased by von Balthasar in Hans Urs von Balthasar, *The Theology of Henri de Lubac: An Overview* (San Francisco: Ignatius, 1991), 88–89.

44. "Defenselessness in the face of the world means above all the relinquishing of a security system that man imposes and controls between the realms of the natural and the supernatural by means of a metaphysical panoramic view of the universe stretching from Alpha (or, rather, Atom) to Omega. For it is absolutely certain that in such a system the supernatural will soon be reduced to a function of the natural." Von Balthasar, *The Moment of Christian Witness*, 137.

wider plan of God in creating the world with a view to its transcendent goal. His goal in doing so is to demythologize the Christian story, to extract and preserve from all the time-bound trappings of Christian narrative and history an essential kernel that "makes sense" of the universe as it appears to the post-Christian mindset. One may wonder whether there is the danger in this approach that Rahner does not leave enough to what Hans Urs von Balthasar has often referred to as the "self-interpreting" character of the incarnation. This term, which derives from the use of the verb *exegeomai*—from which we get the word "exegesis"—used in John 1:18, expresses the conviction that the rationale behind the incarnation cannot be worked out in advance, whether historically nor logically, as an *a priori* condition calling for a certain kind of necessary fulfillment, nor can it be extracted and separated out from the concrete "mythological" mode in which it is historically embodied and embedded (narrative, gospel, liturgy, sacraments), but becomes manifest only by faith-filled engagement with the self-interpreting drama of Christ himself as he fulfills his ministry and lives his personal history as Son of God and Savior. The perennial Christian claim is that in the incarnation we witness what theologian Gerald O'Collins calls special divine action, "divine activity that is distinct from the normal intentions and power that 'God manifests in creating and conserving the universe.'"[45] By drawing the incarnation into such close proximity with the process of cosmic evolution toward self-consciousness and spirit in human nature, Rahner may have unduly paved the way toward an idealist philosophical interpretation of Christianity—already held by Leibniz and so staunchly criticized by Hans Urs von Balthasar—in which "special divine action" is reduced to an epiphenomenon of natural cosmological and historical processes. For Leibniz, says von Balthasar, "the cosmological horizon no longer serves to provide evidence for Christianity, but has instead absorbed Christianity into itself without a trace."[46] According to this idealist interpretation, the indubitable facts upon which Christianity is founded may retain a certain positive role within spatio-temporal history, but "make sense" only as an "outward shell covering the inner religious dimension of mankind."[47] The Christian religion in this scheme "gives man nothing that he would not

---

45. Gerald O'Collins, "Critical Issues," in *The Incarnation: An Interdisciplinary Symposium on the Incarnation of the Son of God*, ed. S. T. Davis, D. Kendall, and G. O'Collins (Oxford: Oxford University Press, 2002), 11; quoting C. Stephen Evans, *The Historical Christ and the Jesus of Faith: The Incarnational Narrative as History* (Oxford: Oxford University Press, 1996), 143.

46. Hans Urs von Balthasar, *Love Alone Is Credible*, trans. D. C. Schindler (San Francisco: Ignatius, 2004), 28.

47. Von Balthasar, *Love Alone Is Credible*, 29.

have been able to get from himself, . . . only it gives it to him more quickly and easily."[48]

In his defense it can be asserted that Rahner purported to know the difference between idealism and realism. To be sure, his foray into the relation between christology and evolution "projected the idea of a possible Incarnation from the formal scheme of a world-evolution which reaches its climax in God's communication of himself." But he acknowledges that such a projection is possible only by virtue of what he knows already from the *fact* of the incarnation. "The *idea* of the God-man and the acknowledgement of Jesus and of no one else as the one, unique and real God-man are two quite different perceptions. Only this second perception, which is one of faith, makes one a Christian."[49] To Rahner's mind, it is just this distinction that lends weight to his proposal that human deification, and with it, the deification of the cosmos embodied and culminated in human beings, does not depend on this or that idea but on the contingent facts of human and cosmic history, that is, depends on a reality at once divine and internal to the world. May we detect here an openness to a supra-rational, more mythological form of theological realism after all? It is not impossible to find in this rather dense closing assertion an implicit admission to that end:

> Within our briefly outlined ground-scheme in which the spirit is not something alien in the material world but is the factor by which this bodily reality itself becomes present to itself, all that has really to be made clear is that only a concrete bodily reality—and not a universal idea—can really save and be eternally valid—and that Christianity cannot really be an "Idealism" if it is properly understood. The act of grasping the concrete reality of this determined man and seeing that it is the reality of the saving God-man is other and more than the *a-priori* projection of the idea of a God-man conceived as the basic ground of a divinized humanity as a whole and as the basic ground in which the world reaches God himself.[50]

---

48. Von Balthasar, *Love Alone Is Credible*, 29, quoting Gotthold Ephraim Lessing (1729–1781).

49. Rahner, "Christology within an Evolutionary View," 187–88.

50. Ibid., 188.

8

Deification and Ordinary Life

Réginald Garrigou-Lagrange was well into his thirties when he published his first essay. So was Henri de Lubac. Karl Rahner was only twenty-two. Admittedly, it was just a simple piece of pious reflection, brief and unpretentious, devotional rather than academic. It asks what the heart of the Christian should be like, and how it is possible to gain real Christ-like love and sacrificing power. In answer it proposes prayer, through which the human person draws near to God, becomes capable of "touching our Creator and Lord," and is subsequently filled with his grace, his Spirit, his love.[1] Such thoughts may seem to have little connection with the more sophisticated Rahner of later renown, with his high-minded Heideggerian terminology, complex scholastic categories, and provocative ecclesial stance. Yet when read in hindsight, this brief reflection from Rahner's youth indicates a conviction and a set of concerns that in point of fact were to mark his lifelong intention as a theologian and priest. Harvey D. Egan, who characterizes Rahner's entire theological project as more sapiential or mystagogal than intellectual or academic, has drawn attention to the "imbalance" present in many early Rahnerian studies, which focused almost exclusively on his philosophical and speculative theology and neglected the pastoral concerns and spiritual dimensions that pervade it throughout.[2] In the words of Rahner's famous exhortation delivered in the name of St. Ignatius of Loyola, which on his eightieth birthday Rahner looked back upon as his best work and the fitting "resumé" of all his theology and life's ideals, his greatest desire was to help souls to attain a direct and immediate experience of God.[3] He wanted his spiritual

1. Karl Rahner, *Sehnsucht nach dem geheimnisvollen Gott: Profil-Bilder-Texte*, ed. H. Vorgrimler (Freiburg: Herder, 1990), 78–80. ET in Karl Rahner, *Spiritual Writings*, ed. P. Endean (Maryknoll, NY: Orbis, 2004), 31–33.

2. H. D. Egan, "Theology and Spirituality," in *The Cambridge Companion to Karl Rahner*, ed. D. Marmion and M. E. Hines (Cambridge: Cambridge University Press, 2005), 13–28.

writings to be regarded "not as secondary by-products of a theology that is sort of an art for art's sake, but at least as important as my specifically theological works."[4] "[B]ehind everything I have done there stands an immediate pastoral and spiritual interest."[5] All of Rahner's theology, and with it, his doctrine of deification under examination here, can only rightly be understood and interpreted in the light of this express pastoral and practical aim, expressed most lucidly and emphatically in his plentiful spiritual writings made up in the main of sermons, retreats, reflections, meditations, and prayers.

Accordingly, this chapter will draw from the wide range of Rahner's spiritual writings from right across his career in order piece by piece to build up a discernible outline of what deification may actually "look like" in the concrete circumstances and actions of temporal human life. Of course, as Rahner himself would point out, deification is never complete this side of the grave. But a divine life has already begun here, and so it is not too much to expect it to take some bodily and historical shape in the form of various personal and communal practices and conscious experiential manifestations. While such elements as prayer, sacramental participation, and ecclesial incorporation obviously feature in Rahner's description of authentic spiritual life, what is most noticeable in his account is the way in which he locates the momentous transformation wrought by union with God in the ordinary things of life: work, routine, suffering, and finally, death. For on account of the incarnation, an event with decisive and ongoing implications, even the most trivial details in the human situation have been drawn into the drama of God's self-bestowal, so that God may indeed be found, in typically Ignatian fashion, in all things.

Having drawn together this outline of Rahner's spiritual theology, in which we shall find deification more often featuring as an implicit rather than explicit theme, we shall offer some brief concluding comments.

God in the Ordinary

As we have seen, it belongs to Rahner's notion of *Vorgriff* that every human experience at the level of the categorical somehow penetrates beyond the categorical and touches the limitless and transcendent. The incarnation of the

---

3. Karl Rahner, "Ignatius of Loyola Speaks to a Modern Jesuit," in K. Rahner and P. Imhof, *Ignatius of Loyola* (London: Collins, 1979), 9–38. See the late Rahner's reflections on this work in Karl Rahner, *Faith in a Wintry Season: Conversations and Interviews with Karl Rahner in the Last Years of His Life*, ed. P. Imhof and H. Biallowons, trans. H. D. Egan (New York: Crossroad, 1991), 104.

4. Rahner, *Faith in a Wintry Season*, 19.

5. Rahner, *Faith in a Wintry Season*, 18.

eternal Word of God has brought it about that the human encounter with absolute mystery takes place precisely within the categorical; it does not call for a departure from the world of sense and temporality. Karen Kilby has shown how "Rahner insists that transcendental experience does not occur *apart from* categorical experience—we do not have an experience of God neat, all on its own, but always only *in* our experiencing of the concrete, categorical realities."[6] This claim stands at certain odds with other assessments that criticize Rahner's theology for being too abstract, individualist, and disconnected from the stuff of everyday life. According to Fergus Kerr, "Rahner's most characteristic theological profundities are embedded in an extremely mentalist–individualist epistemology of unmistakably Cartesian provenance. Central to his whole theology . . . is the possibility for the individual to occupy a standpoint beyond . . . immersion in the bodily, the historical and the institutional. . . ."[7] It seems to me that such a view is justified if one reads only Rahner's more technical dogmatic and philosophical works, especially those from the earlier period of his life, before the Heideggerian resonances waned.[8] But as soon as one enters the world of his spiritual and pastoral writings, it becomes much clearer that Rahner invests not just the sacramental and symbolic but even the most ordinary and routine physical and temporal dimensions of human experience with extraordinary spiritual and salvific value. As Egan explains:

> To Rahner, we weave the fabric of our eternal lives out of our humdrum daily lives. A genuine Christian must have the bold, but often hidden confidence that ordinary daily life is the stuff of authentic life and real Christianity. It is instructive to note how often the words "ordinary," "banal," "humdrum," "routine," and the like show up in Rahner's writings. For him, grace is actually experienced and has its history in the person's everyday existence.[9]

6. Karen Kilby, *Karl Rahner: A Brief Introduction* (New York: Crossroad, 2007), 8.

7. Fergus Kerr, *Theology after Wittgenstein* (Oxford: Blackwell, 1986), 14.

8. In 1974 we find Rahner doubting whether anyone could detect "any Heideggerian influences on me now, aside from some rather abstract philosophical structures that one might problematically call transcendental method." Rahner, *Faith in a Wintry Season*, 16. Similarly in 1979 Rahner in an interview "distanced himself from any 'great influence' of Heidegger on his theology and insisted that Ignatian spirituality was 'more significant and important' in shaping his approach than 'all learned philosophy and theology.'" See M. P. Gallagher, "Ignatian Dimensions of Rahner's Theology," *Louvain Studies* 29 (2004): 77–91 at 77.

9. H. D. Egan, "Theology and Spirituality," 20. See also Egan's book-length study of Rahner's concept of everyday mysticism. H. D. Egan, *Karl Rahner: The Mystic of Everyday Life* (New York: Crossroad, 1998).

Rahner's spiritual writings and sermons offer us numerous examples of the way he presses his hearers to face up to mundane reality rather than try to escape it, and to do so in the belief that grace is there to be experienced where, going by appearances alone, it may seem least evident. Many Christians feel bored and disgusted with their lives, secretly despairing over days and weeks of wasted time, superficial thoughts and acts, empty musings, trivial routines. The perennial temptation is to fill up the void created by such emptiness and despair with frenetic activity, entertainment, and distraction, some of which can present itself in the form of pious pursuits. But Rahner would counsel patience, not flight. It is wrong to think we must abandon the world of the ordinary and routine, for that is just where God has located himself to be found. "God must be sought and found in the things of our world. By regarding our daily duties as something performed for the honor and glory of God we can convert what was hitherto soul-killing monotony to a living worship of God in all our actions. Everyday life must become itself our prayer."[10] It is in the ordinariness of one's own being and existence that one finds "the grace in which God himself dwells in all his immediacy."[11]

These simple thoughts are expressed further with especial energy in a number of sermons for Easter and Ascension. Easter is not simply a past event for Rahner, but carries radical implications for "ordinary" day-to-day existence. "The alleluia is not for what was; Easter proclaims a beginning which has already decided the remotest future. The resurrection means that the beginning of glory has already started."[12] In the death of Jesus, God entered into the innermost center of the world in order to establish his divine life in its deepest depths, with the result that his divine heart pervades all that is, actively bringing it to its final and glorious goal. This is what the church's proclamation of the resurrection means:

> The transfiguration of the world is no ideal, no postulate, but a reality. The history of nature with all its developments and self-transcendence has already—though for the moment only in its first exemplar—reached its unsurpassable culmination: material reality which, wholly transfigured, is for eternity the glorious body of

10. Karl Rahner, *The Content of Faith: The Best of Karl Rahner's Theological Writings*, ed. K. Lehmann and A. Raffelt, trans. H. D. Egan (New York: Crossroad, 1993), 511.

11. Karl Rahner, "Ignatius of Loyola Speaks to a Modern Jesuit," in Karl Rahner and Paul Imhof, *Ignatius of Loyola* (London: Collins, 1979), 15.

12. In Karl Rahner, *The Great Church Year: The Best of Karl Rahner's Homilies, Sermons, and Meditations*, ed. A. Raffelt, trans. H. D. Egan (New York: Crossroad, 1995), 189.

God. The most tremendous and definitive self-transcendence of the material world (through the grace-given power of God alone, of course) has already taken place. It has leapt beyond itself into the infinity of God's spirituality and, in this upward flight into God's immeasurable flame, it has not been consumed but has survived, definitively transfigured.[13]

If the world and all material reality have already been definitively and irrevocably caught up in this drama of transfiguration, then nothing in them can in principle be closed or sealed off from deifying potential. Christ rises and ascends to the Father not to depart from this world, still less to take us away from it, but to seal and confirm the insertion of this world into his own unbounded life:

> [H]e did not rise in order finally to depart from hence, not so that the travail of death which gave birth to him anew might transfer him to the life and light of God and he would leave behind him the dark bosom of the earth empty and without hope. For he rose again on his *body*. That means he has already begun to transform this world into himself. He has accepted the world forever. He has been born again as a child of the earth, but of the transfigured, liberated earth, the earth which in him is eternally confirmed and eternally redeemed from death and futility. . . . When we confess him as having ascended to God's heaven, that is only another expression for the fact that he withdraws from us for awhile the tangible manifestation of his glorified humanity and above all that there is no longer any abyss between God and the world.[14]

We may note in these passages a theme highlighted in the previous chapter, namely, the way materiality features so prominently in Rahner's account of the world's deification. The bodily resurrection of Jesus adumbrates the physical transfiguration of the entire material universe in God. There is no need to leave the world and its categorical limits. To do so would be to run away from ourselves, and from the God who has appropriated our human existence and the world we inhabit as his very own. "We therefore do not need to leave it [the world]. For God's life dwells in it. . . . For in our Lord's resurrection God has shown that he has taken the earth to himself forever."[15] At this point Rahner

13. Rahner, *The Great Church Year*, 190–91.

14. Ibid., 194–96.

quotes from Tertullian's famous axiom: *caro cardo salutis.* "The flesh is the hinge of salvation." He explains:

> The reality beyond all the distress of sin and death is not up yonder; it has come down and dwells in the innermost reality of our flesh. The sublimest religious sentiment of flight from the world would not bring the God of our life and of the salvation of this earth down from the remoteness of his eternity and would not reach him in that other world of his.
>
> But he has come to us himself. He has transformed what we are and what despite everything we still tend to regard as the gloomy earthly residue of our spiritual nature: our flesh.[16]

All this is accomplished fact, given reality. Yet one thing is still needed "for his action, which we can never undo, to become the benediction of our human reality."[17] Even having heard the gospel, many faced with the discord of their own existence may yet lose courage and choose not to face it. Although faith discerns the reality that divine love is at the center of the world and that the risen Christ is the Lord of history, every human being is eventually confronted with the overwhelming appearance that evil reigns and that the world's misery is unending. Again, the answer is not to run away from the apparent absurdity and inevitable suffering of human existence. While it is God alone who can redeem humanity from the ever-present power of death, he does so not from the outside like some superhuman redeemer portrayed in the gnostic myths, but from within the very vulnerability of our mortal existence. Rahner's proclamation of this remarkable dynamic amply illustrates the pastoral spirit in which it is intended:

> He must break open the tomb of our hearts. He must rise from the center of our being also, where he is present as power and as promise. There he is still in movement. There it is still Holy Saturday until the last day which will be the universal Easter of the cosmos. And that resurrection takes place under the freedom of our faith. Even so it is *his* deed. But an action of his which takes place as our own, as an action of loving belief which takes us up into the tremendous

15. Ibid., 196.
16. Ibid., 196–97.
17. Ibid., 197.

movement of all earthly reality toward its own glory, which has begun in Christ's resurrection.[18]

The Drama of Human Experience

When we come across the word "drama" or "dramatic" as a descriptive category in contemporary theology, we are more likely to associate it with the name of Hans Urs von Balthasar than with that of Karl Rahner. Both von Balthasar and Rahner were indebted to Ignatian spirituality for their respective theological worldviews, and excellent studies have been published demonstrating the connections, but would it be appropriate to describe Rahner's theology of human experience as dramatic?[19] Werner Löser has argued that of three main approaches to interpreting the Ignatian *Exercises*—the ascetic, the mystical, and the dramatic—von Balthasar's "dramatic" approach is unique to him. By contrast, Löser associates Rahner with the "mystical" interpretation, which goes back to the seventeenth-century Jesuit Louis Lallemant and has now by and large replaced the "ascetical" one, identifying him as one of its best-known modern-day heirs.[20] Harvey D. Egan has surveyed a number of contemporary Ignatian commentators, from Przywara and Fessard to Bakker and Mendoza, not to mention both Hugo and Karl Rahner. While Egan does not use the words "drama" or "dramatic" in connection with Rahner's Ignatian mysticism, he shows the way Rahner envisages the path through conversion to union with God to be bound up with an interactive movement of procession into the concrete drama of life in the world and return to oneself.

> K. Rahner emphasizes that the response to the ever-present, ever-loving immediacy of God through a personal conversion in faith,

18. Ibid.

19. On von Balthasar, see Werner Löser, "Hans Urs von Balthasar and Ignatius Loyola," *The Way* 44, no. 4 (2005): 115–30; J. Servais, *Théologie des Exercices spirituels: H. U. von Balthasar interprète saint Ignace* (Paris: Culture et verité, 1996); W. Löser, "The Ignatian Exercises in the Work of Hans Urs von Balthasar," in *Hans Urs von Balthasar: His Life and Work*, ed. D. L. Schindler (San Francisco: Ignatius, 1991), 103–22. On Rahner, see M. P. Gallagher, "Ignatian Dimensions of Rahner's Theology," *Louvain Studies* 29 (2004): 77–91; P. Endean, *Karl Rahner and Ignatian Spirituality* (Oxford: Oxford University Press, 2001); A. Zahlauer, *Karl Rahner und sein "produktives Vorbild" Ignatius von Loyola* (Innsbruck: Tyrolia, 1996); H. D. Egan, *Karl Rahner: The Mystic of Everyday Life*, 28–54.

20. Gallagher, "Ignatian Dimensions of Rahner's Theology," 83, mentions an "ascetical emphasis" in Rahner's earliest expositions of Ignatian piety, but confirms a shift to a more mystagogal approach after the 1950s.

hope and love can never be separated from the concrete, historical realization of this conversion through specific action in one's daily life.[21]

To know God and his grace with the mind, even the mind illuminated by revelation and assenting by faith, is not sufficient, or rather, not sufficiently "dramatic." The Christian is more than a mind; she is an incarnate spirit, a person with a body and a history and a life to be integrated into "the transcending adventure of human freedom."[22] Divine realities must therefore be known, as Ignatius himself put it, with "an inner feeling and tasting" (*el sentir y gustar de las cosas internamente*).[23] For Rahner, the experience of grace and the Spirit is not had in splendid isolation from the dramatic and often messy details of mortal existence. Nor is it exclusively confined to the explicit means of grace instituted by God and operative in the Church. In the drama of trying to love God even when we don't feel like it, in the drama of feeling suffocated by life's pressures and unable to escape, in the drama of protracted illness and the looming specter of death, Rahner believes it is possible to taste something of

> he experience of eternity, the experience that spirit is more than a piece of this temporal world, the experience that the meaning of man is not exhausted in the meaning and happiness of this world, the experience of risk and venturesome trust which has no provable justification deducible from mere worldly success, in short and finally: the experience of God, the experience of the descent of the Holy Spirit which became a reality in Christ through his incarnation and his sacrifice on the cross.[24]

In the simple "trivialities" of Jesus' human life "we had everything—everything incarnate: we had God, his mercy, his grace and his nearness. The eternal Word of the Father compressed himself into our flesh."[25] In the same way, the simple "trivialities" of our own lives bear within themselves the same divine riches,

21. H. D. Egan, *The Spiritual Exercises and the Ignatian Mystical Horizon* (St. Louis: Institute of Jesuit Sources, 1976), 14. See also H. D. Egan, *Karl Rahner: The Mystic of Everyday Life*, 28–79.

22. This is the phrase with which Gallagher characterizes Rahner's vision of the life of faith in contrast to viewing faith as simple assent to truth. See Gallagher, "Ignatian Dimensions of Rahner's Theology," 79.

23. Ignatius of Loyola, *Spiritual Exercises* 2, quoted in Gallagher, "Ignatian Dimensions of Rahner's Theology," 78–79.

24. Karl Rahner, *Christian at the Crossroads* (London: Burns & Oates, 1977), 60–61.

25. Rahner, *The Great Church Year*, 202.

even if they are often hidden from our unstudied gaze. As Egan remarks, "In our daily lives we often overlook or take for granted the divine life we in fact dwell within and experience."[26] Would-be Christians need not go off and manufacture some "other" drama with their life, one allegedly more spiritual or more interesting. Their life and actions will yield fruit only when they first accept and begin to take responsibility for the living drama that is their own life now. If I cannot find God in my "daily drudge" (*Alltag*), it is not because God is not there to be found, but because I have allowed myself to be blinded by false appearances:

> When I think of the hours that I spend at your altar or saying your Church's office, then I realize that it's not worldly business that makes my days a drudge, but me—I can change even these sacred actions into hours of drudgery. It's *me* who makes my days drudgery, not the other way around. And thus I realize that if there can ever be a way for me to you, then it leads through my daily drudge. To get away to you without my daily drudge is something I could do only if, in this holy escape, I could leave myself behind.[27]

The discovery of God is not like the discovery of some necessary truth or objective empirical fact. It calls for interpersonal encounter, for action and decision, for surrender. This is why there is no fail-safe "method" or circumstance for encountering God, for it is a meeting involving two freedoms. Depending on the state of the human heart, God can be found—and lost!—in everything.

> My God, if we can lose you in everything—if neither prayer, nor a sacred celebration, nor the silence of the cloister, nor disillusionment about everything in general can of themselves forestall this danger, then even these holy, non-everyday things still belong to the daily drudge.[28]

How is it possible for a person to rescue herself from the dramatic ruin of losing God? If through the blindness and inattention of my heart I can lose God and miss his presence even in those holy means of grace which proclaim him with clarity, if, while immersed in prayer, sacraments, and holy works, I can fall into

---

26. Egan, "Theology and Spirituality," 19.

27. Rahner, *Spiritual Writings*, 46.

28. Ibid., 47.

pride, hypocrisy, and despair, how will I find him in the ordinary drama of life, filled as it is with things and events that seem most unlikely and unsuitable tokens of anything remotely divine? Rahner answers:

> My God, only through you. Only through you can I be an "inward" person. Only through you am I with you within myself even as I am turning outward in order to be among things. Neither *Angst* nor nothingness nor death free me from being lost in the things of the world . . . but only your love, love for you, you who are the goal drawing all things, you who satisfy, you who are sufficient to yourself. . . . In your love, all turning outward to the daily drudge becomes a retreat into your unity, which is eternal life.[29]

True *metanoia*—repentance and conversion—is therefore more often than not accomplished by means of the raw materials necessary for daily social existence: genuine acts of self-criticism, admission of guilt and indolence, request for pardon, rejection of injustice, readiness to confront harsh truths about one's own life, and so on. Compared to the church's sacrament of penance, says Rahner, such ordinary acts "can be just as much salvific events of metanoia, provided that they are recognized (more or less thematically) as God's work and are experienced (again, more or less thematically) as God-given, as the grace of forgiveness and the bestowal of life."[30]

Reflecting on these passages, the question arises whether Rahner overly relativizes the means of grace, which the church has always regarded as divinely privileged and performative acts bearing the objective revelatory and salvific actions of God. At the very least Rahner seems to relegate them to a secondary role, in favor of a more primordial existential encounter with God. God is infinitely beyond all symbolic categories, even those of Christian revelation and dogma: they serve not as ends in themselves but to initiate us into what is ultimately limitless. "The clearest and most lucid formulation, the holiest formula, the classical concentration of the Church's centuries of work in prayer, thought, and struggle about the mysteries of God—these draw their life, then, from the fact that they are beginning and not end, means and not goal, *one* truth that makes freedom for the—ever greater—Truth."[31] Rahner acknowledges that God has provided abundant irrigating waters, "intended to soak the land of the

---

29. Ibid., 49.

30. Rahner, *Christian at the Crossroads*, 76.

31. Karl Rahner, "Current Problems in Christology" (1954), in TI, vol. 1, 149–200 at 149.

soul," in the church, the word, and the sacraments. But these external forms are intended only to awaken and call forth the fountain that arises from within:

> [A]ny appeal from outside to God's name is only an attempt to clarify God's inner promise of himself. . . . [S]uch indoctrinations and such imperatives from without, such channelling of grace from without, are ultimately only of use if they meet the final grace from within.[32]

Such comments give us reason for pause. Is this not too agnostic and deprecatory? Is it not tending too much toward an extreme apophaticism, a mode of theologizing according to which, even in the vision of beatitude, God remains the great unknown, the bottomless abyss, the forever unreachable? Does it not sit at odds with the perennial claim of Christianity that its most central symbols and categories, on account of the fact that they are not just human approximations to the divine but actually God-given, do grant access to the innermost being of God? The humanity of Jesus, the triune name, the ministry of the church, the sacramental elements: when appropriated in faith these very human realities are found to be impregnated with divine presence and power. It is surely true that God can be found anywhere and everywhere. Yet the real question is not simply where *can* God be found, but where does God *want* to be found? Where has he in fact given himself to be found? God's self-limitation to the revealed means of grace is his way of accommodating himself to the limitations of our historical and bodily condition. This is what is meant by sacramentality. In the person of the Word made flesh, and especially in his passion and death, the living God has penetrated the very extremities of creation, so that he can be found even in the dark shadow of godforsakenness and death. But take the light of Christ away, go there alone, and what is left in these experiences but radical ambiguity and doubt?

Rahner was well aware how his doctrine of the immediate experience of God may raise questions concerning the claims of historical revelation. His defense was that he was ultimately concerned for the modern atheist or agnostic who is offended by the particularity of Christianity when it points its finger to certain concrete realities with no apparent connection to this or that person's immediate experience and says: there is God.[33] Yet despite his praiseworthy concern to give a credible answer to this mindset, which Rahner believes poses

---

32. Rahner, "Ignatius of Loyola Speaks to a Modern Jesuit," 16.

33. See the crucial discussion titled "Finding God in the World," in Rahner, *Foundations of Christian Faith: An Introduction to the Idea of Christianity*, trans. W. V. Dych (London: Darton, Longman & Todd, 1978), 81–89.

a real threat to "the historical, revealed religion which Christianity is,"[34] it may be wondered whether his existential spirituality goes too far down the track of pastoral concern into the sphere of doctrinal ambivalence. On the one hand, Rahner's spirituality manifests a profound sense of the incarnational and concrete. "The absolute Logos shall look at me in eternity with the face of a man. Those who theorize on the beatific vision forget this."[35] And as for the church's objective means of grace, as he affirms in one of his Easter sermons, every liturgical celebration of the church "in rite contains the actual reality celebrated."[36] On the other hand, he holds that liturgical and sacramental incorporation in the body of the church is not constitutive for incorporation in Christ, but a potential occasion for it, a contingent situation that is open-ended and in itself indecisive. The Christian is "in direct contact with God and his inspiration (however much it leaves him as a part of the Church and itself belongs to the Church as a community of grace) is not simply imparted through the ecclesiastical apparatus."[37] Prescribed prayers and spiritual disciplines, while not to be regarded as optional extras, are "basically rules for recollection," "intended as helps to effect something approaching an experience of grace. . . ."[38] Rahner explains how in times past, it was often thought that there were two worlds:

> the earthly, profane world in which normal man spent most of his time willy nilly, and a religious world—apprehended as a heterogeneous element, fostered mainly by priests and nuns ("religious people")—which people "in the world" could only with difficulty and in small doses bring to bear on their secular existences.[39]

Now he finds this nature-and-grace dichotomy slowly giving way to a future in which nature and grace, humanity and God, human life and divine life, seem to function as virtually exchangeable terms:

> Today Christianity is slowly learning that it can and must live and understand everything in profane life as a process of salvation (or unsalvation) if it is not to incur a false secularism. . . . Everything that

34. Ibid., 83.
35. Rahner, *The Great Church Year*, 204.
36. Ibid., 192.
37. Rahner, "Ignatius of Loyola Speaks to a Modern Jesuit," 27.
38. Rahner, *Christian at the Crossroads*, 60.
39. Ibid., 82.

is not sin but is freely and responsibly posited is, for the Christian in a state of grace, an event of this grace, a piece of salvation history borne up by the Spirit of God, an acceptance of his eternity.[40]

To Rahner this evolution is a happy sign of the "Copernican revolution" in Christian piety taking place today.

> It consists in the experience that the real depth of the apparently superficial and "worldly" dailiness of life is filled with and can be filled with God and his grace, and that because of this ultimate meaning of apparently secular life, the expressly religious becomes intelligible and practicable for the men [*sic*] of our time.[41]

Whether this shift amounts to a creative appropriation of the mysticism of Ignatius of Loyola or a more or less subtle departure from it remains highly debatable. Rahner does not deny that "expressly religious" practices, if undertaken with authenticity, can certainly illuminate and deepen the "anonymous Christianness of the secular daily round."[42] Yet Gallagher is surely correct in observing that Rahner's "prioritorising of the existential dimension" and "inviting people to trust their experiences of self-transcendence as encounters with God" would come over as "a surprise to Ignatius in his more faith-saturated context."[43] What for Ignatius starts out as a conviction that human beings are capable of touching God our creator and Lord in the dynamic interactive matrix constituted by the enscripturated word (imaginatively engaged) and ordinary daily experience (attentively examined), becomes with Rahner a radically apophatic mystical-experiential convergence of my own being with the ultimately nameless infinity "we call God." Endean summarizes the matter for us perfectly, if disquietingly: "[I]f God in Christ has become human, then, in the words of one of Rahner's early prayers, God has also become human experience."[44]

40. Ibid.
41. Ibid., 83.
42. Ibid.
43. Gallagher, "Ignatian Dimensions of Rahner's Theology," 79.
44. Endean, "Introduction," in Rahner, *Spiritual Writings*, 14.

LOVE AND DEATH

I have offered these critical remarks here rather than later in order to relate them more closely with issues arising from my examination of Rahner's vision of the human experience of God in the drama of everyday life. However, they need not detain us from pressing on now to our final analysis, closely connected with our treatment so far, of the role of suffering love and death in the deification of the human person. How love and death are related in this dynamic will hopefully become clear as our analysis unfolds.

The first point to be made from Rahner's spiritual writings is that love and death both stand out as acts in which divine freedom and human freedom coincide. This possibility is at least quite apparent in the case of love. In a well-known criticism directed toward Rahner by Hans Urs von Balthasar, it was alleged that Rahner wrongly credited love of neighbor with the same value as love for God, though it seems clear now that he rather posited a necessary and vital unity between these two loves—a unity that does not upset the proper order between them—rather than an identification.[45] In any case, what this little controversy brought to the fore was the fact that Rahner regards human acts of genuine love, whether toward God or toward one's neighbor, as a real participation in God's prevenient movement of love toward the world. Some comments taken from a retreat given to seminary students preparing for ordination offer an illustration suitable for our purposes. "[O]ur 'ascending' love to God is always a participation in God's descent to the world."[46] If this is so, and if by God's descent into the world Rahner means "the movement of divine love into the world in Christ, then for this reason it must be a love of God within the world and within the Church."[47] He explains further:

> [T]his love of God is precisely the descending love, the love that communicates itself to the world, the love that, as it were, loses itself in the world, the love that brings about the becoming-flesh of the Word, the love that means the abiding of the eternal Word in his creature, and that therefore also means a divinized world and Church.[48]

45. For a discussion of this controversy, see D. Marmion, "Rahner and His Critics: Revisiting the Dialogue," *Irish Theological Quarterly* 68 (2003): 195–212.

46. Rahner, *Spiritual Writings*, 57.

47. Ibid., 58.

48. Ibid.

This participation by the human person in God's self-emptying love for and in the world gives rise to a form of action normally impossible for human beings. Herein lies the mark of specifically Christian love.

> [T]he Christian, who participates in God's action of descent to the world and of love for this world—a love in which God has accepted the world definitively, for all eternity, as his own-most reality, as the expression of himself—can, in this love, love with a radicality that would not otherwise be possible or imaginable for a human being. Christians can do this despite all indifference, despite all reserve, despite all crucifying death in Christ. No one can turn themselves so radically in love toward the world as the one who does it in this descent of God's—God who has, in Jesus Christ, accepted for always and for eternity the flesh of humanity and thus of the world. . . . [49]

If the death of Christ on Golgotha stands forever as the climax of God's irrevocable movement of unconditional love toward sinful humanity, then every act of human love that participates in this love will necessarily bear a cruciform character. That is, it will involve some form of death experience, some undoing of the self, for the lover.

It is at this point that we may draw into our conversation one or two observations drawn from Rahner's theology of death. We said above that in Rahner's spiritual theology both love and death stand out as acts in which divine freedom and human freedom coincide. This seems a justifiable statement with reference to love, but how can it be said of death? To Rahner's mind, while every human being, including the Christian, has the "right" to fear death (as Rahner himself often urged when asked about his own personal attitude to death),[50] death also presents every human being, believer or not, with a decisive opportunity to undertake the most free and self-transcending act that can be made. For if in death we are forced to surrender every temporal and physical

---

49. Ibid., 59–60.

50. "When I have to go to the dentist, I can find the treatment terrifying from a purely instinctive point of view, and so, in this sense, be afraid of it. But still I can say to myself with my reason: dental care does not kill anyone. But that means that in this case reasonable calm and instinctive fears are already closely bound together. It is similar with regard to the fear of death. No Christian must say that he or she has no fear. One can admit fear, for even Jesus sweated blood on the Mount of Olives in view of his future. Ernst Bloch once said that we must conduct ourselves like the Sioux Indians who at the stake stoically endured all sorts of tortures, including death. I think that is nonsense. If I hurt horribly, I have the right to scream. And I have the right to be afraid, and consequently the right to be afraid of death." Rahner, *Faith in a Wintry Season*, 104. See further Egan, *Karl Rahner: The Mystic of Everyday Life*, 193–95.

good that we have hitherto cherished and desired, we are there finally faced with what lies beyond death as our one and only concrete, eternal, good. In this way surrendering to death can become, more or less explicitly, the ultimate act of surrender to God.

Rahner expresses this idea briefly, but quite pointedly, in a reflection on Elisabeth Kübler-Ross's so-called "fifth stage" in the dying process, namely, the stage of "acquiescence." According to Rahner, Christian theology is clear about the fact that the eternal destiny of a dying person, "which becomes definitive in death," can never be ascertained with certainty from the observable circumstances surrounding the death itself, "but remains the secret of human freedom and of God."[51] Even so, Rahner believes that the simple act of acquiescence to death can contain, implicitly hidden in itself as it were, an act of personal surrender to God.[52] While it is true that physiological and psychological factors may well induce a type of involuntary acquiescence quite apart from the dying person's free decision, the moment of acquiescence to death can, according to Rahner,

> still be the act in which there is a free acceptance on the part of the dying person, in which the person really lets go of himself and of everything to which he had hitherto held on as a particular good in an absolute, free decision; this acquiescence can therefore be an act in which the person surrenders himself to the will of the incomprehensible God, in which, even though perhaps very implicitly, he "repents of his sins" because in this acquiescence he also surrenders those goods to which he had up to that moment culpably adhered in unconditional freedom.[53]

This does not mean that such acquiescence is always and necessarily salvific. But this does not prevent Rahner from holding out hope for a situation "in which God's merciful providence makes it easy for a man to surrender confidently to that incomprehensible mystery which in death man meets more clearly than ever before and which we call God."[54]

When we supplement these somewhat speculative musings with thoughts drawn from some of Rahner's Lenten and Good Friday homilies, a poignant picture emerges according to which death, as an event in which total human

---

51. Rahner, *Christian at the Crossroads*, 84.

52. Ibid., 85.

53. Ibid.

54. Ibid.

surrender to the ultimate good and divine self-communication coincide, becomes the climactic point of the person's deifying union with God. Rahner arrives at this vision by means of a penetrating exploration of Christ's death as God's appropriation of the most dreadful, lonely, yet universal experience of all human beings. "In dying, Jesus stood as a human being before that abyss of death that puts everything into question and renders it impotent."[55] The sheer inexorability with which death approaches each person must not be avoided, but faced in all its threatening terror. The only question is whether one faces it with hope or despair, whether one reacts to it with stoic cynicism or accepts it as a participation in Christ's own agony and death. Precisely in the hopeful acceptance of the inevitable reality of death and its blanketing silence does a person truly embrace the Christian vocation to "take up one's cross" and follow Jesus the crucified Lord. Hope only becomes Christian hope, and thus saving and eternity-creating hope, in the face of this bitter mystery of dying:

> The Christian hope is that God himself with his power will be with us in the abyss of our powerlessness at the moment of death so that not only will life follow death but death itself through God's power becomes our own act by which life is created. Willing self-abandonment is a deed that creates eternity.[56]

But even though death only comes once to each person, the opportunity it presents for hope-filled and "willing self-abandonment" is not limited to that single point. Death is encountered and anticipated in a thousand ways during the course of one's lifetime. For the truth is, as soon as we came to be we began to die.[57] Every moment of involuntary suffering and pain, every hour of dark isolation and godforsakenness, presents an opening for the exercise of "hope against hope," an opportunity for love of God to prove itself in faith. For in these crises of existence, in which what is most agonizing and fearful is not the pain itself but the apparently mocking silence of God, the God who in the cross of Jesus descended to the lowest reaches of creaturely negation is himself hiddenly present, waiting to receive our surrender. "[God] has veiled his love in the stillness of his silence so that our love might reveal itself in faith. He has apparently forsaken us so that we can find him."[58] Our loved ones who have

---

55. Rahner, *The Great Church Year*, 160.

56. Ibid., 162.

57. Ibid., 163.

58. Ibid., 369.

died remind us of this silence, often painfully. Suddenly they are gone, and no longer speak. Yet through this silence,

> they speak to us clearly. They are nearer to us than through all the audible words of love and closeness. Because they have entered into God's life, they remain hidden from us. . . . They live with the boundlessness of God's life and with his love. . . . Be mindful of the dead, O heart. They live. Your own life, the life still hidden even to you, they live unveiled in eternal light.[59]

With these thoughts we come to the conclusion of this chapter. By recourse especially to Rahner's "spiritual" writings, embodied mainly in his sermons, meditations, autobiographical reflections, and retreats, we have gradually built up a picture of the way in which the German Jesuit depicts the deification of the human person in the concrete contours of human life. We have seen how he is concerned to locate the unfolding of deification not in the confines of a sacred realm fenced off from an allegedly separate and unrelated secular existence, nor only in an unforeseeable future, but in the day-to-day experiences of ordinary life, each of which, when closely attended to, is gravid with potential for a self-transcending, dramatic encounter with God. Yet among the range of "ordinary" experiences that comprise human life, none presents a more profound potential for this encounter than death, whether suffered in its numerous forms during the course of one's journey, or in its definitive form at the end of life. Although Rahner continually emphasizes the inseparability of the transcendental and categorical, and the way the former is only reached in and via the latter, there is a sense for him in which death, or more specifically, death with Christ, takes a person beyond the categorical into that infinite and direct immediacy in which God, "nameless and unfathomable, silent and yet near, bestowing himself upon me in his Trinity," is finally known "beyond all concrete imaginings."[60]

59. Ibid., 369–70.

60. Rahner, "Ignatius of Loyola Speaks to a Modern Jesuit," 11.

PART III

Henri de Lubac

9

Deification and the Supernatural

It is impossible to offer an adequate analysis of de Lubac's contribution to the theology of deification in the pre-Conciliar period without attending to his famous _Surnaturel_ (1946), a work that is almost universally acknowledged to have precipitated a theological revolution. In it de Lubac demolished the theory first broached by Thomas di Vio Cajetan and then turned normative in the Thomistic commentatorial tradition that had posited an integral this-worldly end for human beings, commensurate with the innate potencies of human nature, to which the life of grace and the desire for final beatitude could only be envisioned as additional, elicited conditions. In place of this two-tiered anthropology, de Lubac pressed the case for a supernatural finality inscribed within the very being of the human creature, yet a finality whose realization is infinitely, and paradoxically, disproportionate to natural capacity. In presenting de Lubac's thought on this score, I shall avoid rehearsing the well-known story of the fortunes of this controversy right down to the present time, which calls for mastery of an ever-growing body of scholarly literature. Instead I shall try to make sense of de Lubac's theology of the supernatural insofar as it brings to light the theme of deification in his overall theological vision.

Neoplatonist Radicalism?

We may begin by referring to the study of John Milbank in which he presents Henri de Lubac as a key figure in bringing to the notice of twentieth-century catholic thought the essential continuity between "the original and authentic Latin patristic understanding of the operation of grace" (an understanding equally represented by Thomas Aquinas), and "the Greek patristic notion of deification."[1] While for the late medieval and renaissance tradition of scholastic

---

1. John Milbank, _The Suspended Middle: Henri de Lubac and the Debate concerning the Supernatural_ (Grand Rapids: Eerdmans, 2005), 16. The literature discussing de Lubac's _Surnaturel_ is vast. One may

theology, grace is "merely a judicial corrective for sin,"[2] for de Lubac, as for the early Fathers of the church, grace is regarded as a divine power that raises humanity above itself, uniting it to God and thereby bringing about "the ultimate experience of the supernatural."[3] Though the desire for deification is intrinsic to human nature, paradoxically its realization is both "our highest act" and "wholly done for us by God."[4] But it is the character of deification as gift that eventually stands out. In fact, so radical is the gratuity involved, says Milbank, deification is best understood as "a gift to a gift." Through our total transfiguration by the divine light, "we *become* the reception of this light and there is no longer any additional 'natural' recipient of this reception."[5] "This," Milbank suggests, "is perhaps the subtle heart of de Lubac's theology."[6]

Back in an earlier chapter I indicated that the revolutionary character of de Lubac's project in *Surnaturel* is better appreciated when read in light of its intellectual background in French Augustinian Neoplatonism, especially as represented by the philosopher Maurice Blondel. There I also pointed out that far from confounding the distinction between the natural and the supernatural, Blondel rejected the claim that there is fundamentally no difference between "the gifts of the creator" and "the gifts of the incarnation and redemption," or that the natural order *is* supernatural. "[F]or my part I believe that there is an abyss to cross, and in order not to see it one must not *realize in concreto what God is*."[7]

Was this also the way de Lubac understood the relation between creation and deification? If Milbank is correct, it would seem that there is something about de Lubac's construal of deification that is supposedly more radical than anything we find in Blondel. While remaining "in line" with Blondel, says Milbank, de Lubac goes beyond him by positing a "non-ontology," by which Milbank means not that de Lubac refused ontology, but "that he articulated an ontology between the field of pure immanent being proper to philosophy on

---

consult with especial profit the essays in S.-T. Bonino, ed., *Surnaturel: A Controversy at the Heart of Twentieth-Century Thomistic Thought*, trans. R. William and M. Levering (Ave Maria, FL: Sapientia), 2009; see also Nicholas J. Healy, "Henri de Lubac on Nature and Grace: A Note on Some Recent Contributions to the Debate," *Communio* 35, no. 4 (2008): 535–64.

2. Milbank, *The Suspended Middle*, 34.

3. Ibid., 46.

4. Ibid., ix.

5. Ibid., 46–47.

6. Ibid., 47.

7. Quoted by Alexander Dru in the introduction to Maurice Blondel, *Letter on Apologetics and History and Dogma*, trans. A. Dru and I. Trethowan (Grand Rapids: Eerdmans, 1994), 75–76.

the one hand, and the field of the revelatory event proper to theology on the other."[8] It is in the terms of this paradoxical middle ground, in Milbank's view, that de Lubac articulates a vision of human nature's "ontological transformation into as close a likeness with God as is consistent with a persisting created status."[9] On its own this does not seem to represent any radical departure from anything in the earlier tradition. If it appeared revolutionary, it was because catholic theology had in many places been taken over by an ontotheological system and so been severed from its medieval, patristic, and biblical roots.[10] But here and there Milbank gives the impression that de Lubac, in the mode of this "non-ontology," goes beyond the traditional account. From the fact that creation only exists "because of deification," Milbank would have de Lubac conclude—in contrast to the traditional order that has grace "presupposing" or "perfecting" nature—that grace, since it is the cause of creation, presupposes absolutely nothing.[11] This more radical construal would have us envision deification along the lines of an unmodified Plotinian Neoplatonism, where "to be" and "to be God" mean essentially the same thing. The two terms simply indicate two aspects of a single ontological continuum—though perhaps we should say "nonontological" continuum, since the mode in question transcends the positive (or negative) metaphysical categories commonly attributed by natural philosophy on the one hand and dogmatic theology on the other. In any case, it is a continuum, because it offers an account of human being in which being divine constitutes our "latent mystical condition."[12] The final union of God and the human creature is of such a kind that no real distinction between them remains: giver and receiver share one and the same divine existence.

It may be saying too much to claim that this is what Milbank explicitly says. It is an observation made partly in the light of what he has written elsewhere, in which precisely this kind of issue has been noted as problematic.[13]

8. Milbank, *The Suspended Middle*, 5.

9. Ibid., 16.

10. By "ontotheological system" I mean the end product of a theological methodology that subsumes God under philosophical concepts such as being and makes the mysteries of divine revelation answer to controlling criteria established by an allegedly all-sufficient rational framework.

11. Milbank, *The Suspended Middle*, 52, 45.

12. Ibid., 28.

13. See, for example, B. Gallaher, "Graced Creatureliness: Ontological Tension in the Uncreated/ Created Distinction in the Sophiologies of Solov'ev, Bulgakov and Milbank," *Logos: A Journal of Eastern Christian Studies* 47 (2006): 163–90; Reinhard Hütter, "*Desiderium Naturale Visionis Dei–Est autem duplex hominis beatitudo sive felicitas*: Some Observations about Lawrence Feingold's and John Milbank's Recent Interventions in the Debate over the Natural Desire for God," *Nova et Vetera* 5, no. 1 (2007): 81–131. In this article Hütter refers to Milbank's "radicalized Bulgakovian Lubacianism."

That said, it is still possible to point out some statements in *The Suspended Middle* that explicitly head in that direction. Recall the sentence quoted earlier in which is described the beatific transfiguration by divine light: "Here we *become* the reception of this light and there is no longer any additional 'natural' recipient of this reception."[14] We may refer also to Milbank's enthusiasm in finding substantial consonance between de Lubac and Meister Eckhart on this score. To be sure, Milbank acknowledges that some of Eckhart's statements of identity between God and the human soul are "extreme"—on this point he could have cited de Lubac's own mention of this "disquieting feature" in Eckhart's mysticism.[15] Still, Milbank says, de Lubac is able to accommodate such features "in terms of the Origenist *longue durée*." In other words, if to be spirit is not necessarily to be God, it is at least to be "lured to unity with God" and "in some sense already to possess this unity."[16]

This impression that Milbank gives of de Lubac as a Neoplatonist radical is strengthened by his rendition of the unfolding of the *nouvelle théologie* controversy. Milbank argues that de Lubac—with one or two hesitant exceptions—did not go on fully to develop all the implications of his "uncompromising radicalism."[17] Rather, "seeking to square his views with *Humani Generis*," de Lubac in his later works "reduces the natural desire for the supernatural to a negative lack and denies that it in any way positively anticipates the supernatural end."[18] With his (and Hans Urs von Balthasar's) "formal capitulation to papal authority,"[19] de Lubac fails to carry through on the trajectory set by *Surnaturel*, especially in the realm of his ecclesiology which, in Milbank's judgment, remains far too conservative and extrinsicist. His curious criticism on this point is worth noting, if only for the reason that it reveals key aspects of Milbank's underlying agenda:

> There is a failure here to think of all the Church, in her bridal essence, as actively as well as passively Sophianic, as able potentially to meet the Bridegroom with an equal deified response since the Church, as the heavenly divine temple (Jerusalem who always abides with God above), is, one might venture to say, collectively,

14. Milbank, *The Suspended Middle*, 46–47.

15. Henri de Lubac, "Tripartite Anthropology," in idem, *Theology in History*, trans. A. E. Nash (San Francisco: Ignatius, 1996), 184.

16. Milbank, *The Suspended Middle*, 50.

17. Ibid., 48.

18. Ibid., 66.

19. Ibid., 104.

primordially and eschatologically enhypostasized [*sic*] by the Holy Spirit.[20]

In other words, according to Milbank, there is a failure on de Lubac's part, finally, to know the church as an intra-divine donative interplay, "the active/passive (infinitely dynamic yet infinitely replete) *Sophia* which names the Christian Godhead (in its unified essence) as 'goddess.'"[21]

The question that must be asked is whether this account of the Frenchman's early doctrine of deification over-implies its affinity with the more radical, henological Neoplatonism of thinkers in the vein of Plotinus, Proclus, Eriugena, Eckhart, and Trouillard, according to which any meaningful distinction between the natural and the supernatural collapses. Arriving at an answer is not straightforward. On the one hand, as we have seen, de Lubac has been associated with Blondel in an Augustinian Neoplatonism quite distinct from more radical varieties. On the other hand, more conservative critics of de Lubac's thought have alleged its ambiguity and even incoherence at just this point: if human nature is essentially marked by a supernatural finality, then it is human in name only.[22] As its end is realized, its natural distinction from God finally disappears, swallowed up in an all-embracing, univocal, intra-divine exchange, so that, as Milbank has it, no "natural recipient" of divine activity remains.

Distinction and Union

With this problem now clearly posed, it is time to examine more closely what de Lubac himself actually wrote. The following survey of a selection of representative texts will lead me to argue that, in both his early and late works, de Lubac never lost sight of what Blondel called the "abyss," "the radical heterogeneity" that obtains between God and humanity, such that what is required for the passage to divine life is not simply a spontaneous *epistrophe* but a thoroughgoing mortification, death, and rebirth. At the same time, it will bring to light a certain ambiguity in de Lubac's expressions on this matter. It is possible that this ambiguity can be explained by the polemical context of

20. Ibid., 105–6.

21. Ibid., 107.

22. For a summary of the critical literature, see H. Donneaud, "*Surnaturel* through the Fine-Tooth Comb of Traditional Thomism," in *Surnaturel: A Controversy at the Heart of Twentieth-Century Thomistic Thought*, ed. S.-T. Bonino, 41–57; also David Braine, "The Debate Between Henri de Lubac and His Critics," *Nova et Vetera* 6, no. 3 (2008): 543–90.

his writings: their underlying intent to counter an autonomous, positivistic, ahistorical rationalism. It could also be due to their unsystematic, historical, and occasional character. Whatever its causes, this ambiguity leaves the door open for the kind of interpretation Milbank has given, even if our final conclusion is that that interpretation somewhat misses the mark.

To begin our analysis of de Lubac's theology of deification, let us turn to his mature essay "Mysticism and Mystery," an early draft of which was first published in 1965.[23] There is no doubting that de Lubac here proposes the constitutive form and goal of the Christian life in terms of a real union with God. Mysticism for the Christian means "the union with the tripersonal God of Christian revelation, a union realized in Jesus Christ and through his grace."[24] The summit of mystical life consists in "an actual union with the Divinity," a union "possible only through a supernatural grace whose normal setting is the Church and whose normal conditions are the life of faith and the sacraments."[25] St. Paul and especially St. John attest to this mystical union not only as a future hope but as a reality in some way already "mysteriously consummated."[26]

But at this point de Lubac critically takes up the charge that mysticism aims ultimately at identification with the divine in a kind of realized monism. Quoting a line from the famous representative of metaphysical esotericism, René Guénon (1886–1951), he asks, "Does it not, at least as far as those who attempt it are persuaded, lead to 'consciousness of the Identity of Being, permanent throughout all the indefinitely multiple modifications of the unique Existence'?"[27] Yet not only does this question arise from a misunderstanding of what deification really entails; it proposes an experience, claims de Lubac, "very far removed from the Christian point of view."[28]

De Lubac's crucial point of departure by which he distinguishes Christian mysticism from all forms of monism is essentially anthropological. Here he draws upon the distinction made by some of the early Fathers between image and likeness. On the one hand, human nature is "basically the same everywhere. Man, the Scriptures tell us, is created in the image of God." Yet human nature is no static entity, but defined by its divine vocation according to which

23. English translation in Henri de Lubac, *Theological Fragments*, trans. R. H. Balinski (San Francisco: Ignatius, 1989), 35–69. This essay may be taken as an outline in brief of de Lubac's long-wished-for but eventually unrealized plan to compose a lengthy monograph on the subject.

24. De Lubac, "Mysticism and Mystery," 39.

25. Ibid., 43.

26. Ibid., 50.

27. Ibid., 51, quoting R. Guénon, *Le symbolisme de la croix*, 214.

28. De Lubac, "Mysticism and Mystery," 51.

each human being is called to resemble God, "a resemblance that must be consummated in the 'beatific vision.'" While this aspiration is inherent in human nature as a capacity and a desire that "must be described as ontological," it is nevertheless a kind of negative imprint, a God-shaped vacuum in the human heart. De Lubac calls it a "passive power," a faculty only "for receiving, in itself empty and powerless. . . ." While its fulfillment is entirely an immanent experience, the causal agency of its activation is transcendent. There is something strikingly Aristotelian in the way de Lubac defines this desire as an "essential passivity," a "radical passivity." But his rationale is evidently theological. The mystery embodied as gift in Jesus Christ can only be received: "there is no other way of obtaining it."[29]

This remark leads de Lubac to posit four principal characteristics of Christian mysticism. The alert reader will notice the affinity these four marks share with elements in Garrigou-Lagrange's analysis of Christian mysticism. First of all, it is a mysticism of likeness. Even though the divine image is inalienable in every person, "a mysticism based on image *alone* would be an awareness of self, at the deepest part of one's being, without the gracious intervention of God in giving the mystery."[30] Repeating a now well-rehearsed theme in this book, de Lubac relates the traditional teaching that while God is completely present everywhere, he does not dwell in everyone. The divine indwelling for which the Christian yearns involves personal assimilation and loving surrender. Unlike natural mysticism, which tends to be self-focused and atemporal, a mysticism of likeness—even if it contains an element of nostalgia for a lost Paradise—ultimately presses toward an eschatological and as yet not fully realized goal.[31]

Christian mysticism is secondly a mysticism of the holy books (of Scripture), inasmuch as the Scriptures embody in their many-layered depths the mystery who is Christ. "[T]he mystical or spiritual understanding of Scripture and the mystical or spiritual life, are, in the end, the same."[32] The Christian

---

29. Ibid., 51–52.

30. Ibid., 57.

31. Ibid., 57. De Lubac's patristic-inspired distinction between image and likeness, which we shall analyze in greater detail in the penultimate chapter, parallels C. S. Lewis's distinction between "nearness by likeness" and "nearness by approach." In Lewis's analogy, a man standing on the edge of a precipice overlooking a village seems to be very close to it. But only by abandoning his proximate vantage point and descending the long winding track that leads around the cliff and back into the valley can he actually approach the village and eventually reach it in safety. Similarly, "whereas the likeness is given to us—and can be received with or without thanks, can be used or abused—the approach, however initiated and supported by Grace, is something we must do." C. S. Lewis, *The Four Loves* (London: Fontana, 1960), 11.

32. De Lubac, "Mysticism and Mystery," 58.

mystic "has no wish to know a Word of God that resounds only within himself."[33] The deifying anagogy or assimilative ascent that results from spiritual engagement with the text presupposes the lasting constitutive relevance of the concrete providential and elective interventions of God in history.

It is in the third characteristic of Christian mysticism that the traditional and conservative character of de Lubac's doctrine of deification as a union-without-confusion with God most clearly stands out. Christian mysticism is a nuptial mysticism, indissolubly bound to the symbol of spiritual marriage. De Lubac boldly defends the validity and universality of this symbol. This nuptial metaphor is not, he argues,

> as certain theoreticians have said with a trace of disdain, something exoteric, rather vulgar, less appropriate than others to translate the mystical reality. On the contrary, it illustrates an unsurpassable feature of Christian mysticism considered not only in its evolution but also at its highest summit. Because, between the human soul and its God, as in the marriage of the Church and the Lamb, there is always a union, not absorption (whether in one sense or the other). It is, if you wish, a unification and not an identification. It involves mutual love even though all the initiative comes from God.[34]

We must note carefully what de Lubac is saying here. Why is nuptial or marital symbolism especially applicable and appropriate to the Christian mystery? Because the union it entails involves a real reciprocity and mutuality between two subjects who, while truly one, nevertheless maintain their own ontological and personal specificity. De Lubac is not insensitive to the possible misgivings to which such an image may give rise. Does the idea of "spiritual marriage" sufficiently communicate the profundity of the union involved in the mystical process? Does it not retain too much of the idea of duality? But this anxiety, he answers, proceeds from "a false notion of unity." One need only compare the mysterious unity of the holy Trinity, where nevertheless "the distinction of personal Beings is not only maintained but carried to perfection."[35] In an analogous way, the intimate "one flesh" union of spouses in marriage results in a real union of spirit, desire, and will, without any merging of personal subjectivity. De Lubac quotes St. John of the Cross who gives an apposite testimony along these lines:

33. Ibid., 59.
34. Ibid., 60.
35. Ibid., 61.

When we speak of the union of the soul with God, we are not referring to the union that already exists between God and all his creatures, but to the union of the soul with God and its transformation by his love. The transformation takes place, however, only when the soul, through love, resembles that of the Creator. That is why the union is called supernatural. It takes place when two wills, that of the soul and that of God, are in agreement, and one has nothing that repels the other. Thus, when the soul completely rejects in itself all that is repugnant or does not conform to the will of God, it is transformed into God through love.[36]

For de Lubac, this essentially nuptial aspect of Christian mysticism is at once an ecclesial aspect, "since the Incarnation achieves first of all in the Church the marriage of the Word and humanity." There is no disjunction between the individual Christian soul and the universal church, both of whom have the Virgin Mary as their type. To them both the "wondrous exchange" proclaimed by the liturgy is equally applicable.[37]

This nuptial-cum-ecclesial mark of Christian mysticism leads de Lubac to the fourth and final characteristic, which is Trinitarian. The God with whom we have to do is not some generic *Ungrund*, some unspecifiable "original chasm" or "obscure core of being—or nonbeing. . . ."[38] Quoting von Balthasar, he goes on:

The God whom we adore and who wants us to be united with him is not faceless: he has a superior form, an "infinitely determined form." His infinity is not one of dispersion but of concentration: in him all the mystery of the personal Being is condensed. Contemplation may enable man to plumb other depths and abysses, but unless they are explicitly or implicitly depths of the triune, human-divine and ecclesial life, they are either spurious or demonic.[39]

This reference to von Balthasar prompts us to return to the question we have been pursuing. In response to the material I have adduced so far, someone might point out that it all stems from a relatively late period in de Lubac's career. Do not these later expressions confirm, rather than refute, Milbank's

36. Quoted in de Lubac, "Mysticism and Mystery," 62.
37. Ibid.
38. Ibid.
39. Ibid., 63.

thesis that de Lubac, perhaps unduly influenced by von Balthasar's allegedly "Barthian outlook"[40] and residual "Germanic Protestant"[41] mentality, drew back from his earlier, more "radical" theology, and instead adopted a more guarded, conservative position? In answer, defending the validity of this material, it could be recalled that de Lubac equated its content with a longtime driving inspiration: for him it summed up "some of the ideas that, according to my original outline, would have been developed in several volumes."[42] Still, it has to be admitted that, if comments taken from ten years before its publication have any bearing on the matter, de Lubac felt that what he really wanted to say in such a work eluded him. It wasn't that he didn't know the problems he wanted to raise, but that he felt incapable of formulating their solution.[43]

Thus in order to demonstrate more clearly that de Lubac was not so much the radical Milbank seems to imply, it will be necessary to search in his earlier works, preferably prior to *Humani Generis* (1950), for explicit statements that confirm his essential continuity with the Blondelian, Augustinian—and let us add Thomistic—Neoplatonist construal of the human being's mysterious union with God. Our first early example therefore comes from "The Mystery of the Supernatural," published in the journal *Recherches de Science Religieuse* in 1949. The essay represents an important development and extension of certain historical aspects of findings published in *Surnaturel*.[44] In it we find de Lubac exposing the oddity of requiring, for the sake of preserving the gratuity of God's supernatural gift of grace, any abstract entity known as *pure nature*. Human nature as it has been created by God and in fact is, is always already supernaturally graced in some way. At first blush, this sounds as though de Lubac takes creation and deification to be equivalent realities. Indeed, he speaks of "a real parallelism" between the first gift, the gift of being, "and the second gift, completely distinct from it: the ontological call to deification, which will make man 'a new creature.'"[45] Conceptually, we are of course bound to divide

40. Milbank, *The Suspended Middle*, 74.

41. Ibid., 66.

42. De Lubac, *At the Service of the Church: Henri de Lubac Reflects on the Circumstances That Occasioned His Writings*, trans. A. E. Englund (San Francisco: Ignatius, 1993), 113.

43. Ibid.

44. In his comments on Etienne Gilson's letters, de Lubac notes that this article was approved by the Roman censors. "It was not a recapitulation nor a clarification of the book *Surnaturel*, but an enlargement. . . ." He argues for the essential harmony between the article and *Humani Generis*, even suggesting that the encyclical was "demonstrably inspired" by it in that, following the article, it "avoided invoking the so-called theory of 'pure nature' that a number of theologians wanted the encyclical to validate." *Letters of Etienne Gilson to Henri de Lubac: Annotated by Father de Lubac*, trans. M. E. Hamilton (San Francisco: Ignatius, 1988), 98–99 n. 1.

the "moments" of being graced into two: first I am given (natural) being, then I am given (supernatural) finality. "That is an unavoidable process of dissociation and exposition, given the nature of human intelligence. . . ."[46] Yet however much we are bound to begin with this twofold conception, we are bound not to remain there. The gift of being, far from simply forming the necessary background for what follows, is itself imbued with mystery.

> For this gift is wholly within me, and nothing of what I am is without it. It is for me incomparably more *gift* than all external, superadded gifts that can then be made by men. If I want to remedy a little the weakness of my own language without risking the impossible effort to correct it thoroughly, I should thus say that, through creation, God has given me to myself.[47]

What de Lubac seems to be saying is that there is something about creation itself, something about the gift of "natural" existence, that is overwhelmingly "supernatural" and gratuitous. It is as though de Lubac would have us see in the human *esse* or act of existence an unexpected irruption of infinite divine energy, limited and temporarily rendered finite only by the boundary set by the specificity of its not being God. Precisely in my "thatness," even before my "what" or "what-for," precisely in the fact that "I am" instead of "am not," I am a unique, willed instance of the infinitely generous, creative activity of God, with the result that "God is more interior to me than I am to myself." Moreover, this interiority of God in me, at a level prior to any "second act" activity on my part, always already and simultaneously stamps me with a supernatural finality. Which means that "my being created" or begun and "my being finalized" do not represent two acts, two moments, two conditions, but "a twofold miracle of gratuity whose power no analogy drawn from human gifts can express."[48]

But before jumping to any conclusions, it is important to notice one or two key qualifying terms in the sentences above. Although creation and deification are formally and structurally parallel, although they are given together in the very summoning of my being into existence, they are nevertheless "completely distinct." Although our requirement that they be conceptually two does not *per se* make them actually or separately two—as certain theologians from Lombard to Bonaventure to Dante had maintained[49]—they are nevertheless "twofold." De

---

45. De Lubac, "The Mystery of the Supernatural" (1949), in *Theology in History*, 299.
46. Ibid., 300.
47. Ibid.
48. Ibid., 302.

Lubac is keen to jettison the Neoscholastic theory of "two ends" (*fines duo*), but he nonetheless retains the adjective "twofold" (*duplex*) as an indispensable means of expressing an irreducible categorical distinction:

> I must carefully distinguish and always maintain a twofold gratuity, a twofold divine gift, and therefore, if one may say so, a twofold divine freedom. There are here, as it were, two successive planes, like two landings without any communication from the bottom one to the one above. A twofold ontological passage, doubly impassable to the creature without the twofold initiative that arouses and calls him. . . . Between the existent nature and the supernatural to which God destines it, the distance is as great, the abyss is as profound, the heterogeneity is as radical as between being and nonbeing.[50]

With such language as "abyss" and "radical heterogeneity" it is impossible not to hear direct strains of Blondel's 1932 letter to de Lubac quoted earlier. In upholding the capacity of human nature for God, the theologian clearly does not want to supernaturalize the natural sphere, as though it were ontologically congenital to God or contained some kind of divine seed. "Considered in itself," he iterates, "there is not, let us repeat, the least supernatural element in it."[51] Having said that, it is not possible simply to consider nature "in itself" without reference to its intrinsic finality. Human beings are summoned into being by the one who is also their end, an end that is at once utterly disproportionate to their capacities and their only apt fulfillment. De Lubac admits that we are in the realm of paradox, contradiction, antinomy. "Such antinomies do not surprise us. They arise from any mystery."[52] The mystery of the relation between creation and deification is akin to other Christian mysteries: the mystery of the Son's consubstantiality with and generation from the Father, the mystery of divine grace and human freedom, the mystery of an eternal creator and a temporal creation, the mystery of a divine man and a human God. The trick is to hold both together, in the transcendent darkness of faith, without excluding one or the other. In this sense it is quite appropriate to speak, with von Balthasar and Milbank, of a "suspended middle."

---

49. See J.-P. Torrell, "Nature and Grace in Thomas Aquinas," in *Surnaturel: A Controversy at the Heart of Twentieth-Century Thomistic Thought*, ed. S.-T. Bonino, 155–88 at 157–58.

50. De Lubac, "The Mystery of the Supernatural" (1949), 302.

51. Ibid., 303.

52. Ibid., 308.

A Necessary Mortification

The final question now remains to ask to what extent the transformation necessary for the human passage to beatitude is a mortification, and if a mortification, whether that is due to the character of human nature itself or to the consequences of sin. Earlier I asserted that like Blondel, de Lubac believed that what is required for the passage to divine life is not simply a spontaneous *epistrophe* but a thoroughgoing mortification, death, and rebirth. In his 1965 *The Mystery of the Supernatural*, de Lubac explicitly made reference to Blondel on this score. "Man, by his deliberate intention, can only rise to the heights of his spontaneous aspiration by annihilating his self-will and establishing in himself the opposite will, the will to mortification." And again, "No man can see God without dying."[53] True enough, Blondel was in these very Jansenist-sounding remarks reflecting upon human nature as marked by sin. Yet it remains true, says de Lubac, "that the passage to the supernatural order, even for an innocent and healthy nature, could never take place without some kind of death."[54] "Between nature as it exists and the supernatural for which God destines it, the distance is as great, the difference as radical, as that between being and non-being: for to pass from one to the other is not merely to pass into 'more being,' but to pass to a different type of being. It is a crossing, by grace, of an impassable barrier."[55]

Lest anyone think we are restricting ourselves to de Lubac's later writings, let us also cite some earlier works. In 1949, referring to this same ontological requalification, de Lubac quotes the biblical idea of a new creation, one that is "without common measure with the first creation. . . . [T]his gift constitutes for nature a real *sublimation*, a real *exaltation* above itself, in brief, a real *deification*."[56] Earlier still, in his 1938 *Catholicisme*, de Lubac pursues this theme in the final pages of the book with rhetorical passion. The whole mystery of Christ is a mystery not only of resurrection, but also of death. "Pasch means passing over. It is a transmutation of the whole being, a complete separation from oneself which no one can hope to evade. It is a denial of all natural values in their natural existence and a renunciation even of all that had previously raised the individual above himself."[57] The terrible shadow of the cross must encompass everything human, dimming all natural light. Only through the painful way of

---

53. Henri de Lubac, *The Mystery of the Supernatural* (1965), trans. R. Sheed (New York: Crossroad, 1998), 29.

54. Ibid., 28.

55. Ibid., 83.

56. De Lubac, "The Mystery of the Supernatural" (1949), 303.

57. Henri de Lubac, *Catholicism*, trans. L. C. Sheppard (London: Burns & Oates, 1950), 209.

negation can what is human attain its proper glory. Participation in the agony of the Son's kenosis and sacrifice is the efficacious means to union with the Father.

> There is no smooth transition from a natural love to a supernatural love. To find himself man must lose himself. . . . *Exodus* and *ecstasy* are governed by the same law. If no one may escape from humanity, humanity whole and entire must die to itself in each of its members so as to live transfigured in God.[58]

It is not difficult to see how these comments give rise to the question about the integrity of the human nature redeemed in Christ. The issue touches upon the mutual relation between the theology of the cross (event-theology) and the theology of the incarnation (being-theology).[59] De Lubac was well versed in the Chalcedonian logic according to which the human nature assumed by the Word in the hypostatic union undergoes a profound modal qualification, a real *communicatio idiomatum*, while nevertheless retaining unchanged its fundamental natural principle (*logos*). Yet the mystery of Christ's death seems to force upon this metaphysical vision a dilemma of far-reaching theological scope. How does Christ's activity on the cross illuminate and modify what we know about being human? Why must this nature which has been deified in an inseparable personal union with the divine nature die? And if it must, what does this mean for all the members of humanity who are united as one in him, the second Adam?

The answer to these questions is crucial, because on them depends the answer to the question: What precisely is redeemed? Who or what is the object of salvation? It is here that a purely dialectical theology is in danger of overdetermining grace to the detriment of nature and thereby obliterating the relation between creation and redemption. If the "new creation" has no connection whatsoever with the "old creation," then the incarnation—the eternal Word's assumption of a nature defined by, among other things, its finitude and creatureliness—is a docetic myth. If it is true, as Philip McCosker has supposed, that "ultimately the way one configures the 'and' between nature and grace in a Christian way depends on the way one configures the 'and' between humanity and divinity in Christ . . . ,"[60] then both the Nestorian and Apollinarian errors must equally be avoided. The theology of the cross,

---

58. Ibid., 210.

59. See Joseph Ratzinger, *Introduction to Christianity*, trans. J. R. Foster (San Francisco: Ignatius, 2004), 228–30.

without losing its critical function, drives us back to the problem of being, "[f]or without being grace vanishes. . . ."[61] With Christ, of course, one and the same person is the subject of human and divine activity. Yet in articulating this mystery we must still distinguish between what it means to be human and what it means to be God, a task in which we may be helped by categories from Plotinian and Proclean Neoplatonism, all the while mindful of its lack of any doctrine of creation and thus of any sense of how multiplicity and difference may be accorded a relative yet positive ontological character. The great patristic doctors of deification—the Cappadocians, Maximus the Confessor, John of Damascus—argued that the synthesis achieved in deification is not a *henad* but a union, or in biblical terms, a reconciliation. For them the transfiguration of humanity effected in Christ is a modal qualification, an elevation at the level of *tropos* rather than *logos*, but precisely thereby an affirmation, restitution, and renovation of *logos*. Or as Thomas Aquinas might put it, in Christ the *state* of his human nature is modified; the *principle* of his human nature remains the same as ours. The resulting theandric union is therefore a composite reality in which certain far-reaching ontological distinctions—and differences—irreducibly remain.

But I think it is still possible to argue that, perhaps despite himself, de Lubac meant nothing more than this, combined with the recognition that the Christian life consists in living *metanoia*. In a lecture given to fellow priests at the *Semaine sociale* in Paris in 1947, de Lubac repeated numerous expressions word for word from this last page of *Catholicisme*, adding however one or two vital comments that reveal his essential congruity with St. Thomas. Emphasizing the need for supernatural agency in the full actualization of human nature, he writes: "Whatever therefore might be the natural progress gained, even in moral values, whatever might be the new idea elaborated, something else must intervene in order to confer on all this its definitive value: a transfiguration, incommensurate with all natural transformations."[62] This transformation does not spell the destruction of nature. "The bonds are real and close between nature and the supernatural, since it is the first that weaves, so to speak, the body of the second. . . ."[63] Even so,

---

60. Philip McCosker, "Middle Muddle?" *Reviews in Religion and Theology* 13, no. 3 (2006): 362–70 at 368.

61. G. Narcisse, "The Supernatural in Contemporary Theology," in *Surnaturel: A Controversy at the Heart of Twentieth-Century Thomistic Thought*, ed. S.-T. Bonino, 295–309 at 308.

62. "La Recherche d'un homme nouveau," in de Lubac, *At the Service of the Church*, 243.

63. De Lubac, *At the Service of the Church*, 244.

It is not a question of passing over into a new degree in the same order. The *supernatural* is not a higher, more beautiful, richer or more fruitful nature. It is not, as is sometimes said today through a poor neologism, an overnature. It is the irruption of a totally different principle. A sudden opening of a kind of fourth dimension, without proportion of any kind with all the steps provided in natural dimensions.[64]

Does this mean human beings can or should make no effort to prepare the way for this irruption? Is there no more proximate goal for human nature, no good one can "do" to anticipate or advance the advent of ultimate happiness? De Lubac does not let us off the hook so easily. Some inner compulsion or calling drives us forward, even if, in the end, we can only wait with open hands:

Let man, therefore, confident of divine assistance, take responsibility once again for the work of the six days. Let him prolong it throughout the seventh day. Let him be bold, victorious, inventive. . . . But the eighth day, on which alone everything is brought to completion and renewed, is the day of the Lord: man can only receive it. Let him pursue, as long as the world lasts, the activities of Prometheus: let him light in every century a new fire, the material basis for new human strides, new problems and new anguish. But at the same time, let him beg for the descent of the unique Fire without whose burning nothing could be purified, consumed, saved, eternalized: *Emitte Spiritum tuum et creabuntur, et renovabis faciem terrae. . . .*[65]

To draw our findings in this chapter on de Lubac's doctrine of deification together into a brief conclusion, it appears that although Milbank may have been justified in highlighting certain ambiguities in the theological writings of Henri de Lubac, his main achievement is to have drawn attention to the way deification features as a key motif in the Jesuit's theological vision. De Lubac reconfigures the more speculative scholastic doctrines of nature and grace in the more fluid terms provided by the patristic doctrine of deification and the contemporary mode of historical exegesis. He recovers from Aquinas, along

---

64. Ibid., 243–44.

65. De Lubac, *At the Service of the Church*, 244.

with a vast range of traditional sources, a fresh and compelling understanding of the human vocation as progressive participation in God.

How faithful this vision was to the sources cited as its authorities, how conceptually unified it was within the ambit of normative doctrine, and how different it was from existing Neothomist accounts remain questions that scholars will no doubt continue to pursue. But as far as I can tell at least, Milbank's attempt to cast de Lubac in the form of a would-be radical who subsequently suffered a collapse in nerve makes more of the evidence than a modest appraisal would allow.

10

Deification and Ecclesial
Concorporation

In the opening chapters I remarked that Henri de Lubac's first book, written at the age of forty-two, was *Catholicism: The Social Aspects of Dogma*. As the subtitle suggests, *Catholicism* elucidates the constitutively social and communal aspects of Christianity. Despite the fact that de Lubac himself prized the exploration of the Christian mystery and the subsequent elaboration of theology in an irenic, inclusive mode, in contrast to the turbulent and unbalancing anti-positions characteristic of more polemical theology, *Catholicism* was at least partly occasioned by longstanding criticisms to the effect that Christianity is hopelessly individualistic, spiritualizing, and otherworldly, and thereby undervalues and even undermines the goods of temporal human society. It would be fair to read it as de Lubac's attempt to answer the polemically loaded charge: "How can a religion which apparently is uninterested in our terrestrial future and in human fellowship offer an ideal which can still attract the men of today?"[1] In formulating his response, de Lubac was well aware that, although Christianity is in truth irreducibly social and historical, the answer to the campaign against individualism, particularly in the form of the increasingly popular Marxist solution, could never lie in reducing the Christian gospel to a social program. As he would explain a little later in *Le Drame de l'humanisme athée* (1944), Auguste Comte's attempt to separate off the more humanistic "social genius" of institutional "Catholicism" from the originally theocentric and monotheistic spirit of "Christianity" was false and ill-founded.[2]

---

1. Henri de Lubac, "Introduction" in idem, *Catholicism: Christ and the Common Destiny of Man*, trans. L. C. Sheppard (London: Burns and Oates, 1950), xiii (translation made from the fourth French edition (1947).

2. The ET is from the seventh French edition (1983): *The Drama of Atheist Humanism*, trans. E. M. Riley et al. (San Francisco: Ignatius, 1995).

By deifying the social group, Comptian-type social philosophies end up in an anti-personalistic cult of "sociocracy," in other words, in "sociolatry," in which the individual person amounts to no more than "a mere abstraction."[3]

On the other hand, there is no such thing as an individual Christian soul. Humanity has been created as a corporate unity, consisting as it were in a single body. Only as a single body will it be saved. The fragmentation of humanity into innumerable isolated units, far from being natural, is a consequence of sin. The gratuitous redemption of humanity must consequently take the form of a reunification. In the words of St. Paul and St. Irenaeus, humanity must be altogether "recapitulated" (Eph. 1:10). Herein lies the deep connection between creation, christology, and ecclesiology. The Logos takes his body from the one, corporate body that is creaturely humanity. Indeed, his incarnation was not a simple *corporatio*, an embodiment, but a *concorporatio*, a mysterious bodily incorporation of all humanity into himself so as to form "one new man" (Eph. 2:15). The church in all its various dimensions—spiritual, sacramental, hierarchical—is essentially a kind of vast, living extension of this divine humanity. Christianity is universal not only in the sense that Jesus Christ is the Savior of all but also in the sense that *all of humanity* finds salvation in Jesus Christ. All human beings—believers and unbelievers, past, present, and future—have therefore been implicated and touched by the incarnation, whose reality and effects are irreversible. Only if these propositions are true, de Lubac would argue, can the church consequently be the dynamic social and historical matrix in which humanity's unifying and finally deifying drama unfolds.

In the 1930s, such ideas were regarded by the dominant Neoscholasticism of the day as either novel and therefore suspicious, or else tinged with a certain quaint obsolescence. Post-Tridentine ecclesiology had to a great extent been conditioned by anti-Protestant apologetic concerns, and made to harmonize with a largely individualistic interpretation of the beatific vision according to which the overt sociality of the church, essential perhaps for the wayfarer, eventually faded away in the light of a one-on-one heavenly affair.[4] To many, a return to the more social ecclesiology of the Fathers signaled a step backwards toward a fluid world of theological naïveté and conceptual uncertainty. As Brian Daley observes,

---

3. De Lubac, *The Drama of Atheist Humanism*, 193, 248, 261.

4. See B.-D. de la Soujeole, *Le Sacrement de la communion: Essai d'ecclésiologie fondamentale* (Paris: Cerf, 1998): 13–54; J.-M. R. Tillard, *Chair de l'Église, chair du Christ: Aux sources de ecclésiologie de communion* (Paris: Cerf, 1992), 7–8.

> The patristic project . . . seemed to be an invitation to step off into a world of exotic symbolism, of collectivist ecclesiology and trendy social projects, of subjectivity and conceptual impermanence: into that very rejection of propositionally formulated truth that had been the core of the modernist spirit.[5]

But for those increasingly steeping themselves in the Fathers, perhaps following the lead of the great nineteenth-century dogmatists Möhler, Kuhn, and Scheeben, or for those especially considering the thought of the Fathers as it comes to bear on ecclesiology, such as we find it in Emil Mersch's massive study on Christ's mystical body, a work that de Lubac explicitly credited for shaping his own views,[6] this was a familiar language, biblical and liturgical in inspiration, universal and cosmic in scope.[7] Besides the plethora of passages from the Fathers quoted within the main body of *Catholicism*, de Lubac appends some fifty-five extracts from figures as old as Ignatius, Hermas, and Hilary, as diverse as Eusebius, Maximus, and Julian, as obscure as Adelman, Baldwin, and Claudianus, as new as Newman, Miel, and Cournot, and as controversial as Origen, von Hügel, and Teilhard. De Lubac's theological retrieval of the Fathers of the great pre-medieval tradition especially was considered and deliberate, but not intentionally provocative. "I seek only to understand them, and listen to what they have to tell us, since they are our Fathers in the Faith and since they received from the Church of their time the means to nourish the Church of our times as well."[8] What we adapt ourselves to in reading the Fathers this way is less the speculations of pre-Christian philosophy than the inspired spirit of Peter, John, and Paul. Such an approach involved a noticeable shift away from the polemically motivated ecclesiology that had prevailed since the sixteenth century. Along with Jean Daniélou, Yves Congar, and the other "new" theologians of the 1930s and 1940s, de Lubac

5. Brian Daley, "The *Nouvelle Théologie* and the Patristic Revival: Sources, Symbols and the Science of Theology," *International Journal of Systematic Theology* 7, no. 4 (2005): 362–82 at 367.

6. "The informed reader will notice that we owe much to Fr. Mersch." De Lubac, *Catholicism*, Introduction, 211 n. 6; referring to Emil Mersch, *Le Corps mystique du Christ: Études de théologie historiques* (1936); ET: *The Whole Christ: The historical development of the doctrine of the mystical body in scripture and tradition*, trans. J. R. Kelly (Milwaukee: Bruce, 1938).

7. See Daley, "The *Nouvelle Théologie* and the Patristic Revival," 362–82. On the importance of the Tübingen school for twentieth-century ecclesiology, see D. J. Dietrich and M. J. Himes, *The Legacy of the Tübingen School: The Relevance of Nineteenth-Century Theology for the Twenty-First Century* (New York: Crossroad, 1997); M. J. Himes, *Ongoing Incarnation: Johann Adam Möhler and the Beginning of Modern Ecclesiology* (New York: Crossroad, 1997).

8. De Lubac, "Introduction" in idem, *Catholicism*, xix.

looked to the Bible and to the church Fathers for a different, unequivocally metaphorical set of concepts to describe the church: it was the Body of Christ, identified with his risen humanity through his "mystical" or sacramental body present in the eucharist; it was the new form of God's pilgrim people, in damaged yet real continuity with ancient Israel, whom God had chosen once and for all; it was the Bride of Christ, as Origen and Gregory of Nyssa had discovered in their reading of the Song of Songs. It was, in other words, not only a human society, with all the objectifiable, institutional features, all the boundaries of membership and ranking societies must have; it was also a sign, present through all the changes of human history and pointing to the eschatological kingdom, a sacrament—as *Lumen Gentium* would put it—that already makes real, in a veiled yet life-giving way, the thing it signifies.[9]

Our study of de Lubac's doctrine of deification in this chapter calls for a closer investigation of a number of these central ecclesiological themes as they are elaborated first in *Catholicism* and then in numerous subsequent works. We shall begin by focusing on the simultaneously corporate and christological character of the church as it is summed up in the *concorporatio* theme which de Lubac finds in Hilary of Poitiers. Next, we shall examine the sacramental character of the church, with particular reference to the way in which the eucharist serves as a means of deification precisely in its unificatory function and in its constitutive character as a communion not first of holy people but in holy things. Finally, we shall show how all these elements presuppose and imply the necessarily physical and bodily character of deification, a reality iterated by the key term "mystical body."

Deification as *Concorporatio*

Foremost among the articles of Christian faith concerning the church stands the confession of her fundamental unity: "I believe in *one*, holy, catholic and apostolic church." Like her sanctity, this unity is supernatural. It is not the result of moral achievement or sociological consensus, but represents a divine endowment and is a consequence of her origin in and relation to the one true God. But as de Lubac asserts in the very opening page of *Catholicism*, this supernatural unity of the church "supposes a previous natural unity, the

9. Daley, "The *Nouvelle Théologie* and the Patristic Revival," 380.

unity of the human race." For the Fathers of the church, the human race constitutes a single numerical whole, created by God as a corporate unity, fallen in Adam as a corporate unity, and redeemed in the new Adam as a corporate unity. For them, "the lost sheep of the Gospel that the Good Shepherd brings back to the fold is no other than the whole of human nature." However diverse the range of images and metaphors employed to express this unity, their meanings all point to "a concrete nature," demonstrating that corporate humanity was in the view of the Fathers "a genuine reality."[10] Just as God is one and undivided, so is his image in man. What Gregory of Nyssa taught concerning this "divine monogenism" in the fourth century was echoed by Ruysbroeck in the fourteenth:

> It is in reference to this eternal image that we have all been created. It is to be found essentially and personally in all men; each one possesses it whole and entire and undivided, and all together have no more than one. In this way we are all one, intimately united in our eternal image, which is the image of God and in all of us the source of our life and of our creation.[11]

The "Adam" of the Genesis narrative is therefore a universal figure. He is one person and he is himself, yet in himself he incorporates the whole human race, just as Christ, the second Adam, similarly embodies all humanity. But this corporate unity of humanity in Adam is difficult to discern, for sin, which is essentially divisive, has brought about its shattering and fragmentation. "Satan has broken us up."[12] Empirical humanity, the human race as we know and experience it in the darkness of unbelief, is humanity divided. De Lubac cites Augustine's symbolical interpretation of Adam's name in this light. "A" stands for ἀνατολή, meaning east. "D" stands for δύσις ἡλίου, meaning west. The second "A" stands for ἄρκτος, meaning north. And "M" stands for μεσημβρία, meaning south. With his very name indicating the four points of the compass, "Adam himself is therefore now spread out over the whole face of the earth. Originally one, he has fallen, and, breaking up as it were, he has filled the whole earth with the pieces."[13]

What do these and such-like reflections have to do with deification? Or with the church? They tell us that the redemption, being a work of restoration,

10. De Lubac, *Catholicism*, 1.

11. De Lubac, *Catholicism*, 3.

12. De Lubac, *Catholicism*, 5, quoting Cyril of Alexandria.

13. De Lubac, *Catholicism*, 5.

"will appear to us by that very fact as the recovery of a lost unity—the recovery of supernatural unity of man with God, but equally of the unity of men among themselves."[14] If deification means union with God, it necessarily also means union with human beings, or rather, the unification of all human beings in a single, undivided humanity.

It is at this point that de Lubac inserts his findings from St. Hilary (d. 367) on the theme of *concorporatio*. But before seeing what he does with them, some background comments are in order. The term *corporatus*, translating the Greek ἐνσώματος, has a history of use long preceding the time of Hilary. It went back at least to the second-century Bishop Melito of Sardis (fl. c. 170), for whom it functioned as a vital anti-gnostic, anti-docetic term in service of affirming the physical reality of the divine Word's incarnation.[15] Jesus is none other than the incorporeal Logos who "has woven for himself a body from our form."[16] When Hilary, in whom Latin christology "found its first comprehensive description,"[17] later took up the substantive *corporatio*, he used it widely in his writings with the simple meaning of embodiment, but also enriched it further with his deeply Trinitarian, kenotic, and ecclesiological theology of the incarnation. The incarnation of the Word is indeed a real embodiment, a real *corporatio*; this is Hilary's constant refrain. However, Christ's body also possesses a universal, inclusive character. For this, Hilary uses the term *concorporatio*. In becoming human the Word assumed an already-existing common humanity. But this metaphysical fact is ordered and directed toward the establishment of a very new reality. Since Christ is truly God, his incorporation of human nature cannot but bring about a dynamic transformation of that humanity into something uniquely and utterly new. To speak of the incarnation as a *concorporatio*, then, is to recognize in its lineaments the foundation of a new humanity, fully contained in Christ's actual bodily reality, so that in its growth and destiny, the growth and destiny of all humanity is effectually embodied and revealed. For Hilary, this fact is confirmed in part by Jesus' lack of human paternity: not just his body, but all human flesh has inchoately become his home in the womb of the Virgin:

14. De Lubac, *Catholicism*, 6.

15. See Aloys Grillmeier, *Christ in Christian Tradition: From the Apostolic Age to Chalcedon (AD 451)*, trans. J. S. Bowdon (London: Mowbray, 1965), 111–14; Henry Chadwick, "A Latin Epitome of Melito's Homily on the Pascha," *Journal of Theological Studies* 11, no. 1 (1960): 76–82.

16. Melito of Sardis, *Fragment* 14, from the Latin translation quoted by Grillmeier, *Christ in Christian Tradition*, 114.

17. Grillmeier, *Christ in Christian Tradition*, 313.

By his own power—the power of God—which overshadowed her, he sowed the beginning of his body, and entered on the first stage of his life in the flesh. He did this so that by his Incarnation he might take to himself from the Virgin the fleshly nature, and that through this commingling there might come into being a hallowed body of all humanity; so that through that body which he was pleased to assume, all mankind might be hidden in him, and he in return, through his unseen existence, might be reproduced in all.[18]

But not only is the body of Jesus the body of all humanity. It is also a glorious body; indeed, it is the body of God. By assuming humanity, the divine Son adds humanity to his divinity, transfiguring it whole and entire into divinity.[19] In Christ, creation witnesses the advent of a deified human nature of which all human beings are the primary and common benefactors. This nature

began in him with his human birth, so that all he obtains is on behalf of that nature which before was not God, since after the mystery of the economy God is all in all. It is, therefore, we who are the gainers, we who are promoted, for we shall be conformed to the glory of the body of God.[20]

---

18. Hilary of Poitiers, *De Trinitate* II, 24 (NPNF 9, 59). On the relation of these texts to Hilary's doctrine of deification, see P. T. Wild, *The Divinization of Man According to Saint Hilary of Poitiers* (Mundelein, IL: Saint Mary of the Lake Seminary, 1950).

19. Hilary, *De Trinitate* XI, 40–42 (NPNF 9, 214–15).

20. Hilary, *De Trinitate* XI, 49 (NPNF 9, 217). In a manifest concern to avoid any association with the so-called "physical" doctrine of redemption ascribed by many nineteenth- and twentieth-century western theologians to the Greek Fathers, Wild plays down the significance of these and similar passages in Hilary's theology of the incarnation. "These texts do not force us to admit a universal incarnation, but in the absence of contrary texts they would strongly incline us to do so. Although it is true that in these places Hilary closely resembles the Eastern Fathers who like Athanasius do not at all times clearly distinguish between Christ and Christians, he nevertheless gives us sufficient proof that he teaches no incarnation of God with a universal man." Wild, *The Divinization of Man*, 62. For an alternative view almost exactly contemporaneous with the publication of Henri de Lubac's *Catholicism*, see Emil Mersch, "Filii in Filio," *Nouvelle Revue Théologique* 65 (1938): 551–82, 681–702, 809–30. Mersch argues from the Fathers that the plenitude of Christ's humanity exceeds the physical boundaries of his earthly, pre-glorified body. In fact one can already detect this notion in the New Testament, as noted by Yves Congar: "In the thought of St. Paul, it is the personal body of the risen Christ which comes first. Nevertheless, this body has a role and a value for the entire world; through it, Christ is the principle of a new creation." Yves Congar, "Peut-on definer l'Eglise? Destin et valeur de quatre notions qui s'offrent à la faire," in J. Leclercq, *L'homme, l'oeuvre et ses amis* (Paris and Tournai: Casterman, 1961), 233–54 at 240.

Here then is the theology that de Lubac wants to evoke in his brief reference to Hilary's notion of *concorporatio*. Returning to the text of *Catholicism* we read:

> For the Word did not merely take a human body; his Incarnation was not a simple *corporatio*, but, as St Hilary says, a *concorporatio*. He incorporated himself in our humanity, and incorporated it in himself. . . . In making a human nature, it is *human nature* that he united to himself, that he enclosed in himself, and it is the latter, whole and entire, that in some sort he uses as a body. *Naturam in se universae carnis adsumpsit.* Whole and entire he will bear it then to Calvary, whole and entire will he raise it from the dead, whole and entire he will save it.[21]

A critical ecclesiological implication of this doctrine immediately suggests itself. For Hilary, the term *concorporatio*, especially as used in his *Tractates on the Psalms*, as well as designating Christ in his bodily universality, also designates the church.[22] De Lubac proposes a similar reciprocal analogy. Just as Jesus "took the elements of his body from our race" in such a way that "his human nature is not like to ours only in an ideal way" but is in fact "our own nature," so in like manner with the church, "it is humanity that provides it with a body."[23] What can be said of Christ can in many cases be said equally of the church. Each is "a center, an atmosphere, a whole world even, in which man and God, man and man, are in communion and achieve union."[24] This is not to say that the church is all divine. De Lubac explicitly repudiates ecclesiological monophysitism. But as in christology, neither the divine nor human dimensions can be dissociated without fatal consequences.[25] If Christianity is to have any meaning, any real universality for the human race scattered through time and space, then what we find in Christ we must also encounter in the church. And what do we encounter therein? Completed humanity, deified humanity, "the form that humanity must put on in order finally to be itself."[26] How can it be otherwise, if what Gregory of Nyssa says is true, that "he who beholds

21. De Lubac, *Catholicism*, 7.

22. See Wild, *The Divinization of Man*, 61, 73–81; A. Fierro, *Sobre la Gloria en San Hilario: Una sintesis doctrinal sobre la noción biblica de «doxa»*, Analecta Gregoriana 144 (Rome: Libreria editrice dell' Univ. Gregoriana, 1964), 121–80.

23. De Lubac, *Catholicism*, 149.

24. Ibid., 11.

25. Ibid., 27–28.

26. Ibid., 157.

the Church, really beholds Christ"?[27] De Lubac goes so far as to attribute a kind of *communicatio idiomatum* between the deified humanity of Christ and the church.[28] Such bold predications are permissible ultimately in the light of the final reality, yet between means and end the relationship is not merely extrinsic. Even now in the church, as in Christ, "man's desires and God's have their meeting-place. . . ."[29] And just as every detail in Christ's human life is charged with salvific value and power, so too, nothing that belongs to the church by nature, from her historical contingency to her hierarchical structure, is incidental to her deifying, sacramental character. "If Christ is the sacrament of God, the Church is for us the sacrament of Christ; she represents him, in the full and ancient meaning of the term, she really makes him present. She not only carries on his work, but she is his very continuation. . . ."[30]

In this way de Lubac makes it clear that the body of Christ which is the church is not radically other than the body of Christ incarnate, crucified, and risen. There is essentially only "one new humanity," one pattern of fullness and perfection. Humanity is organically one by virtue of its "divine structure." The church's calling is to embody that pristine, theogenetic unity which human beings have lost, and to restore and complete it.[31] Here we are at the heart and center of de Lubac's idea of the church as the *locus deificandi*. Being a supernatural, corporate union of humanity with God in the one body of Christ, deification is essentially and irreducibly ecclesial. This does not empty the intrinsic differentiation that obtains between the many members of the church of its meaning and value. De Lubac affirms simultaneously both union and distinction in the church by recourse to Maximus the Confessor's mystagogical meditations on the divine liturgy. In the communion of nature established in the church, difference is not so much removed as it is rendered transparent and fruitful:

> Men, women, children, profoundly divided in nationality, race, language, walk of life, work, knowledge, rank or means . . . all these she recreates in the Spirit. On all in the same measure she imprints a divine character. All receive of her a single nature which cannot be divided and by reason of which their many and deep differences can no longer be held in account.[32]

27. Gregory of Nyssa, *Cant.* 13, quoted by de Lubac, *Catholicism*, 26.

28. De Lubac, *Catholicism*, 26.

29. Ibid., 156.

30. Ibid., 28.

31. Ibid., 16.

In these and in numerous other affirmations related to the *concorporatio* theme, de Lubac makes clear his conviction that the church is the divinely instituted and necessary organ of salvation in the world, inasmuch as she actually is humanity inscribed with the form of Christ. Long before Rahner's problematic presentation of an anonymous Christianity according to which, as we have seen, the church's proclamation and liturgical embodiment of the gospel seem sometimes only to function as occasions for making explicit that which is already implicitly present and real in the human condition, de Lubac also considers the question of an "implicit" Christianity, a notion that seems to be required by the fact that saving grace is available and operative outside the boundaries of the visible church.

> Since salvation is made accessible to those who are called (no longer with good reason) "unbelievers," is not the necessity for their belonging to the visible Church diminished to such an extent that it vanishes altogether? By what right henceforward is any obligation of entering the Church imposed upon them? It is not sufficient answer to say: the obligation devolves only on one who encounters the Church.[33]

The positive command to be baptized and believe the gospel, binding as it is, does not in itself furnish a harmonious rationale by which to make sense of the church's requisite missionary vocation on the one hand and the real possibility of salvation for non-Christians on the other. Do not these two apparently irreconcilable facts call for the notion of an implicit Christianity, or something like Rahner's "unthematic" Christianity? And if so, does that notion not call into question the obligatory character of a person's coming to profess an "explicit" Christian faith? As de Lubac asks, "If an implicit Christianity is sufficient for the salvation of one who knows no other, why should we go in quest of an explicit one?"[34]

32. Maximus the Confessor, *Mystagogia* 1, quoted by de Lubac, *Catholicism*, 16. For a more detailed analysis of Maximus' ecclesiology and liturgical metaphysics, see Adam G. Cooper, *The Body in Saint Maximus the Confessor* (Oxford: Oxford University Press, 2005), 165–205.

33. De Lubac, *Catholicism*, 109. For a critique of Rahner's theory of anonymous Christianity, see Hans Urs von Balthasar, *The Moment of Christian Witness*, trans. R. Beckley (San Francisco: Ignatius, 1969), 100–13. However, Karen Kilby has argued that to the degree that von Balthasar's critique depends on a foundationalist reading of Rahner's theology, it tends toward caricature and misrepresentation. See Karen Kilby, *Karl Rahner: Theology and Philosophy* (London: Routledge, 2004), 116–19.

34. De Lubac, *Catholicism*, 110.

In answer, de Lubac steers us away from inquisitive speculations concerning the eternal fate of this or that individual, and draws us back to a consideration of the essentially social and corporate unity of humanity. "The human race is one. By our fundamental nature and still more in virtue of our common destiny we are members of the same body." Salvation of the members of this body is contingent upon the salvation of the body itself, and the salvation of the body itself "consists in its receiving the form of Christ." But what else is the church than the body of humanity which has received the form of Christ? And thus, as St. Augustine has put it, "In her alone mankind is re-fashioned and re-created."[35]

For de Lubac, this means that any religious form or mystical sentiment that in principle or practice does not lead toward a *sequela Christi*—a following of Christ—is one that has failed to attain its proper goal. "Outside Christianity nothing attains its end, that only end, towards which, unknowingly, all human desires, all human endeavours, are in movement: the embrace of God in Christ."[36] With this reference to a dynamic movement "unknowingly" present in all human activity, it may be wondered whether de Lubac is indicating something similar to Rahner's unspecified, unthematic trajectory of transcendence. But de Lubac is much bolder and more confident than Rahner in identifying the church as the concrete place or locale ("here") in which this "embrace of God in Christ" may be existentially encountered and fulfilled:

> Cities expand yet are always closed societies, they combine together but only to fight more bitterly with one another, and beneath their outward unity there is always the personal enmity of the souls within them. But here is that divine house built upon the rock *in qua,* according to that marvellous formula of the Vatican Council, *veluti in domo Dei viventis, fideles omnes unius fidei et caritatis vinculo continerentur.* Here is the marriage house in which heaven is joined to earth. Here is the household in which all are gathered together to eat of the Lamb; here is the place of true sacrifice.[37]

---

35. De Lubac, *Catholicism*, 111. Quoting from Augustine, *Ep.* 118.

36. De Lubac, *Catholicism*, 112.

37. Ibid., 113. The Latin translates: "in which . . . all the faithful should be linked by the bond of one faith and charity." *Dogmatic Constitution on the Church of Christ*, Session IV, Vatican I (1870); text and translation in *Decrees of the Ecumenical Councils*, vol. 2, ed. N. P. Tanner (London: Sheed & Ward, 1990), 811.

In a later theological commentary and reflection on the Dogmatic Constitution *Lumen Gentium*, de Lubac confirms this fundamental ecclesiocentrism by drawing an important distinction between the anonymous Christian "found in diverse milieux where, one way or another, the light of the gospel has penetrated," and a so-called anonymous or implicit *Christianity* to which the preaching of the gospel adds nothing new but which is simply rendered explicit by it and so left "essentially unchanged."[38]

In this connection, it is interesting to observe that, in this same work just quoted dating from after the Council, in which he could have been tempted to name Rahner as the specific target of this critique, de Lubac irenically draws on Rahner in support of his argument for the efficacious and utterly surprising newness of the Christ event: "Christianity . . . is the herald of an entirely new, entirely other, dimension of human existence. . . . God has *assaulted* this world so constituted. He offers to its anxious search an issue in his own infinity."[39] This quote recalls de Lubac's constant insistence upon the radically unexacted and surprising character of the supernatural: the Christ event entails a rupture, a new beginning, a profound conversion in the depths of human being. At the same time we may note a qualification made by de Lubac concerning the relativity of this novel humanity inaugurated by Christ. The New Testament repeatedly designates the human being incorporated into Christ a "new creation" (2 Cor. 5:17; Gal. 6:13), heralding Christ's intended renewal of "all things" and the foundation of a new heaven and earth (2 Cor. 5:17; 2 Pet. 3:13; Rev. 21:1-5). But is this to be taken as a creation all over again, a kind of "plan B" consequent to some inherent failing in the first? De Lubac argues that "the novelty of Christianity consists in its being a transfiguration rather than a fresh creation."[40] In fact what arrives on the scene in the historical reality of the Christian religion is not new at all, but somehow older than creation itself. Early witnesses speak of the church as existing before all creation, not as some "transcendent hypostasis," but as creation's true pattern and goal, "a mystery surpassing its outward manifestations."[41] On the one hand, her present form is provisional, as Pope Pius XI affirmed: "men were not made for the Church, but the Church was made for men." On the other hand, she is not just a means to unite humanity to God, "but she is herself the end, that is to say, the union in its consummation."[42] Between the means and the end there is not just "an extrinsic

---

38. De Lubac, *The Church: Paradox and Mystery*, trans. J. R. Dunne (Shannon, Ireland: Ecclesia, 1969), 87.

39. Ibid., 93 n. 78, quoting Karl Rahner, *Mystique terrestre et mystique chrétienne de l'avenir* (1961).

40. De Lubac, *Catholicism*, 19.

41. Ibid., 21.

relationship." Rather we are dealing with "two states of the same body."[43] In short, there is finally only one creation, which, by virtue of its incorporation in the God-man Christ, remains forever "new."

COMMUNION IN HOLY THINGS

Especially since the Second Vatican Council, it has been common to refer to the church in terms of "the people of God." If the church has in history sometimes looked and acted like a monarchical political empire, it is in truth more fundamentally a pilgrim assembly, the Spirit-filled *qahal* of the living God, on route to its true and heavenly homeland. Combining with the people-of-God theme there has been a parallel development in what may called a *communio* ecclesiology or "ecclesiology of communion,"[44] which draws not only on the New Testament theology of *koinonia* but on a revitalization of Trinitarian theology that structures the church in constitutive dependence upon the economically immanent *circumincession* of the divine persons. There is no doubt that among the seminal works of theology that laid the foundations for this conciliar renewal in ecclesiology ranks Henri de Lubac's *Catholicism.*

However, it wasn't until his research for *Corpus Mysticum* and its publication after the war that de Lubac first investigated in detail a much-neglected facet proper to a fully catholic ecclesiology of communion, without which it risks losing the objective ground upon which the communion among the faithful and with God is founded.[45] And yet despite its importance, this facet, which has to do with the meaning of the phrase *sanctorum communio* in the third article of the Apostles' Creed, has barely received the attention it deserves, being overshadowed particularly in the postconciliar era by the more popular "people of God" ecclesiology.[46] In his later years de Lubac was known to express numerous regrets about an increasing muddying of the waters in

42. Ibid., 25.

43. Ibid., 27.

44. "This ecclesiology of communion [espoused by de Lubac] became the real core of Vatican II's teaching on the Church, the novel and at the same time the original element in what the Council wanted to give us." Joseph Ratzinger, *Church, Ecumenism, and Politics: New Essays in Ecclesiology* (New York: Crossroad, 1988), 7.

45. The earliest evidence that I can find that indicates de Lubac's awareness of the question, with reference to Kattenbusch's study, is de Lubac, "Communauté et communion," in *La Communauté Français: Cahiers d'études communautaires*, vol. 2, ed. F. Perroux and J. Madaule (Paris: Presses Universitaires de France, 1942); ET: "Christian Community and Sacramental Communion," in de Lubac, *Theological Fragments*, trans. R. H. Balinski (San Francisco: Ignatius, 1989), 71–75.

catholic theology in general.[47] In one place in particular he mentions the failure on the part of twentieth-century catechetical teaching to take up this ancient and original locus as a kind of corrective balance to more socializing ecclesiological trends. The time has come, he said, "for emphasizing all the depth of the original meaning of the *communio sanctorum*—not for erasing or blurring the derived meaning, which is inherent in the original one, but for demonstrating its unique and necessary foundation."[48] But what is its original meaning? And why is this so important?

De Lubac first addressed the question of the meaning of *sanctorum communio* in *Corpus Mysticum* in his treatment of the word *communio*, translating the Greek words σύναξις or κοινωνία.[49] His attention was drawn by a number of studies from as early as 1894 to a range of early Christian witnesses in which *communio sanctorum*, commonly taken as a kind of creedal exposition of the preceding "holy catholic church" and translated accordingly as "communion of saints," is rather understood as "communion in holy things" and refers to the sacraments or, more specifically, to the eucharist.[50] Up until the turn of the twentieth century the phrase *sanctorum communio* in the Apostles' Creed was thought to have originated in Gaul some time around the middle of the fifth century. Interpretations of the formulation almost invariably understood *sanctorum* as the genitive of *sancti*, meaning "saints" or "holy persons." But then a passage was discovered in the writings of Bishop Nicetas of Remesiana (d. c. 420) that suggested an earlier Greek background for the phrase, such that the corresponding Greek formulation would read τῶν ἁγίων κοινωνία. While it is grammatically feasible to read the genitive τῶν ἁγίων as a collective masculine ("of holy people"), normally, when intending the term κοινωνία to

---

46. By contrast the question of the *sanctorum communio* has aroused no little discussion among liturgical scholars and historical theologians. Key studies include F. J. Badcock, "*Sanctorum Communio* as an Article in the Creed," *Journal of Theological Studies* 21, no. 1 (1920): 106–26; Werner Elert, *Eucharist and Fellowship in the First Four Centuries*, trans. N. E. Nagel (Saint Louis: Concordia, 1966 [orig. 1954]); S. Benko, *The Meaning of "Sanctorum Communio"* (London: SCM, 1964); J. N. D. Kelly, *Early Christian Creeds* (Harlow, UK: Longman, 1972, 3rd ed.), 388–97.

47. For a number of quite candid criticisms see de Lubac, *At the Service of the Church*, 140–51; also C. J. Walsh, "Henri de Lubac in Connecticut: Unpublished conferences on renewal in the postconciliar period," *Communio* 23 (1996): 786–805.

48. De Lubac, "Sanctorum Communio," in idem, *Theological Fragments*, 11–34, at 26.

49. De Lubac, *Corpus Mysticum: The Eucharist and the Church in the Middle Ages*, trans. G. Simmonds et al. (Notre Dame: University of Notre Dame Press, 2006), 20–21 (translated from the 2nd French ed. of 1949).

50. De Lubac, *Corpus Mysticum*, 20–21 nn. 53–54, citing Badcock, Morin, and Kattenbusch respectively.

speak of a fellowship among persons, the predominant pattern in early Greek texts is to use a prefix (such as μετά, εἰς, or πρός) followed by the noun in the appropriate case. Unless suggested otherwise by context, κοινωνία with the genitive normally indicates a fellowship in *things*, rather than in *persons*. Thus a more precise interpretation of the creedal formula τῶν ἁγίων κοινωνία or *sanctorum communio* is to understand it as referring to a communion or participation *in holy things*.

Of course a purely grammatical argument needs to be supported by additional evidence. What are the holy things (τὰ ἅγια) to which the phrase refers? Testimonies from early Christian liturgies and liturgical catechesis furnish numerous examples that indicate the holy things to be the body and blood of Christ offered and administered in the eucharist. Referring to the moment after the Lord's Prayer in the eucharistic liturgy of mid-fourth-century Jerusalem, Cyril of Jerusalem comments:

> After this the priest says, "Holy things to holy people." Holy are the gifts presented, since they have been visited by the Holy Spirit; holy also are you, having been deemed worthy by the Holy Spirit. The holy things therefore correspond to the holy persons.[51]

One may also mention certain negative testimonies that, in the context of ecclesial discipline, refer to the exclusion of persons from communion in the holy things. What these witnesses tell us is that, in the understanding of the early Christians, fellowship in the church was constituted and mediated by participation in the eucharist. Inclusion or exclusion from the communion of the saints was effected by inclusion or exclusion from communion in holy things, that is, the holy rites and actions culminating in the reception of Christ's body and blood. De Lubac affirms the judgment of Fr. Jacques-Joseph Duguet (1649–1732) in his *Conférences ecclésiastiques*:

> [I]n the ancient custom of the Church there was no separation between reconciliation and participation in the sacraments, and when penitents were judged to have been made righteous, they were given the Eucharist, in such a way that communion signified both one and the other. . . .[52]

51. Cyril of Jerusalem, *Mystagogical Catecheses* V, 19. ET: *St. Cyril of Jerusalem's Lectures on the Christian Sacraments: The Procatechesis and the Five Mystagogical Catecheses*, ed. F. L. Cross (London: SPCK, 1951), 78.

52. Quoted by de Lubac, *Corpus Mysticum*, 18.

This understanding of participation in holy things as constitutive of fellowship in the ecclesial body of Christ seems to have been present from very early on in the Christian liturgy. In the late first- or early second-century text of the *Didache*, again in the context of commentary on the eucharistic liturgy, we encounter the warning: "Let no one eat or drink from your Eucharist except those who have been baptised in the name of the Lord. For the Lord also spoke concerning this, 'Do not give what is holy to dogs.'"[53] Here the author expressly applies τὸ ἅγιον from Matt. 7:6 to the consecrated eucharistic elements. The implication is clear enough: participation in the holy things—the holy body and blood of the Lord—effectively constitutes a real fellowship and unity among the participants.[54] The ecclesial κοινωνία among the saints is caused by, and ontologically dependent upon, the sacramental κοινωνία in holy things.

De Lubac's aim in developing this theme is not to play one translation off against the other. In fact he finds the two aspects indivisibly interlocked. The bulk of evidence from the early church indicates that the communion of saints is

> simultaneously and indivisibly described as *communion of the sacraments* and *the society or fellowship of the blessed*, that is to say, it is the communion of saints in its current sense, or communion with the saints or among the saints—*one fellowship in communion*—in the common sharing in the sacrament, in the *holy things* (= *holy mysteries*) and through the effect of this participation.[55]

However, the discovery and elaboration of these texts seems to occasion a subtle new emphasis in de Lubac's writings on ecclesiology that had not been as sharply spelled out in *Catholicism*. The emphasis relates to the causal relation between the sacramental mysteries or "communion in holy things" on the one hand and the church or "communion of the saints" on the other. In *Catholicism*, de Lubac seems to envisage a mutually reciprocal causal relation between the

---

53. *Didache* 9, 5.

54. Similarly, the neuter plural τὰ μυστήρια in 1 Cor. 4:1 suggested to early Christian exegetes a reference to the gospel and sacraments (or the Sacrament of the Altar in particular), which together comprise the holy gifts or holy things with which Paul and his fellow Apostles had been solemnly entrusted by the Lord and of which they had been appointed administering servants and stewards. For a study of its exegesis in Origen, see J. L. Kovacs, "'Servant of Christ' and 'Steward of the Mysteries of God': The Purpose of a Pauline Letter according to Origen's *Homilies on 1 Corinthians*," in *In Dominico Eloquio / In Lordly Eloquence: Essays on Patristic Exegesis in Honor of Robert L. Wilken*, ed. Paul Blowers et al. (Grand Rapids: Eerdmans, 2002), 147–71.

55. De Lubac, *Corpus Mysticum*, 21.

eucharist and the church, since they are both *corpus Christi*. In this way the causality of the sacraments is seen to depend in large part upon their social context. Quoting Matthias Scheeben on this score, de Lubac asserts that their performative power lies not so much in the supernatural efficacy of this or that rite or action as in the existence of a certain kind of society within which such rites and actions are conferred with meaning.[56] True enough, "it is still in view of the Church that this efficacy is bestowed upon them," yet it remains the case that "the sacraments derive their efficacy from the Church. . . ."[57] But having engaged with the *sanctorum communio* question, de Lubac seems here and there to envision some form of asymmetry in the relationship between holy things and holy people, with the priority resting in the *sacra* or holy things. "It is communication among the saints (*sancti*) that results from their common participation in the sacrament, in the holy mysteries (*sancta*)."[58] There is nothing that suggests he felt any need to rescind his earlier expressions, still less to correct them. Typically he wants to hold both together in paradoxical tension: both church and eucharist "are remade each day by each other."[59] But in later writings a clear emphasis emerges. He argues that the "holy things" interpretation of the creedal *sanctorum communio*, besides being historically accurate, is entirely in keeping with the "*objective* turn of mind" that has always characterized the orthodox Christian gospel proclaimed in its integrity and confessed in faith.

> From beginning to end, it is the announcement of a divine reality concerning man's salvation and of the divine deeds that bring about this salvation. Thus, it always deals with the objective conditions of salvation, not with its subjective appropriation.[60]

True enough, the subjective appropriation "is envisaged in its cause." But the primary sense contained and expressed in the confession of the *sanctorum communio* is of an objective reality designating "the source from which the Christian receives his personal saintliness. . . ."[61] Only thereby does there

---

56. De Lubac, *Catholicism*, 32.

57. Ibid., 33.

58. De Lubac, "Christian Community and Sacramental Communion," in idem, *Theological Fragments*, 72.

59. Ibid., 75.

60. Ibid., 75.

follow, as effect from cause, a communion or *communicatio* among the saints. "It is through the *communio sanctorum* that the *communicatio sancti Spiritus*, the communication of the Spirit of Christ, is brought about."[62] And again, "The communion of saints is not an effect that is exterior to the sacrament; it cannot be detached from it. It is the definition of its fruitfulness. . . . The Eucharist makes the Church, it completes it."[63] For this reason de Lubac calls the eucharist "the sacrament of sacraments," for it is precisely on account of these holy things that there is present in the church, and through the church in the world, "a deifying virtue."[64]

BODILY DEIFICATION

It is now time to consider the place this particular ecclesiology of communion or participation "in holy things" holds in our wider account of de Lubac's understanding of deification. This will become clear as we consider it in broader relation to what we may describe as the constitutively corporeal character of deification according to de Lubac's theology. As we have seen, the words *corpus Christi*, body of Christ, are applicable to both the eucharist and the church. Communion in the one effects and constitutes communion in the other. "To communicate sacramentally or receive the body of Christ in one's self is to incorporate oneself into Christ."[65] De Lubac draws attention to the contrast, often related by the Fathers, between the ordinary assimilation of food by the body and what happens in eucharistic communion. When I eat ordinary food, I assimilate it to myself, to my body. When I eat the body of Christ, I myself am assimilated to him, to his body. "We do not assimilate the nourishment from the Eucharist; it assimilates us. We receive life by entering into union with Christ: *incorporetur ut vivificetur*."[66] For de Lubac this is no rhetorical game. "Through the Eucharist each person is truly placed within the one body."[67] To draw out de Lubac's meaning further we are able to utilize again the christological concept of *concorporatio*. This being "placed within the one body," this insertion that takes place through communion in the holy things administered in the

61. De Lubac, "Sanctorum Communio," in idem, *Theological Fragments*, 16.

62. Ibid., 19.

63. Ibid., 24.

64. Ibid., 31, quoting Jean Daniélou.

65. De Lubac, "Christian Community and Sacramental Communion," in idem, *Theological Fragments*, 74.

66. Ibid., 74.

67. De Lubac, *Corpus Mysticum*, 23.

eucharist, is surely nothing else than a mystical *concorporatio*. Its possibility depends on the mysterious but real continuity that obtains between the triple intersecting "modes" of the one body—the one *concorporatio*—of Christ: the historic, the eucharistic, and the ecclesial. In the economy of the ecclesial body of Christ, the incarnate Word passes into his church. But this passage is itself "prepared, or even prefigured by an earlier passing, that of the Church into Christ: is the Church not in fact the greater body from which Christ drew his body?"[68] As we have seen in the doctrine of *concorporatio*, in the incarnation, humanity furnishes a body for the Word. Now, in the eucharist, the Word furnishes his body, transformed by his passion and resurrection, for humanity. The universal *concorporatio* realized by Christ is now made concretely accessible in the form of its liturgical and ecclesial actualization. De Lubac is especially struck by a passage along these lines from Candidus, the ninth-century monk of Fulda and successor of Rabanus Maurus:

> "Take and eat." That is, Gentiles, make up my body, which you already are. This is the body which is given for you. What he took from that mass of the human race, he broke by his passion, and raised up after breaking . . . . Therefore what he took from us he handed over for us. You are to "eat," that is, perfect the body of the Church, so that, whole and perfect, she may become the one bread, with Christ as its head. . . . Bread, therefore, is the body of Christ, which he took from the body, the Church.[69]

Such sentiments presuppose the decidedly *physical* character of sacramental and ecclesial communion with Christ and, in him, with the holy Trinity. This remark calls for qualification. In *Catholicism* de Lubac had urged resistance to any pressure to conceive the final unity of the church with God as either a "physical" or a "merely moral" union. "The analogies that these opposed conceptions evoke lead inevitably to so many confused ideas. . . ."[70] Our participation in the divine nature is rather a union of love, a "Trinitarian" union, and therefore necessarily a social and collective union. Yet as he goes on to argue, the social character of salvation is bound up with its bodily character in such a way that, according to theological tradition, there stand two conditions to final happiness: the resurrection of the body and the completion of the

68. Ibid., 24.

69. Candidus of Fulda, *De passione Domini* 5–6, quoted by de Lubac, *Corpus Mysticum*, 24 (in italics, modified here).

70. De Lubac, *Catholicism*, 51.

number of the elect.[71] It is the corporeal character of deification that requires not only the resurrection of individual bodies, but of all bodies united in the one body, whose full stature is only realized in perfection at the *parousia*. De Lubac approves St. Thomas's doctrine of the kingdom of God as "nothing else than the well-ordered society of those who enjoy the vision of God."[72] But what does this mean? The human being is an integrated unity, such that the soul alone is not perfect without the body. Moreover, the body is the medium of human communication and social interaction. Both these unities—soul and body, and body and society—are essential to human existence, development, and final well-being. Thus the soul separated from the body at death suffers a double isolation: from its own body, and from other body-persons. Only at the resurrection of all bodies is this isolation ultimately resolved. But this resolution is already anticipated precisely in the deifying *concorporatio* performatively embodied in the eucharist:

> [The soul] is separated from its body and so it is also cut off, in some sort, from the natural medium through which it communicates with its fellows. And is it not true to say, too, that according to traditional teaching the Eucharist by incorporating us in Christ, that is to say, by uniting us to him, and in him to all our brethren, makes us ready for the resurrection to a glorious immortality?[73]

Only in this embodied, social form will the history of salvation be complete, "the history of the penetration of humanity by Christ."[74]

De Lubac's development of this point seems to be paralleled further on in *Catholicism* in his chapter on "Person and Society." Just as the separated soul suffers a "twofold" isolation, so the fallen human being faces a "twofold" obstacle barring his way to the Promised Land. Corresponding to the soul separated from its own body is "egoism," while corresponding to the soul separated from other body-persons is "individuality." The first is a moral obstacle; the second, however, is metaphysical.[75] Deification concerns both. Their resolution depends upon the human person's bodily incorporation into a communion of love in which his or her personhood is established and realized in all its God-intended

71. Ibid., 60.
72. Ibid., 59.
73. Ibid., 60.
74. Ibid., 66.
75. Ibid., 189.

nobility. For man by himself, morally wounded and metaphysically bounded, the goal is unreachable.

> But what is impossible to mere man becomes possible to man made divine. . . . Christ, by completing humanity in himself, at the same time made us all complete—but in God. Thus we can say, in the end, taking up again St Paul's εἰς and St Augustine's *una persona*, that we are fully persons only within the Person of the Son, by whom and with whom we share in the circumincession of the Trinity.[76]

Of course, language like this can easily become the target of criticisms that would label it as "pie in the sky." How can it be said with any plausibility that the eucharist celebrated by very ordinary priests in lowly suburban and rural parishes anticipates and effectively embodies such high-minded supernatural realities? De Lubac is conscious of the Marxist temptation to take social transformation into one's own hands, to transpose into the natural order this vision of the supernatural. But an equally dangerous temptation is so to separate this supernatural vision from the natural world that faith, exercised well enough in heavenly realities, is prevented from bearing fruit in love. Again, it is only by retaining the bodily and social dimension that faith is rescued from disincarnate gnostic fancies. "Charity has not to become inhuman in order to remain supernatural; like the supernatural itself it can only be understood as incarnate."[77] This explains why, if the faith-filled determination of the Christian fails, "he will feel it as a wound in his own flesh."[78]

Throughout this chapter we have seen how the intelligibility of de Lubac's doctrine of deification depends upon a christocentric ecclesiology of communion according to which the body of Christ and the body which is his church are inseparably related in a kind of *communicatio idiomatum*. Unlike its christological counterpart, however, the reciprocal predication of properties between Christ and the church is not meant to be undertaken with dogmatic exactitude. Still less ought one attempt to achieve a precise, mathematically symmetrical system. As de Lubac envisages it, and as he finds it in the teaching of the great Fathers of the church, it rather possesses a character and function more heuristic, evangelical, and meditative, arising as it were out of the dynamism of a lively, searching faith elicited and expressed through contemplative exegesis of the holy Scriptures and liturgical praxis.

76. Ibid., 189.
77. Ibid., 207.
78. Ibid., 208.

Having said that, in a careful study Susan Wood has argued that de Lubac in his later works himself occasionally attenuated the applicability of such imagery, alert to its liability to give rise to certain theological misappropriations. "The image of the Church as a body is ambivalent, making, as it does, a single organism of Jesus Christ and his Church, but signifying at the same time the subjection of the members to the head."[79] Wood's own critique of de Lubac's analogy between Christ's union with the church and the union of the divine and human in Christ goes somewhat further.

> On the one hand, if the Church is joined to Christ as humanity is joined to divinity, this results in a hypostatic unity. In this instance the relationship between Christ and the Church could not be free, resulting in an orthodox Christology but in a heterodox ecclesiology. If, on the other hand, the Church is joined to Christ in a covenantal relationship, this results in a Nestorian Christology as the *anthropos* is joined to the *Logos*. Because in this case the unity of the Logos-anthropos is intrinsically covenantal, the corresponding Christology is adoptionist.[80]

The key to the right use of analogous statements about Christ and the church seems to lie in reading them eschatologically. Wood acknowledges de Lubac's awareness of this fact already at the time of *Catholicism* when, in a passage we have already commented on, he describes the church as "that mysterious structure which will become fully a reality only at the end time: no longer is she a means to unite humanity in God, but she is herself the end, that is to say, that union in its consummation."[81] What finally matters, and this point stands behind all that has been argued in this chapter, is that both the divine and human elements in the church be held together, as Wood states, "in all their paradoxical tension. . . ." Only in this way is it possible to avoid "a merely secular and sociological understanding of the Church as institution." Just as Christ's physical humanity is the sacrament of God, so the church—in both her bodily (holy things) and social (holy persons) dimensions—is the sacrament of Christ and as such the place of deification in world history. It is entirely appropriate to speak in this exalted way of the church since to do so "is never to

79. See Susan. K. Wood, *Spiritual Exegesis and the Church in the Theology of Henri de Lubac* (Grand Rapids: Eerdmans, 1998), 84, quoting de Lubac, *The Church: Paradox and Mystery*, trans. J. R. Dunne (New York: Ecclesia, 1969), 24.

80. Wood, *Spiritual Exegesis and the Church*, 86.

81. De Lubac, *Catholicism*, 25, referred to by Wood, *Spiritual Exegesis and the Church*, 82.

speak of the Church alone or to let our vision stop short at the Church, but to consider the Church always in relation to Christ."[82]

82. Wood, *Spiritual Exegesis and the Church*, 106.

11

Deification and Assimilation to God

In their explorations of the meaning of *theosis* or the gift that enables human beings to become *koinonoi* in the divine nature (2 Pet. 1:4), the early Fathers of the church had recourse to two main ideas, expressed in two key terms. The first idea was expressed in the term μέθεξις, understood in the sense of an ontological participation and transformation, while the second idea was expressed in the term ὁμοίωσις, understood in the sense of a profound personal and moral assimilation.[1] In some ways, the second of the two terms proved the more basic and foundational, opening up to the imagination a more concrete range of possibilities for lived spiritual praxis, and able to be conceptually integrated with already-existing schemas of moral pedagogy. This was partly because the term already had long roots in the Platonic moral tradition, in which the goal of the life lived in pursuit of wisdom and flight from this world was understood to be "assimilation to God as far as possible" (ὁμοίωσις θεῷ κατὰ τὸ δυνατόν).[2] But more importantly, it also had roots in the biblical tradition, in which, at least in the reading given by some exegetes, such assimilation to God was regarded as the God-given ideal for every human being who, fashioned according to the divine εἰκών or "image," was also from the beginning designed to attain ὁμοίωσις or "likeness" to God (Gen. 1:26–27 LXX).

Even a cursory reading of Henri de Lubac's writings makes it clear that this classic patristic and medieval distinction between the image and likeness of God constitutes one of the main structural paradigms of his theology, standing beneath his articulation of the relation between created human nature and its

1. See Norman Russell, *The Doctrine of Deification in the Greek Patristic Tradition* (Oxford: Oxford University Press, 2004), 2.

2. *Theaetetus* 176b. The first formal definition of deification in the Christian tradition, given by Dionysius the Areopagite (fifth–sixth c.), echoes this Platonic formula: "Θέωσις is the attaining of likeness to God and union with him as far as possible." *Ecclesiastical Hierarchy* I, 3 (PG 3, 376A).

vocation to deification. The image of God inscribed in the human person constitutes "a kind of secret call" to the supernatural fullness of life with Christ.[3] What is less clear without a more focused analysis is the way de Lubac importantly links this distinction to two other vital binary pairings of his theology, namely, the distinction between letter and spirit in his articulation of God's scriptural and historical economies, and the distinction between soul and spirit in his tripartite anthropology. It is the purpose of this penultimate chapter to expound the main points in de Lubac's teaching in each of these areas, to relate them to one another by analyzing their relative convergence, and to outline their role and interaction in the movement of the human person toward deifying assimilation to God.

IMAGE AND LIKENESS

It is surely no accident that de Lubac's earliest reading in the Greek Fathers, often snatched in free time during his formative years of exile in Britain—especially in Canterbury and Jersey in the second period after the war between 1919 and 1923—was of the *Adversus haereses* of Irenaeus of Lyons, a work of seminal paramountcy in the history of Christian thought for all sorts of reasons, but not least for its creative adoption and development of the image and likeness distinction.[4]

The distinction itself presupposes acceptance of a particular line of Old Testament interpretation that not all the Fathers of the church, not to mention modern exegetes, have found apparent or convincing. Some background comment on this question is called for. In their juxtaposition in Gen. 1:26, the Hebrew terms *tselem* and *demuth*, customarily translated "image" and "likeness" respectively, are commonly regarded as virtual synonyms. Being added to *tselem* "as an explanatory qualification," Walter Eichrodt explains, the only possible purpose of *demuth* "is to exclude the idea of an actual copy of God, and to

---

3. Henri de Lubac, *The Church: Paradox and Mystery*, trans. J. R. Dunne (Shannon, Ireland: Ecclesia, 1969), 72.

4. Although Irenaeus was a bishop in Gaul, and his writings mostly survive only in Latin and Armenian translations, he originally came from Asia Minor, wrote in Greek his native tongue, and is commonly counted among the Greek Apologists. See further Johannes Quasten, *Patrology*, vol. 1 (Allen, TX: Christian Classics, nd), 287–93. On the image/likeness distinction in Irenaeus, see Eric Osborn, *Irenaeus of Lyons* (Cambridge: Cambridge University Press, 2001), 211–31; Jean Daniélou, *Gospel Message and Hellenistic Culture: A History of Early Christian Doctrine Before the Council of Nicaea*, vol. 2 (London: Darton, Longman & Todd, 1973), 398–408; Gustaf Wingren, *Man and the Incarnation: A Study in the Biblical Theology of Irenaeus*, trans. R. Mackenzie (Edinburgh: Oliver & Boyd, 1959), 14–26.

limit the concept to one of similarity."[5] When later the biblical author wants to refer to man's creation, the term *demuth* suffices, without any mention of *tselem* (Gen. 5:1), and when referring to Seth's resemblance to Adam, the Hebrew text reverses the two terms, placing *demuth* first (Gen. 5:3).

But among those Fathers who made something of the distinction, it must first be noted that they were in the main studying and expounding the old Greek translation of the Hebrew Scriptures, in which the translators had already—and inevitably—exercised some interpretative license. In the two verses of Genesis 5 just mentioned, the Septuagint translators had omitted the term ὁμοίωσις or "likeness" and used only the term εἰκών or "image," in this way harmonizing the text with the slight but to their mind important differences in the two programmatic formulae of Gen. 1:26-27.[6] For there, in the initial intention to create *anthropos*, expressed in the self-deliberation of God in the first person plural, there is mention of both terms:

Let us make man in our *image* and *likeness*. (Gen. 1:26 LXX)

In the very next verse, however, when it comes to reporting the fulfillment of this design, there is only mention of the word "image":

And God created man,
in the *image* of God he created him,
male and female he created them. (Gen. 1:27 LXX)

It was to this subtle verbal difference between the original divine plan and its concrete execution that the early Fathers, for whom no detail in the scriptural text was ever incidental, directed their studied and devout attention. Why, they would have asked, is there no mention of "likeness" in the actual execution of the divine plan? What is it, and how is it distinct from "image"? Is it extrinsic

5. Walter Eichrodt, *Theology of the Old Testament*, vol. 2 (London: SCM, 1967), 123. Von Rad explains the two terms thus: "the second [term] interprets the first by underlining the idea of correspondence and similarity. . . ." Gerhard von Rad, *Old Testament Theology*, vol. 1, trans. D. G. Stalker (New York: Harper & Row, 1962), 144–45.

6. For a brief précis of the meaning of the term in the LXX, see J. Schneider, "ὁμοίωσις," in *Theological Dictionary of the New Testament*, vol. 5, ed. G. Friedrich and G. W. Bromiley (Grand Rapids: Eerdmans, 1967), 190–91.

to human nature, or is it rather some crucial qualification, ultimately intended by God and proper to the ideal form of humanity, but not initially given in its fullness and so held out as a goal to be attained? Reading the Old Testament through the lens of the Christ event and subsequent Christian experience, the Fathers found in the distinction between the two formulae a subtle adumbration of God's deifying pedagogy for human beings through history which would begin with their establishment in being and, through a dynamic cooperative venture of two freedoms, lead eventually to a fully transforming assimilation into his inner Trinitarian life. While Philo had noticed the textual distinction, and on it based his doctrine of double creation, the one ideal and spiritual, the other actual and material, Irenaeus is the first Christian thinker to develop this interpretation with any deep theological promise, integrating it with his christocentric doctrine of recapitulation.[7] The *locus classicus* is in the fifth book of *Adversus haereses*, though it is widely acknowledged that in other passages the distinction is not always as clear-cut.[8] The image of God in the human person corresponds to her physical constitution with its natural intellectual powers. As such, the human person is imperfect. Only by the outpouring of the Spirit of God does man additionally receive similitude or likeness to God.[9] Yet between the two is not just a relation of addition. The word εἰκών for Irenaeus bespeaks a christological determination. To be fashioned according to this archetype is to be inscribed with a dynamic calling toward a christoform destiny. The person who bears this image finally becomes "like" God when, through the Spirit, she is transfigured in the light of the Father which shines in the flesh of Christ.[10]

---

7. On Philonic exegesis of this passage, see David T. Runia, *Philo of Alexandria and the* Timaeus *of Plato* (Leiden: Brill, 1986), 334–40; R. Mcl. Wilson, "The Early History of the Exegesis of Gen 1:26," *Studia Patristica* 1, no. 1 (1957): 420–37. Other Fathers who developed the image/likeness distinction in their theology include Clement of Alexandria, *Stromateis* 2.22; Origen, *De principiis* 3.6.1; Diadochus of Photike, *Capita* 89; Evagrius Ponticus, *Ep. ad Mel.* 12; Maximus Confessor, *Ambigua ad Iohannem* 7 (PG 91, 1084AB) et al. For further patristic references and theological commentary, see Adam G. Cooper, *The Body in Saint Maximus the Confessor: Holy Flesh, Wholly Deified* (Oxford: Oxford University Press, 2005), 95–102; A.-G. Hamann, *L'homme, image de Dieu: Essai d'une anthropologie chrétienne dans l'Église des cinq premiers siécles* (Paris: Desclée, 1987); Vladimir Lossky, "The Theology of the Image," in idem, *In the Image and Likeness of God* (London and Oxford: Mowbray, 1974), 125–39; A. H. Armstrong, "Image and Similitude in Augustine," *Revue des études augustiniennes* 10 (1964): 125–45. For wider discussion of the topic, especially in its relation to the human sciences, see the essays in P. Bühler, ed., *Humain à l'image de Dieu* (Geneva: Labor et Fides, 1989).

8. See J. Fantino, *L'homme, image de Dieu chez S. Irénée de Lyon* (Paris: Cerf, 1986); also Osborn, *Irenaeus of Lyons*, 211–14.

9. Irenaeus, *Adversus haereses* 5.6.1.

10. Irenaeus, *Adversus haereses* 5.6.1; 5.9.2–3; 5.12.4; 5.16.12; 5.36.1–3.

From this initial contact in England with the theology of Irenaeus, which de Lubac himself later regarded as a kind of fortunate "seduction,"[11] it is possible to propose a development in the prominence this distinction plays in the Jesuit's thought. Although it was only in his first years as a professor that de Lubac studied the Greek Fathers "in a more methodical and coherent manner,"[12] already on the first page in his early work *Catholicism* we find him distinguishing between "the natural dignity of man" on the one hand and "the supernatural dignity of the baptised" on the other, a pairing that, as O'Sullivan rightly notes, corresponds to the image and likeness distinction.[13] Further on, de Lubac shows how the distinction functions in Irenaeus's "supernatural evolutionism," according to which humanity progresses toward likeness to God under the guidance of a historically worked-out divine pedagogy. Little by little, by a "gradual education" culminating in the appearance of God the Word in the reality of the flesh, the human creature is integrated into and conducted toward his divine destiny.[14]

In subsequent works the metaphor is used with increasing explicitness and depth. In 1942, in a talk given to chaplains of the *Chantiers de la jeunesse*, de Lubac expressly states the relation between the two terms, giving a brief summary of their respective content:

> For the Fathers of the Church, man, created in the image of God, that is, with those divine prerogatives of reason, freedom, immortality, and the right of dominion over nature, is made with a view to the likeness of God, which is the perfection of this image. This means that he is destined to live eternally with God, to enter into the internal movement of the Trinitarian life and to take all creation with him.[15]

11. "When I returned from the war of 1914–1919, during the first semester of 1920, spent at Canterbury, the *Confessions* of Saint Augustine and the three last books of the *Adversus haereses* by Saint Irenaeus had seduced me." Henri de Lubac, *At the Service of the Church: Henri de Lubac Reflects on the Circumstances That Occasioned His Writings*, trans. Anne Elizabeth Englund (San Francisco: Ignatius, 1993), 64–65.

12. De Lubac, *At the Service of the Church*, 65. De Lubac was appointed Professor of Fundamental Theology in the School of Catholic Theology at Lyons in 1929. We can only imagine how the city's ancient connection with Saint Irenaeus must have touched him.

13. Henri de Lubac, *Catholicism: Christ and the Common Destiny of Man*, trans. Dom Christopher Butler (London: Burns & Oates, 1950), 1; cf. Noel O'Sullivan, *Christ and Creation: Christology as the Key to Interpreting the Theology of Creation in the Works of Henri de Lubac* (Bern: Peter Lang, 2009), 175.

14. De Lubac, *Catholicism*, 128–29.

In 1944, in *The Drama of Atheist Humanism*, the meaning of the image of God in human beings is again described in terms of the prerogatives of reason, freedom, immortality, and dominion over nature, while likeness to God (*la divine ressemblance*) constitutes the perfection toward which such prerogatives, being open-ended, are directed.[16]

By the time we come to *Surnaturel* in 1946, the preparatory studies for which were already initiated by de Lubac as early as 1931, the distinction is well established, forming the point of departure for the second part and shaping de Lubac's entire approach to the question of the natural human desire for supernatural fulfillment.[17] Between the human being's gratuitous γένεσις in the image of God and his gratuitous τελείωσις in the likeness of God lies "a space" (*un écart*) constituted by the operations of human free will, a space experienced as a "trial" or test (*une épreuve*).[18] It is within this space that the drama of the human vocation toward the intrinsically inscribed supernatural finality unfolds. Still a further development occurs in his restatement of the *Surnaturel* thesis in the 1949 essay "Le Mystère du Surnaturel."[19] Here, in addition to the common anthropological qualities contained in the idea of image already adduced, de Lubac stresses the mysterious incomprehensibility of the created human spirit:

> One doctrine dear to the Fathers of the Church was that man is in the image of God not only through his intelligence, his freedom, his immortality, his dominion over nature, but also and especially, in the final analysis, through what is incomprehensible in him.[20]

His point in this and similar paragraphs is to underpin the radically paradoxical character of human nature. If in its creatureliness humanity possesses within itself this profound *abyssum*, if human nature is indeed defined by its very indefinability, how much more is it the case when that nature is

---

15. This quote, which O'Sullivan calls "The 1942 Definition," is reproduced from O'Sullivan, *Christ and Creation*, 174.

16. See O'Sullivan, *Christ and Creation*, 175–26.

17. Henri de Lubac, *Surnaturel: Études Historiques* (Paris: Aubier, 1946), 189–212.

18. De Lubac, *Surnaturel*, 189.

19. Henri de Lubac, "Le Mystère du Surnaturel," *Recherches de Science Religieuse* 36 (1949): 80–121.

20. ET in Henri de Lubac, "The Mystery of the Supernatural," in idem, *Theology in History*, trans. A. E. Nash (San Francisco: Ignatius, 1996), 314.

assimilated to God, who is absolute mystery and infinite *abyssus*? To be created in God's image with a view to attain divine likeness means that the human person is nothing other than a being with a beginning but no end, a being that realizes itself only by surpassing itself.

This emphasis is a crucial one inasmuch as one element in the tradition conceives the deifying acquisition of likeness to God only as a restoration of the pristine clarity of the divine image, a return, that is, to original nakedness. This tradition identifies the "garments of skin" with which Adam and Eve were clothed after their expulsion from Paradise as symbolic of the sinful accretions that obscure and overlay the purity of the image of God in humanity.[21] And so in his treatise on virginity, Gregory of Nyssa admonishes, "Next we must divest ourselves of those coverings of our nakedness, the garments of skins, namely the mind of the flesh. . . ."[22] Gregory repeatedly makes the point that the skins are "dead" or made from the skin of "dead animals."[23] In his reflections on the account in Exodus of Moses before the burning bush we read,

> Sandaled feet cannot ascend that height where the light of truth is seen, but the *dead* and earthly covering of skins, which was placed around our nature at the beginning when we were found naked because of our disobedience to the divine will, must be removed from the feet of the soul.[24]

And again, "Circumcision means the removal of the *dead* skins which we put on when we had been stripped of the supernatural life after the transgression."[25] Or referring to the original pristine state of man he notes, "naked he was then of his covering of *dead* skins."[26]

---

21. See Adam G. Cooper, "Marriage and 'The Garments of Skin' in Irenaeus and the Greek Fathers," *Communio* 33 (Summer 2006): 215–37.

22. Gregory of Nyssa, *De virginitate* 12 (SC 119, 422). "The mind of the flesh" (τὸ φρόνημα τῆς σαρκὸς) is taken from Rom. 8:6-7, in which St. Paul equates it with that aspect of human nature which opposes God and so engenders death: "The mind of the flesh is death. . . . [It] is at enmity with God; it does not submit to God's law, nor can it do so."

23. See the editors' comments in Gregory of Nyssa, *The Life of Moses*, trans. and ed. A. J. Malherbe and E. Ferguson (New York: Paulist, 1978), 160 n. 29.

24. Gregory of Nyssa, *De vita Mosis* II, 22 (PG 44, 333A). ET: Gregory of Nyssa, *The Life of Moses*, 59.

25. Gregory of Nyssa, *Orationes de beatitudinibus* 8 (PG 44, 1292B).

26. *De virginitate* 12 (SC 119, 416–18). See also *De virginitate* 12 (SC 119, 420), speaking of Adam and Eve after the fall: "after that they covered themselves with the skin of *dead* animals."

Nowhere in these passages does Gregory explicitly equate the garments of skin with human bodies *per se*. The garments seem rather to be taken as the conditions that go with empirical bodily existence, to be put off in the soul's return to God. These include everything added to human nature created in God's image that links it to the animal world and marks it off from the intellectual, immortal sphere. Such features include the passions, sexual differentiation, marital procreation, and above all, mortality (thus the emphasis on "dead" skins). Yet this approach contains two problematic tendencies. First, it favors a Neoplatonic conception of the preexistent soul's fall and its terrestrial incorporation. Second, it conceives the human soul or *nous* as essentially divine, so that its ascent to God is nothing but a return to what it is by nature. Having summarized this tradition, which makes much of "la métaphor de la dénudation" and the need for a simplification or subtraction, de Lubac contrasts it with the idea of grace as "surajouté," that is, something added over and above nature to elevate it to the divine realm.[27] Are we then faced with two opposing traditions, one that conceives deification or the attainment of likeness to God a subtraction, the other an addition?

The resolution of this impasse as de Lubac explains is found in an aspect of the patristic doctrine of the *admirabile commercium* or wonderful exchange (*échange*). It is true that the human creature must put off the defiling garments of sin and so return to that state of nakedness again in which its soul reflects, as a mirror, the image of God. But this is only the first stage. The second stage consists in its being clothed with another garment, which the Scriptures and the liturgy refer to as a garment of "purity, light, and glory," a "nuptial robe," a "garment of incorruptibility," "the mantle of the Spirit," indeed, Christ himself.[28] Only in this conferral of "a totally gratuitous participation in the unique Πνεῦμα" do human beings obtain their perfection, the image arrived at the divine likeness.[29] Thus, paradoxically, between the beginning and end, between the formation of the human person in God's image and her arrival at God's likeness, there is both an organic link and an infinite incommensurability.

This paradoxical conception of the relationship between the "two gifts" is underscored by the parallels de Lubac continually draws between nature and grace on the one hand, and image and likeness on the other. "Nature and grace are nearly the same as image and likeness to God."[30] On the one hand we find discontinuity and incommensurability. The "second gift," namely,

27. De Lubac, *Surnaturel*, 378–82.

28. De Lubac, *Surnaturel*, 383–86.

29. Ibid., 385–86.

30. Ibid., 367.

"the ontological call to deification," is "utterly distinct from the first," namely, the gift of being at creation.[31] Nothing in nature, considered in and of itself, predisposes it for its ultimate end. De Lubac quotes the emphatic denial of Maximus the Confessor to the same end: "nothing created is capable of deification," that is, of deifying itself by an unfolding realization of its natural powers.[32] The passage from image to likeness, from one gift to another, is not automatic but implies an interactive synergy of human and divine freedom, a dialogic interplay of natural human activity and humble surrender to supernatural divine activity.[33] In sum, "No more than creation itself is the necessary consequence of something that preceded it, then, is the supernatural gift a simple *sequela creationis.*"[34]

On the other hand, we find continuity and correspondence. The first gift brings into being not just a higher animal in the order of other natures, but a spiritual being, whose *nous* possesses "une tendance active"[35] or natural desire that directs him beyond the created order toward a supernatural fulfillment that is already somehow "interior to his proper nature as spirit."[36] Between his creation in the image of God and his attainment of likeness to God there is an "organic link [*un lien organique*], in the sense that man is made in the image of God in view of arriving one day at his likeness, or, to use another metaphor from Origen, in the sense that man is by nature the temple of God, destined to receive his glory."[37]

We shall soon enough explore further de Lubac's understanding of the uniqueness of the human spirit, but to be noted in conclusion of this section is the way its dynamic directedness toward union with God parallels the dynamic directedness of the image toward assimilation to God. Yet when certain ancient Fathers and especially certain medievals affirmed this dynamism operative in the image and likeness distinction, as de Lubac subsequently found necessary to qualify, "they were in no sense intending to affirm by this that this 'likeness'

---

31. De Lubac, "Le Mystère du Surnaturel," 101. ET: "The Mystery of the Supernatural," in *Theology in History*, 299.

32. De Lubac, *Surnaturel*, 367. Quoting Maximus Confessor, *Quaestiones ad Thalassium* 22, 93–94 (PG 90, 721A; CCSG 7, 141).

33. See Aaron Riches, "Church, Eucharist, and Predestination in Barth and De Lubac: Convergence and Divergence in *Communio*," *Communio* 35 (2008): 565–98.

34. De Lubac, "Le Mystère du Surnaturel," 104. ET: "The Mystery of the Supernatural," in *Theology in History*, 302.

35. De Lubac, *Surnaturel*, 367.

36. Ibid., 387.

37. Ibid., 475. Citing Origen, *In Mattheum* 16.23 (PG 13, 1453B).

was of the same nature as the 'image,' that it had nothing specific to add to it, or that it was not superior in kind, and the object of a further totally free gift."[38] Nor does the distinction imply that nature lacks "its own proper stability and its own definite structure."[39] The point to keep clear is that the structure of human nature, being defined by the divine imprint, is not self-enclosed, nor can that nature be defined simply along the lines of other created natures. It was Cajetan's error, like Denys the Carthusian (1407–1471) before him, "to see in the human *spirit* no more than the *human* spirit. Like Denys, he turned that spirit back upon itself, enclosing it in 'its own species' in the same way as the lower natures. . . ."[40] An assessment of human nature that accepts as its starting point not simply a graduated hierarchy of being but the Christian doctrines of creation and redemption knows that God has created human beings for a divine end, and that this supernatural *telos* constitutes a "secret call" in the heart of every human person:

> There must therefore be—however one is to explain it—something in man that prepares him for this end and for its revelation. One way of putting it would be to say, as Irenaeus, Origen, and others did, that God created man in his own image in view of their meeting. Deep in human nature (and so in every man) the image of God is imprinted, that is, a quality that constitutes in it—and even without it—a kind of secret call to the object of the full and supernatural revelation brought by Christ.[41]

SOUL AND SPIRIT

All created beings bear in themselves some "trace" or reflection of God, yet only human beings (and angels) resemble God "by way of an image."[42] We mentioned in the section above that one of the important characteristics de Lubac came to add to his description of the image of God in human beings was the characteristic of incomprehensibility, and it is precisely in this incomprehensibility, expressed in their openness to the infinite, that human beings most closely approximate their maker. Here the anthropological distinction between body and soul on the one hand, and spirit on the other,

38. De Lubac, *The Mystery of the Supernatural*, 31.

39. Ibid., 31–32.

40. Ibid., 144.

41. De Lubac, *The Church: Paradox and Mystery*, 72.

42. De Lubac, *The Mystery of the Supernatural*, 108. Cf. Thomas Aquinas, ST I, 93, 6.

comes especially into play. Unlike the image and likeness distinction, we are not dealing with such a strict relation between soul on the one hand and spirit on the other. In fact, it is not really possible to draw a neat parallel between image and soul, and spirit and likeness.[43] Yet there are similarities, and within the category "spirit" especially we have something akin to the dynamism we have encountered in the image and likeness idea.

We can hardly in this limited context do justice to de Lubac's profound interest in the human spirit. "Everywhere in his writing, Fr. De Lubac delights in the word 'spirit.'"[44] We shall therefore limit ourselves to a few main passages and ideas. De Lubac's own point of departure for an in-depth study of this subject arises from the tripartite anthropological formula of St. Paul in 1 Thess. 5:23: "May the God of peace make you perfect and holy, and may your entire being, spirit, soul and body, be kept safe and blameless for the coming of our Lord Jesus Christ."[45] Despite all the "elasticity" and "fluidity" of Pauline anthropological terminology, de Lubac finds the apostle clearly distinguishing here an element in man that is indicative of his fundamental openness to the Spirit of God. His analysis of this term in the theology of the Fathers, especially of Irenaeus and Origen, without avoiding obvious variations and subtle differences, enables several broad conclusions to be drawn. According to the Fathers, soul and spirit, or even *nous* and spirit, are not mere equivalents. The human being is not simply a bipartite soul and body composite, but properly a tripartite unity, whose "third" element, the "higher part" of soul, forms the crucial "point of contact" between the human person and God's indwelling Spirit.[46] Neither body and soul alone, nor spirit alone, represents humanity in its perfection. Only "the mixture and union of all these things," as Irenaeus puts it, completes the image in likeness to God.[47] The dimension of spirit, in other words, is crucially linked to the attainment of deifying likeness to God.

Admittedly, with such terms we are dealing with something ambiguous and difficult to pin down—no verbal fiction to be sure, yet something more than another aspect or "faculty" of human personality. This spirit which is in every human person is somehow more than the person, something, we might

43. This has been amply demonstrated by O'Sullivan, *Christ and Creation*, 195–201.

44. Eric de Moulins-Beaufort, "The Spiritual Man in the Thought of Henri de Lubac," *Communio* 25 (1998): 287–302 at 291.

45. Henri de Lubac, "Tripartite Anthropology," in idem, *Theology in History*, trans. A. E. Nash (San Francisco: Ignatius, 1996), 117–200.

46. De Lubac, "Tripartite Anthropology," 140.

47. Irenaeus, *Adversus haereses* 5.6.1.

even say, divine; yet it is not just another way of speaking of the Spirit who is God.[48] Rather it amounts to something very much like what we have been describing so far as "the image of God," a real participation dynamically ordered toward deifying assimilation to God. Unlike soul or body, "it does not appear completely like a constituent part of man as such"; indeed, as de Lubac observes, it is more "in man" than it is "of man."[49] Summarizing the fundamental idea as he finds it in Origen, "spirit" may be thought of as a kind of guarantee assuring

> a certain hidden transcendence of the man over himself, a certain opening, a certain received continuity between man and God. Not that there is the least identity of essence between the one and the other (like Irenaeus, like Clement, Origen is an implacable adversary of this pantheism of the pseudo-Gnostics); but it is, at the heart of man, the privileged place, always intact, of their encounter.[50]

De Lubac traces in detail the intellectual evolution of this idea. It is too detailed for us to follow here, but with reference to a number of other passages in his writings we can draw out a number of applicable points that bear upon our study of the image and likeness distinction and the journey of humanity's deifying assimilation to God. Our question is to what extent this "spiritual" character of the human creature, by which there is present a kind of nascent anticipation of its supernatural end, is different from those conceptions of human nature that posit it as somehow essentially divine. How, in other words, does the created-ness of the human spirit qualify its movement toward fulfillment?

De Lubac specifies two ancient anthropologies, one pagan and the other Christian, that both fall short of accounting adequately for the actual reality that the human being is. According to the pagan account, divinity and immortality are virtually synonymous. "[J]ust as there was no real immortality except for divine natures, so also there was no 'returning' to God for any soul that was not already divine in essence."[51] Acceptance of this doctrine of humanity's "needy"

---

48. Having observed the fluency in the language employed by the Bible and the Fathers in this connection, O'Sullivan concludes: "In any case, what can be established with certainty is that there is something in man, which is the spark of the divine life, a spark that can only be fully ignited by the Holy Spirit, which is other than man, and which we call 'spirit.' Because it is not part of man, its gratuity is therefore safeguarded." O'Sullivan, *Christ and Creation*, 200–201.

49. De Lubac, "Tripartite Anthropology," 129.

50. Ibid., 141.

nature meant that resignation, not hope and desire, was regarded as the proper attitude of the soul closed within its own natural limits.

> That the [classical pagan philosophers] lacked hope was primarily because the very idea of a *sursum* and a superabundance, the idea of an order incommensurate with nature, the idea of something radically new, something we might call an "invention of being," the idea of a gift coming gratuitously from above to raise up that needy nature, at once satisfying its longings and transforming it—such an idea remains wholly foreign to all whose minds have not been touched by the light of revelation.[52]

Whether de Lubac's assessment here fully represents every strand in classical thought is perhaps debatable. One may recall for example the way Plato envisions *eros*, neither divine nor fully human in itself, carrying the soul toward the contemplation of archetypal beauty as on a pair of wings.[53] Whatever *eros* is in this description, it is no mere "craving" or "neediness," nor does it harmonize morally with an attitude of hopeless resignation.[54] Nevertheless, the Jesuit's primary point remains relevant: in many ancient schemes, God and humanity are felt to inhabit two different and even opposing worlds, each set within its own proper limits. In an anthropology of this sort, "deification" can only bear connotations of a fundamental hubris on the human side, a desire to overstep one's proper bounds, an attempt to supernaturalize one's inherently created, mortal nature and make it consubstantial with God.

The second anthropology, also inadequate in its own way, is found in Christian tradition, and is most notably associated with the name of Gregory of Nyssa. Here de Lubac considers the idea arising from Gregory's eschatological speculations according to which human beatitude consists in a "perpetual progress," an eternal *epektasis* or infinite stretching of human capacities in harmony with the infinitude of the object of desire.[55] It is the doctrine of the

51. De Lubac, *The Mystery of the Supernatural*, 126.

52. Ibid., 130.

53. Plato, *Phaedrus* 248–53; cf. *Symposium* 206–12.

54. See further Josef Pieper, *Divine Madness: Plato's Case Against Secular Humanism*, trans. L. Krauth (San Francisco: Ignatius, 1995).

55. On this theme see Paul Plass, "Transcendent Time and Eternity in Gregory of Nyssa," *Vigiliae Christianae* 34 (1980): 180–92; E. Ferguson, "God's infinity and man's mutability: Perpetual progress according to Gregory of Nyssa," *Greek Orthodox Theological Review* 18, no. 1–2 (1973): 59–78; Jean

eternal "incompleteness" of the human person, whose perfection consists in a never-ending, spiraling advance toward the good. Yet this idea of beatitude as a "universal gyration," as it was sometimes characterized, fitting as it may be within a strictly Neoplatonic framework, does not do justice to the interpersonal and immediate character of the Christian's deifying vision of and union with God. The Christ of the Gospels teaches us that "universal gyration is not the ultimate reality."[56] Moreover, a being whose fulfillment lay forever out of its reach would never be happy. The restless heart would never "be still" in its knowledge of God; the thirsty soul would remain forever unsated.

Having pointed out the inadequacies of this thesis, however, de Lubac draws out certain merits in it that shed important light on our inquiry into the nature of the human spirit. The merit of the idea of beatitude as a perpetual progress, in contrast to the anthropology of classical antiquity, lies in the way it rejects any idea of "a closed and static natural happiness."[57] It further underscores the infinite incomprehensibility of God, his nature as wholly other, and thus in turn the incomprehensibility of the human person whose very being, created in the image of this same God, is in the end also infinitely expanded by God as its object of knowing and loving. This vision stands as an important counterpoint to the secularizing anthropology of modern naturalism, which exalts this-worldly human progress and advance as an ultimate value, disavowing any intrinsic connection with or ordering toward transcendence or otherworldly happiness. In contrast to this view,

> it is *within* the one and only beatitude, within the joy of God, that an advance used to be seen in the past, and not merely an advance, but as St. Bernard went so far as to say, following the Fathers, a desire, a seeking: "And the happy finding does not by any means strike out [*extundit*] holy desire, but stretches it out [*extendit*]. Is the consummation of joy the destruction of desire? . . . Gladness will be filled, but there will be no end of desire, nor, for the same reason, of seeking."[58]

Daniélou, *Platonisme et théologie mystique: Essai sur le doctrine spirituelle de Saint Grégoire de Nysse* (Paris: Aubier, 1944).

56. De Lubac, *The Mystery of the Supernatural*, 204.

57. De Lubac, *The Mystery of the Supernatural*, 199.

58. Ibid., 206.

This line of inquiry and comparison contributes directly to de Lubac's thesis that the human spirit is what it is only by infinitely transcending itself. Between its creation and its beatitude, both of which are in the order of divine gift, stands a dynamic correspondence. The human person stands in the unique situation of "a spirit which is to become subject and agent of an act of knowledge for which it has no natural equipment, and which is thus to be fulfilled by getting beyond itself."[59] Commenting on this theme as it is expounded variously from Bonaventure and Bernard to Bérulle and Blondel, de Lubac writes:

> Hence every spirit, whether in a body or not, enjoys certain privileges which, making him "in the image of" the Creator, make him at the same time superior to the whole order of the universe.[60]

> [T]here is something in man, a certain capacity for the infinite, which makes it impossible to consider him one of those beings whose whole nature and destiny are inscribed within the cosmos.[61]

> Congenitally, the end of the spiritual creature is something that surpasses the powers of his nature or any other created nature; and this is because the spiritual creature has a direct relationship with God which results from its origins.[62]

Note again in this last passage in particular the vital connection: the human end, which we have been describing as likeness to God or deification, springs somehow from humanity's special beginning as a being created directly by God with God's own "hands," as Irenaeus characterizes the Son and the Spirit, and in his own image. This divine immediacy to humanity in the act of creation is not incidental to human being, but internal to it, constitutive of it. And thus, as Eric de Moulins-Beaufort rightly states, "Union with God, when it is achieved, springs from a place that runs deeper than the distinction of the faculties—the very place, indeed, wherein man springs from his source, God."[63] The actions springing from intellect and will "translate a movement which is prior to them,"

59. Ibid., 102, quoting from an article by Père A.-R. Motte in *Bulletin Thomiste* 4 (1934–36).
60. De Lubac, *The Mystery of the Supernatural*, 104.
61. Ibid., 110.
62. Ibid., 111.
63. De Moulins-Beaufort, "The Spiritual Man in the Thought of Henri de Lubac," 289.

a divinely initiated movement present deep in humanity as spirit, image, call, and echo.[64] There is no neutral ground, an uncommitted space from which people may sit back and objectively contemplate the various paths open to them. The human person is already gratuitously constituted as spirit, as image called to and destined for likeness to her creator. Whether and how she attains that gratuitously bestowed destiny is a matter decided by the action of living history, that is, by her level of consenting incorporation into the divine drama of salvation history.

LETTER AND SPIRIT

These comments bring us to a second distinction standing in parallel to that between image and likeness. Worked out in de Lubac's hermeneutical theology, especially in *Histoire et esprit* of 1950 and the magisterial four-volume work *Exégèse médiévale* (1959–63), it is broadly speaking the distinction between the letter and spirit of Scripture. This distinction, which lies at the heart of the Christian understanding of history, and indeed is determinative for all Christian theology, is itself expressive of a series of vital relations between the old and the new covenants, between prefigurement and fulfillment, shadow and reality, between the apparently disparate narrative events of salvation history and their inner unity, meaning, and salvific purpose.

The twentieth century witnessed a widespread renewal of interest in the tradition of spiritual exegesis developed in the early church and commonly exercised until the dissociation of spirituality, exegesis, and theology in the high middle ages and the arrival of a "scientific" and critical exegesis in the renaissance. In her study of spiritual exegesis in de Lubac's theology, Wood points out how its advent coincided not only with the revival of patristic studies, but also with the *nouvelle théologie* and its concern to avoid the errors of extrinsicism on the one side and historicism on the other.[65] To the mind of Blondel, she explains further, whose criticism of these two errors was so influential for de Lubac, extrinsicism focuses too exclusively on the fact that God has spoken or acted, without taking into account the dynamic variables of human agency in revelation. Such an approach "leads to an absolutism uninterested in the internal criticism of texts or the work of the historian."[66]

---

64. Ibid., 292.

65. Susan K. Wood, *Spiritual Exegesis and the Church in the Theology of Henri de Lubac* (Grand Rapids: Eerdmans, 1998), 17–24.

66. Ibid., 20.

The problem with historicism on the other hand is its exclusive interest in empirically verifiable data and its rejection of any interpretive principle exterior to or transcendent of those data. Spiritual exegesis by contrast avoids both these pitfalls "because the spiritual senses are grounded in the literal or historical sense."[67] In other words, spiritual exegesis presupposes the unity of divine revelation and its historic mediation. Furthermore, and related to this, spiritual exegesis "is consistent with the concept of Christ as both the object and the mediator of revelation."[68] Everything in Scripture, even the least detail, is somehow related to Christ and directed toward him. "Consequently, he is, so to speak, its whole exegesis."[69]

As well as corresponding to de Lubac's own christocentric approach to theology, this emphasis indicates something about the nature of the relationship between the so-called letter and the spirit. "Literal" and "spiritual" indicate two kinds of meanings, "and these two meanings have the same kind of relationship to each other as do the Old and New testaments to each other."[70] The "letter" of Scripture indicates its historical foundation, the facts themselves, which, as de Lubac tirelessly argues, are never repudiated or trivialized by the great representatives of this tradition.[71] This letter represents the embodiment of a pedagogical strategy on God's part whose goal lies on a deeper level, the level of spirit. Only in the person and work of Christ is this goal attained; only by his Spirit is this inner meaning of the letter or the trajectory of saving history discerned.

As far as terminology goes, the "letter" of Scripture is on a par with type, figure, image, and shadow, each of which is ordered, as preparation, toward a union with some kind of original or archetypal reality.

> For the Christian there exist two successive "testaments," which are not primarily or even essentially two books, but two "Economies," two "Dispensations," two "Covenants," which have given birth to

---

67. Ibid., 21.

68. Ibid., 22–23.

69. Henri de Lubac, *Medieval Exegesis*, vol. 1, trans. M. Sebanc (Grand Rapids: Eerdmans, 1998), 237.

70. Ibid., 225.

71. De Lubac observes that *littera* is essentially synonymous with *historia*, which in the interpretation of Scripture constitutes "the universal *foundation*." "The redemption has not been accomplished in the imagination, but in time and in factual reality. It has been prepared, since the creation of the world, by a sequence of historical events, related in a collection of chronicles whose veracity we cannot put into doubt without putting our patrimony at risk and without damaging our own foundations." Henri de Lubac, *Medieval Exegesis*, vol. 2, trans. E. M. Macierowski (Grand Rapids: Eerdmans, 2000), 47.

two peoples, to two orders, established by God one after the other in order to regulate man's relationship with him. The goal of the one that is prior in time is to prepare the way for the second.[72]

Yet the relationship between the letter and its fulfillment at the level of spirit is not extrinsic: one cannot extract from the letter some demythologized inner content, purged of the symbolic trappings peculiar to history, culture, literary form, and human agency. Nor is it possible, once one has attained the level of spirit or reality, simply to discard the letter as redundant or obsolete. "The spirit is not separated from the letter. At first, it is contained and hidden in the letter. The letter is good and necessary, because it leads to the spirit. The letter is its instrument and servant."[73] Just as the relation between the two testaments is one of both continuity and discontinuity, so the relationship between letter and spirit involves continuity and discontinuity in a manner akin to the inner, "organic" relationship between image and likeness. And so referring to the two testaments, de Lubac writes: "The second arises from the first and does not repudiate it. The second does not destroy the first. In fulfilling it, it gives new life and renews it. It transfigures it. It subsumes it into itself. In a word, it changes its letter into spirit."[74] Or again, this time from *Histoire et esprit:*

The spirit does not wish to harm the letter. It does not wish to "destroy the text." If the reality of the visible world is a figure for the invisible world, then the reality of biblical history will also be a figure for the things of salvation and will serve as the "foundation."[75]

If we are familiar with this kind of terminology, it is because it echoes what has become for catholic theology the axiomatic statement on the relationship between nature and grace: *gratia non destruit sed supponit ac perficit naturam,* that is, grace does not destroy nature, but presupposes and perfects it.

But we have wanted to bring out this letter-and-spirit distinction not simply to add to other studies in this area,[76] but to relate it to our inquiry concerning de Lubac's doctrine of deification, the fulfillment of creation in

---

72. De Lubac, *Medieval Exegesis,* vol. 1, 227.

73. Ibid., 226.

74. Ibid., 228.

75. Henri de Lubac, *History and Spirit: The Understanding of Scripture according to Origen,* trans. A. E. Nash (San Francisco: Ignatius, 2007), 104.

the image of God in a deifying assimilation in likeness to God. It is in this connection that we may point out the relation, originally indicated by Origen, between the multileveled structure of Scripture and the bipartite or especially tripartite composition of the human person:

> Just as visible and invisible things are related to each other—the earth and heaven, the flesh and the soul, the body and the spirit—and just as the world results from their very connections: so we [must] believe also that Holy Scripture is a composite of visible and invisible things. It is in fact composed, as it were, of a body, that is, the body of the letter that is seen; of a soul, the interior sense that one discovers in it; and of a spirit, in the sense that it contains, too, certain heavenly things within it, as the Apostle says to the Hebrews.[77]

For the tradition of spiritual exegesis, therefore, each "sense" of Scripture corresponds to an aspect of the human structure, or rather to the ever more perfect human soul in progressive stages along its spiritual journey. Scripture and the human person have "one and the same structure," "the same inspiration"; indeed, "one and the same divine breath gives birth to them and never ceases to animate them."[78] The moral sense, which most closely relates to the literal, corresponds to "a kind of anatomy and physiology of the soul that, in principle at least, was not pre-supposing revelation."[79] At this level, without the eyes of faith and the illumination that comes from the indwelling Spirit of God, readers of Scripture cannot penetrate beyond the letter, where they are confronted by disparate conglomerations of events and a moral code aimed at modifying their external behavior. But by attending to the inner meaning of Scripture, by not stopping at the external letter with its advice concerning the moral conduct of the body but, in faith, penetrating to its mystical heart, the Spirit-enlightened soul encounters Christ the Logos himself who, in a mystical union, transforms it and draws it toward its perfection. At this level, the mystical and spiritual senses correspond respectively first to "a salvation history of the

76. For further reading, see D. Grumett, *De Lubac: A Guide for the Perplexed* (London: T. & T. Clark, 2007), 75–94.

77. Origen, *Hom.Lev* 5, 1. cf. Heb. 8:5. Quoted by de Lubac, *History and Spirit*, 189. See also Origen, *De principiis* 4.2.4; *Hom.Num* 9.7; *Hom.Lev* 5.1.

78. De Lubac, *History and Spirit*, 398.

79. Ibid., 164.

soul in function of the salvation of mankind by Christ . . ." and finally to an interpretation that "deepens it, interiorizes, and completes it by applying it."[80]

From what we have seen so far, it is not difficult to correlate this spiritual encounter with the Logos in Scripture to the dramatic pedagogical journey by which the image of God in humanity is interiorly renovated by the Spirit.[81] Though de Lubac rarely makes the connection explicit, the language he uses to describe this transforming process closely mirrors the language he uses to describe the passage from image to likeness. For example, the path from the letter toward a spiritual understanding of Scripture, which is nothing less than a path of conversion,

> is a unique movement, which, beginning with initial incredulity, is raised by faith to the summits of a spiritual life whose end is not here on earth. Its unfurling is coextensive with the gift of the Spirit, with the progress of charity. . . . The newness of the understanding is correlative with the "newness of life." To pass on to the spiritual understanding is thus to pass on to the "new man," who never ceases to be renewed *de claritate in claritatem* (from glory to glory).[82]

Commenting on the relationship between the *typos* or figure on the one hand and its fulfillment or eschatological realization on the other, de Lubac remarks that we are dealing not merely with an external resemblance but an "inner continuity" and "ontological bond." This is because it is the "same divine Will that is at work on both sides, pursuing from stage to stage one and the same Plan—that Plan which is the whole subject of the Bible."[83] Or again, discussing how Origen, in relating hermeneutics to his threefold dynamic anthropology, distinguishes between the soul made in the image of God and its higher part, the ἡγεμονικόν or πνεῦμα, de Lubac writes:

> It is in this "spirit of each man" that "the Spirit of God" can come to dwell. It is there, on this high place, in this intimate retreat, that the soul receives its Savior at its table, while waiting to go take part in the banquet he will offer it in the kingdom of heaven.[84]

80. Ibid., 164.
81. Ibid., 163–64.
82. Ibid., 448.
83. Ibid., 462.

In still one more passage, de Lubac comments on the way the tradition of spiritual exegesis likens Scripture to a mirror, a metaphor we discussed earlier in relation to the soul or image of God in the human being.

> In this mirror we learn to know our nature and our destiny; in it we also see the different stages through which we have passed since creation, the beautiful and the ugly features of our internal face. It shows us the truth of our being by pointing out its relation to the Creator. It is a living mirror, a living and efficacious Word, a sword penetrating at the juncture of soul and spirit, which makes our secret thoughts appear and reveals to us our heart.[85]

But the reflection that takes place between the soul and Scripture is reciprocally illuminating. Through the exchange of living experience and meditation on the Word, an ever-increasing likeness to God finally emerges. And what does this likeness look like? "All this teaching of the Scripture, all this strength which shapes me to the divine likeness, is summarized in a single word: charity."[86]

In moving toward some concluding remarks the question might be asked whether all these structural forms can be reconciled without discrepancy. Image and likeness; letter and spirit; twofold, threefold, or even fourfold senses of Scripture; body and soul; body, soul, and spirit: are we not simply playing with words, contriving distinctions and connections—for good heuristic reasons of course—where there are in actual fact none to be made?

As far as scriptural interpretation is concerned, asserts de Lubac, "the essential division" in the end will be "neither threefold nor fourfold. There are in Scripture, fundamentally, only two senses: the literal and the spiritual, and these senses themselves are in continuity, not in opposition."[87] In a similar way, we may add, human beings, however they be composed, have only one final perfection, toward which their whole creaturely structure is directed. The letter of Scripture, like the image of God in humanity, contains, or better, *is* by definition, a dynamic directedness toward this single divine end. The spiritual

---

84. Ibid., 180–81.

85. De Lubac, *Medieval Exegesis*, vol. 2, 142.

86. De Lubac, *Medieval Exegesis*, vol. 2, 141.

87. De Lubac, *History and Spirit*, 205.

interpretation of Scripture calls for and brings about the spiritualization of the human person, by which we mean an interiorization of the Spirit of Christ who is the author of Scripture and impregnates its every word. Only the Spirit of God knows the thoughts of God, and only the spiritual person can receive them. Thus, as de Lubac quotes von Balthasar, "To enter into the spirit of Scripture means, in the end, to learn to know what is inside God, to appropriate the thoughts of God about the world."[88]

The meaning and purpose of Scripture is therefore fulfilled when the reader herself, by interiorizing its message and allowing her life to be assimilated to its divine content, becomes a living "word of God," "God going about in the flesh," as Clement of Alexandria once put it.[89] But since this passage is also a movement of *metanoia*, it cannot be attained by sheer effort of will but only by a redemptive and Spirit-wrought gift of grace. Just as "the divine resemblance is something to be realised, through the action of the Holy Spirit, by man's dependence on the redeeming Incarnation,"[90] so too, in order for us to assimilate Scripture's divine content, to be likened to the Word present in the words, it is necessary that that same Word become personally present in us, "that we ourselves be recreated in him, that the New Man be created in us." This is the special task of the Spirit, who fulfills this role in the sacramental community which is the church.[91] It is there, in the communion of saints for which human beings have been made and in which therefore they find their intrinsic fulfillment, that the Holy Spirit "brings the man who lives according to the spirit dwelling in him" into deifying communion with the triune God.[92] Of the vast number of passages and among the chorus of witnesses marshaled by de Lubac along these lines, we need only offer the briefest sampling:

> The pure soul, the holy soul, the faithful soul is such only "within the Church." . . . The whole life of the Christian flows from the "mystical fecundity of the Church." . . . It is in "the home of the present Church," says Potho of Prüm, a home "created in the image of God," that souls acquire the divine likeness. . . . All that is accomplished in

---

88. Hans Urs von Balthasar, quoted by de Lubac, *History and Spirit*, 449.

89. Clement of Alexandria, *Stromateis* 7.16.101 (SC 428, 304).

90. Henri de Lubac, "Mysticism and Mystery," in idem, *Theological Fragments*, trans. R. H. Balinski (San Francisco: Ignatius, 1989), 35–69 at 52.

91. De Lubac, *History and Spirit*, 363–34.

92. De Moulins-Beaufort, "The Spiritual Man in the Thought of Henri de Lubac," 299.

the Church herself had no other end. Everything is consummated in the inner man.[93]

Who is the primary actor in all this? God, the creator and deifier, or humanity, the created and deified? As intimated by the structure of the incarnation, we are obviously dealing with a theandric synergy. And yet, as we have also seen in this chapter, creation and deification both bear the nature of gift. We quoted already from Maximus the Confessor: "nothing natural is capable of deification." Or again, "We suffer, we do not achieve, our deification, since it is beyond nature." These words, quoted by de Lubac in *Surnaturel*,[94] capture a sentiment native to an old strand in Christian spiritual tradition, which de Lubac expresses with increasing boldness in later works.[95] It is also a point that bears upon the reciprocal character of the believer's engagement with the Spirit-filled words of Scripture, by which the image, "suffering" as it were the infiltrating action of the performative word, step by step attains to its God-ordained likeness. De Lubac leaves it to Paul Claudel to describe how this dynamic unfolds, and with his wisdom it seems fitting for us also to conclude:

> Now . . . it is no longer we who are acting; it is these words, once having been introduced, which act within us, releasing the spirit of which they have been made, the meaning and sonority included within them, and which veritably become spirit and life, and action-producing words. They belong to a place beyond our mental control; there is a certain irresistible force of authority and order in them. But they have ceased to be exterior; they have become ourselves. *And the Word was made flesh and dwelt among us:* one must understand the whole captivating, appropriating power of these two words: *in nobis.*[96]

---

93. De Lubac, *Medieval Exegesis*, vol. 2, 135–38.

94. De Lubac, *Surnaturel*, 366–67.

95. "Speaking of 'man's divinization through grace' Fr. Teilhard de Chardin rightly remarked: 'This is more than a simple union; it is a process of transformation during which all that human activity can do is prepare itself, and accept, humbly.' Put in another way—we need not be afraid of words—humility is a *passive* virtue. . . ." Henri de Lubac, *A Brief Catechesis on Nature and Grace*, trans. R. Arnande (San Francisco: Ignatius, 1984), 55–56; and again: "The supernatural, one might say, is that divine element which man's effort cannot reach (no self-divinization!). . . ." Ibid., 41.

96. Paul Claudel, quoted by de Lubac, *Medieval Exegesis*, vol. 2, 140.

Conclusion

The doctrine of deification consists essentially in the proposition that humanity is made for God. By nature and calling, human beings are properly ordered to loving union with God the Father through a gracious adoption constituted by the Holy Spirit in the crucified and risen flesh of Jesus Christ the incarnate Son. Such a union, which tradition has regarded as nothing less than the human creature's becoming God by grace, utterly transcends human capabilities, yet only this destiny fulfills human beings and brings them the fullness of joy they, by virtue of their creation, naturally and universally seek.

This book has shown that this doctrine of deification occupied a central place in the theologies of three major thinkers in twentieth-century western Catholicism: Réginald Garrigou-Lagrange, Karl Rahner, and Henri de Lubac. While all three authors share a common understanding of deification as human participation in the divine life of the Holy Trinity, they articulate this reality in distinct ways. What again were the main lines of thought?

After providing some broad-brushstroke background illuminating the origins of the *ressourcement* revival of the doctrine, and a brief biographical introduction to each author, I set out by showing how Garrigou-Lagrange understood deification as possessing a structural analogy to the hypostatic union, in which the human nature of Christ is assumed by the person of the divine Logos in such a way that it has no "personality" of its own as such. So fully and intimately does God, who is essentially diffusive goodness, communicate himself in the incarnation that the human "personality" of Christ is effaced, without his human nature in any way being diminished. In a similar way, human beings are deified, or receive God's intimate self-communication, to the degree that they efface themselves or "depersonalize" their own ego. Just as the deprivation of the dimension of personal existence renders Christ's humanity more absolutely open to the deifying influence of the divine Logos, so too does the Christian realize deification in a dramatic and ecstatic self-mortification.

I then went on to show how this structural analogy between the hypostatic union and the deification of the justified serves as a critical criterion by which to judge true from false mysticisms. Here I noted the way the Dominican significantly qualified the now widely controverted idea of "pure nature" by

217

affirming its hypothetical character. Empirically speaking, in fact, there is no pure nature. Rather, every human being lives always and actually in accountable relation to her ultimate end, toward which she either is or is not decisively oriented by her concrete acts of will. If the actual state of human beings is either one of mortal sin or grace, and if progress in deification consists only in cruciform self-mortification and self-effacement, then there can be no indifference or neutrality with regard to the ultimate end. One is always either one step closer to, or one step further away from, final beatitude. Moreover, that final beatitude is no disembodied mental act. It is a real experience or "quasi" experience of God, an intimate interpersonal union, a real participation in the divine nature through which the human soul is "totally transformed."

In the fourth chapter I expounded Garrigou-Lagrange's understanding of deification as involving a real indwelling of God the Trinity in the believer, and the believer in God. Garrigou-Lagrange was critical of any tendency to divorce the realities of revelation and faith from the life of spiritual experience. Inspired by the mysticism of deification being championed by the saints of old and by colleagues such as Ambrose Gardeil and Juan Arintero, he cultivated an affective spirituality intimately wedded to the mysterious reality of the divine indwelling. Sanctifying grace must be understood not simply as some gift distinct from God, but as somehow including, or implying, the self-gift of the giver. That giver is a Trinity of Father, Son, and Holy Spirit, in union with whom the human person discovers the summit of being, thought, and love. The Christian is a dwelling place or glorious temple for this Holy Trinity. In deifying the human person, God does not just produce created effects in him, or only communicate supernatural gifts, but establishes his home and through the gifts of love and knowledge assimilates the Christian to himself. In this sense it is possible to regard deification as a reality the Christian "suffers" or experiences more than one he actuates or brings about. Garrigou-Lagrange makes much of the "passive state," advanced by Louis de Chardon, in which God the supreme lover, accomplishing much more in us than could ever be achieved by even the most perfect act on our part, thoroughly penetrates the whole person, destroying nothing. This motif of passivity, or active receptivity, besides being of interest in recent developments in personalism and theological metaphysics,[1] also surfaces in my exposition of the theology of Henri de Lubac, suggesting it as an important and unexpected point of contact between the two figures, as well as a focal point for further research. It echoes the profound

---

1. See, for example, W. Norris Clarke, *Person and Being* (Milwaukee: Marquette University Press 1993); D. L. Schindler, "Norris Clarke on Person, Being and St. Thomas," *Communio* 20, no. 3 (1993): 580–92; idem, "The Person: Philosophy, Theology, and Receptivity," *Communio* 21, no. 1 (1994): 172–90.

insight of Maximus the Confessor when he taught that deification is wholly experienced or "suffered" gratuitously, and in no way flows from the actuation of native human powers.

In chapter 5, focus turned to a more technical aspect in Garrigou-Lagrange's doctrine of deification, namely, the question of causality, a question that also occupied the mind of Karl Rahner. Is deification precipitated by a causal agency native to human nature? And if not, how can God actuate deification in human beings without human nature undergoing any essential change and so ceasing to be what it is? Anticipating how Rahner would come to approach these questions, I showed how Garrigou-Lagrange responded to them with the Thomistic notion of grace as the seed of glory, that is, the already-present but not yet fully realized principle of a transfiguring activity by which the human being comes to know and love God as God knows and loves himself. Sanctifying grace, caused exteriorly by God, is itself an intrinsic formal cause of deification, and so is a real participation in the divine essence. Unlike Rahner and de Lubac, who always tended to emphasize grace in its uncreated aspect, Garrigou-Lagrange did not hold that deifying grace is uncreated. Yet neither is it for him some kind of intermediary or *tertium quid*. Rather it assimilates us immediately and intimately to God, interiorly, as God is in himself. In its perfect realization, it is the formal cause of a constitutive activity of a finite being that is effectively the same as the constitutive activity of God. I concluded my treatment of Garrigou-Lagrange's theology by drawing attention to the remarkable effect of deifying grace according to which human and divine activity finally become indistinguishable.

In chapter 6 I turned to an analysis of Karl Rahner's doctrine of deification. In contrast to what we found in Garrigou-Lagrange, deification features as a more explicit theme in Rahner's thought, though it is somewhat obscured and overlaid by the more sophisticated language and dialectical conceptual schema that Rahner adopted from modern transcendental philosophy. One of the primary categories of that philosophy is that of experience, which in Rahner's worldview always has a double aspect, the categorical and the transcendental, the thematic and the unthematic or absolute. The human spirit is marked by its radical openness to the absolute, and it is in this transcendental experience that deification properly takes place.

On the face of it, it looks as though Rahner took this philosophical schema as the fundamental starting point for his theology. Yet I also made the point that Rahner in fact intended his anthropology to be radically theological. So that when he says "man," he is referring to a reality that can be known and understood in truth only in terms of its ultimate fulfillment which lies in God, who is absolute mystery. If grace, understood as God's utterly free and unexacted self-communication, is the all-encompassing intention standing behind the whole of created history, then human nature, as the dynamic summit of that history, possesses in its ontological makeup a fundamental openness to God's self-communication. Deification consists in the nexus of the two.

For Rahner, it is decisive for an understanding of God's self-communication to grasp that the divine giver in his own being is also the gift. Grace, in other words, is God's self-gift. At first glance this seems to echo what we encountered in the thought of Garrigou-Lagrange. Yet as I went on to explain, for Rahner the New Testament testifies to grace primarily as an uncreated reality; it is in some respect God himself. It is also an intrinsic, formal cause of our deification, not an extrinsic, efficient cause. This being the case, Rahner seems committed to the idea that God himself is the formal cause of human deification, which amounts to saying that in human fulfillment the divine nature becomes the innermost formally constitutive being of the human person. But Rahner qualifies this affirmation by adding that God acts in this way without in any way losing himself or limiting his transcendence. Moreover, the act is one of "communication," which presupposes the real and ongoing otherness of communicated and communicatee.

In chapter 7 I examined Rahner's evolutionary christology, according to which Christ in the incarnation is envisioned as the pinnacle of cosmic evolution toward spirit and the definitive moment of God's self-communication in and to creation. All finite reality is marked by an inner impulse toward this consummating goal. The history of the cosmos unfolds as the dialectic of God's ever more complete self-communication and creation's ever more complete acceptance of it, climaxing irrevocably in the double-sided event of Christ. This gave rise to a series of critical remarks questioning whether this approach tends to eclipse the uniqueness of Jesus and the significance of his atoning death. While Rahner distinguished the case of Jesus from the way deification unfolds in other human beings, the difference seems to be more one of degree than of kind. Rahner's postulation of human nature's radical orientation to grace puts him on side with de Lubac in opposition to Garrigou-Lagrange, who continued to defend the "two-end" theory of human nature. But his speculative christology tends to relativize the Christ event, making of it a categorical moment that does not in fact bring into effect anything new, but simply occasions transcendental experience. This approach distances him from de Lubac, for whom the definitive and unprecedented newness of the incarnation and the Chalcedonian dogma of Christ's humanity and its qualitative difference from the grace given to all other human beings precludes any easy harmonization of evolutionary doctrine with Christian theology.

With these critical remarks having cast a shadow over aspects of Rahner's speculative theology, the eighth chapter affirmed the especially valuable contribution Rahner made to the topic of deification through his more pastoral and spiritual writings. In his "existential spirituality" and mysticism of the everyday, Rahner invested not just the sacramental and expressly symbolic but even the most ordinary and routine physical and temporal dimensions of human experience with extraordinary spiritual and salvific potential. In his Easter sermons Rahner proclaimed that the transfiguration of the world, set in motion by the resurrection of Christ from the dead, is no mere postulate but a dynamic reality. The self-transcendence of the material world has already begun in Jesus. Rahner makes much of the bodily and physical implications of this fact. The bodily resurrection of Jesus adumbrates the physical transfiguration of the entire material universe in God. We do not therefore need to leave the world to find God. The most trivial human or mundane realities are pregnant with divine presence and activity, if only we entrust ourselves to our experiences of self-transcendence. But here again I pointed out problems with this approach, especially in the way it tends to relativize the church and the sacramental means of grace, which orthodox Christianity has always privileged as special God-ordained locales, so to speak, of divine self-communication.

Finally, I moved on to consider the doctrine of deification as expounded in the theological writings of Henri de Lubac. Although he was born before Rahner I placed him third in the sequence of analysis in order to highlight my proposal that his exposition of deification best coheres with the grand sweep of catholic tradition and with the christocentric and ecclesiocentric vision for human fulfillment advanced by Vatican II. I began in chapter 9 by visiting the well-known debate famously precipitated by the 1946 publication of de Lubac's *Surnaturel*. Here I weighed and found wanting certain interpretations of de Lubac's theology that do not sufficiently recognize the continuing distinction—even "abyss"—that de Lubac affirmed, like Blondel, between nature and the supernatural. Far from confusing the two gifts of being and beatitude, de Lubac sought to hold them together in inseparable but unconfused union. His preference for nuptial symbolism to characterize the union between God and the human person makes clear his conviction that deification entails a real reciprocity and mutuality between two subjects who, while truly one, nevertheless maintain their own ontological specificity. While de Lubac rejected the "two end" theory of human nature defended by Baroque Thomism, he nevertheless maintained the adjective "twofold" as a necessary characterization of the gratuity involved in the human being's passage from created finite existence to participated infinite existence.

If Garrigou-Lagrange is open to the criticism of envisioning deification too much as a union between the individual soul and God, and if Rahner is open to the criticism of making too much of individual gnosis and of relativizing the church as the sacramental *locus deificandi*, the tenth chapter on the notion of deification as ecclesial *concorporatio* can be taken as de Lubac's defining answer to the weaknesses of both. Here we find the lineaments of a much-needed sociology of deification, from which one could begin to trace more definitely the social "shape" of Trinitarian life in history. Anticipating the *communio* anthropology and ecclesiology of later decades, not to mention forms of *communio* Trinitarian theology, de Lubac took up the patristic ideas of corporate humanity, recapitulated and recreated in Christ and his body, the church. Attributing a kind of *communicatio idiomatum* between Christ and the church, de Lubac urged that there is only one new humanity, one pattern of fullness and perfection, such that deification is essentially and irreducibly ecclesial. Just as Christ's physical humanity is the sacrament of God, so the church, in both her sacramental and social dimensions, is the sacrament of Christ and the place of deification in the world. Thus between the means to deification and its fulfillment there is not an extrinsic relationship, as though the church and its grace-filled resources were simply so many external helps to be eventually discarded on arrival at the goal. Rather there is an intrinsic relation between means and end, like two states or modes of the one body.

The last chapter, chapter 11, unpacked a series of vital binary relations in de Lubac's theology whose basic paradigm is found in the longstanding anthropological distinction between the image and likeness of God. If the image of God in human beings constitutes a kind of "secret call" to the supernatural life, likeness to God refers to the unfolding passage of this vocation toward assimilation with God. This distinction adds to the ontological structural composition of human nature a profoundly historical, dynamic, and pedagogical dimension, within which the synergy of human and divine freedom plays a crucial role. The image-and-likeness distinction also corresponds somewhat to the tripartite structure of the human person, in whom the third element, spirit, in distinction from the body and soul composite, functions as the interior point of contact with God and the guarantee assuring a certain hidden transcendence of human beings over themselves. Humanity's end in deification or likeness to God springs from its beginning, that is, from its special, immediate creation by God as intelligent spirit.

A third binary structure, just as dynamic, is found in the distinction between letter and spirit, worked out in de Lubac's profound retrieval of patristic and medieval spiritual exegesis of Scripture. The letter of Scripture represents the embodiment of a pedagogical strategy on God's part whose goal, lying on the level of spirit, is finally attained in humanity's union with Christ. Engagement with Scripture has as its purpose the faith-filled penetration of the letter through to its inner heart, the personal assimilation of, or rather, self-assimilation to, its Spirit-filled content. The plot and purpose of the story of Scripture is fulfilled when the reader herself, by interiorizing its message and allowing her life to be assimilated to its divine content, herself becomes a living word of God. It was in the context of my treatment of this idea that I raised again the fruitful and intriguing issue, first discussed in the chapters on Garrigou-Lagrange, of the relative passivity of the human person and the incapacity of her natural powers in the final surrender to deification. By passivity, de Lubac, in harmony with the thought of Maximus the Confessor and the venerable tradition invoked by Garrigou-Lagrange, does not mean inaction. Rather, human action reaches its zenith in what von Balthasar called a "letting be," a humble surrender to divine love. Since the words of Scripture are performative divine words, once they are introduced at the level of spirit they act on and in us, thereby, as it were, becoming flesh in us. In these ways, in the end, we "suffer" or undergo deification or assimilation to God more than we achieve it.

CRITICAL PERSPECTIVES

In expounding the theology of deification as we have found it in these three authors, this book has purposely avoided getting too heavily locked within certain polemical lines of argument that continue to dominate theological literature concerning their personal roles in the so-called nature-and-grace debate. Yet obviously this debate is pertinent to the way each author understood what it means for human beings to become God by grace. What then are some of the main questions currently in dispute, relevant to our authors, which I have left unresolved?

The first set of questions is suggested by a prominent debate between two groupings of contemporary interlocutors. One group consists in a number of North American Neothomists, who find in de Lubac's account of natural desire for supernatural beatitude a revival of the error of Michael Baius (1513–1589).[2]

---

2. Baius held that grace was somehow a necessary complement to human nature.

Furthermore, they find in de Lubac's insistence on the indefinability of human nature—in that it is created spirit open and called to the infinite—an insufficient affirmation of knowable ends proportionate to knowable natural powers. De Lubac is thus accused of a double emptying: he has emptied grace of its absolute gratuity, and he has emptied the category of "nature" of any definitive content distinguishable from its "hot-wiring" to beatitude, rendering it an ontological "nought" or "vacuole." Critics who have raised these allegations include Romanus Cessario, Lawrence Feingold, Reinhard Hütter, Steven A. Long, and Guy Mansini.[3]

The other group, active especially in England, may be called the anti-extrinsicists. Strongly supportive of de Lubac's theological vision, they have launched a trenchant offensive against the Neothomists, not just by way of exegetical argument over what Aquinas really taught on the relevant questions, but also by highlighting the insidious historical, cultural, and political effects that have been entailed by the hypothetical construction of "pure nature," that is, a human nature defined without fundamental reference either to actual history or to Christ and his deifying grace. By cordoning off the natural from the supernatural and reason from faith, the Neothomists are accused of sanctioning a secularizing worldview that overdetermines the category of human nature and pretends nature and the world to be knowable in abstraction from their actual christoform end. Significant voices in this group include Conor Cunningham, John Milbank, Nicholas Healy, and Aaron Riches.[4]

Without going into the details of this controversy, some of which have been touched on here and there along the way throughout this book, it is nonetheless important to consider whether and how it impacts my reading of our three theologians and to what extent it bears upon the judicious

---

3. Romanus Cessario, "Duplex Ordo Cognitionis," in *Reason and the Reasons of Faith*, ed. Paul J. Griffiths and Reinhard Hütter (New York: T. & T. Clark, 2005), 327–38; Lawrence Feingold, *The Natural Desire to See God According to St. Thomas Aquinas and His Interpreters* (Naples, FL: Sapientia, 2010); Reinhard Hütter, "*Desiderium Naturale Visionis Dei—Est autem duplex hominis beatitude sive felicitas:* Some Observations about Lawrence Feingold's and John Milbank's Recent Interventions in the Debate over the Natural Desire to See God," *Nova et Vetera* 5 (2007): 81–131; Steven A. Long, *Natura Pura: On the Recovery of Nature in the Doctrine of Grace* (New York: Fordham University Press, 2010); Guy Mansini, "Henri de Lubac, the Natural Desire to See God, and Pure Nature," *Gregorianum* 83, no. 1 (2002): 89–109.

4. Conor Cunningham, "*Natura Pura*, the Invention of the Anti-Christ: A Week with No Sabbath," *Communio* 37 (2010): 243–54; John Milbank, *The Suspended Middle: Henri de Lubac and the Debate Concerning the Supernatural* (Grand Rapids: Eerdmans, 2005); Nicholas J. Healy, "Henri de Lubac on Nature and Grace: A Note on Some Recent Contributions to the Debate," *Communio* 35 (2008): 535–64; Aaron Riches, "Christology and Anti-Humanism," *Modern Theology* 29, no. 3 (2013): 311–37.

appropriation and development of elements in their respective doctrines of deification. Among many of the questions raised by the anti-extrinsicists, one in particular seems to me to be of most relevance to the concerns of this book: Is the definitive meaning and purpose of humanity and the universe found in the God who transcends history or in the transcendent God who himself has a history in Jesus Christ? Or to put the question in a more Thomistic form: Can either nature or grace be adequately understood without reference to the incarnation and the saving work of Jesus Christ? Both questions make it clear that the doctrine of deification carries profound implications for our understanding of the relationship between metaphysics and history, between the necessary and contingent, between being and existence. If deification involves the theandric coincidence of both spheres in a union without confusion, and if this union is both the appropriate and actual end for which creation and history exist, then it appears that any attempt to comprehend nature and created being without reference to the actual, historical, and contingent presence in nature and created being of its divine creative principle (the incarnate Logos), can only short-circuit understanding and interrupt our knowing involvement in our own deifying drama. As Frederick Wilhelmsen once astutely observed, "intelligibility is played through as an act before thought through as a conclusion. . . . Every insight into reality . . . demands our situating ourselves within the reality which is subsequently penetrated intellectually."[5]

According to Earl Muller, the consensus in scholarship from Chenu and Gilson right down to the contemporary Neothomists of today holds that, despite a few dissenting voices that argue that Aquinas comprehended all reality—both human and divine—only in the light of Christ the incarnate Word, in the end the angelic doctor believed that both nature and grace possess their own structure and laws independent of history and to which their actual manifestations in history necessarily conform.[6] Whether or not this is true, the doctrine of deification—to the extent that it discerns and maintains the intrinsic link between anthropology and christology, cosmology and eschatology—presents a legitimate and indeed vital challenge to the hegemony of every kind of abstract ontotheological naturalism in metaphysics and theology. In any case, these questions point up the weakness of any proposal that would try to characterize deification along lines that are insufficiently christocentric, historical, and concrete. This is why Garrigou-

5. Frederick D. Wilhelmsen, *The Paradoxical Structure of Existence* (Albany, NY: Preserving Christian Publications, 1991), 160.

6. Earl Muller, "Creation as Existential Contingency: A Response," *The Saint Anselm Journal* 1, no. 1 (2003): 65–78.

Lagrange's doctrine of deification sits rather uneasily in his overall thought, sharply demarcated as it is from a mathematically watertight philosophical system confined to dealing with the necessary and immutable.

A second set of questions of a related but slightly different sort are suggested by a brief but systematic critique raised against all three of our authors by Jesuit Peter Ryan. In comparing the approaches of Garrigou-Lagrange, de Lubac, and Rahner to the problem of how the beatific vision can properly fulfill human nature and yet remain gratuitous, Ryan proposed "friendship with God" to be an obvious missing link in all three accounts.[7] According to Ryan, human nature is not in fact essentially oriented toward supernatural fulfillment, but only toward "ever great fulfilment in various human goods."[8] He rejects Augustine's notion of the *cor inquietum*, also embraced by Aquinas, unapologetically adopting instead a two-tiered vision of human nature according to which the beatific vision is not a fulfillment of human nature as such "but of human *persons* insofar as they share in the *divine* nature."[9]

Ryan's critique holds merit in one or two points. First, there is much to be said for a well-developed theology of friendship, inasmuch as it highlights the interpersonal character of deification. As Livio Melina has so beautifully stated,

> Friendship permits us to maintain the full transcendence of the gift, while also showing its progressive interiorization, just as in the experience of love the lover is transformed by affective union with the beloved, whose imprint, the principle of a specific form of knowledge by connaturality, is borne more and more deeply by the beloved.[10]

But notice the presence in this statement of an important element missing in Ryan's account, yet foremost in both Garrigou-Lagrange and de Lubac: the nuptial analogy, which alone among all creaturely relations—filiality included—fittingly embodies the kind of divine–human intimacy deification entails.

Ryan is also right to emphasize that it is *persons* who are deified, not natures. On this point all our theologians could use more systematic

---

7. Peter F. Ryan, "How Can the Beatific Vision both Fulfill Human Nature and Be Utterly Gratuitous?" *Gregorianum* 83, no. 4 (2002): 717–54.

8. Ibid., 748.

9. Ibid., 751.

10. Livio Melina, *The Epiphany of Love: Toward a Theological Understanding of Christian Action* (Grand Rapids: Eerdmans, 2010), 153.

development along the lines provided by Trinitarian personalism, a theology of the body, and a metaphysics of love. Resources for such a task can readily be found in the works of such personalist thinkers as Maurice Nédoncelle, Karol Wojtyla, and Hans Urs von Balthasar, who have each conceptualized interpersonal reciprocity and the dramatic "we" of deifying theandric communion in rich and fruitful terms.[11]

But Ryan's attempt to construct a Christian doctrine of deification employing the two-tiered anthropology of Germain Grisez and the Neoclassicist (New Natural Law) school associated with him is fraught with problems. This school specifically set out to develop a nonheteronomous, reason-based moral system, conducive to Catholic moral teaching, but exclusive of all reference to a supernatural end. Introducing a Kantian-like division between nature and person, it effectively tends toward a deistic view of ethics, in which the natural and supernatural orders are self-contained and only extrinsically juxtaposed.[12]

A further weakness in Ryan's proposed reconstruction is that his theology of friendship is devoid of any reference to merit. This omission points up an issue in the theologies of all three of our theologians: an insufficiently developed doctrine of sin. An adequate doctrine of both sin and merit is an essential safeguard against a Pelagianizing doctrine of deification on the one hand and a false separation between salvation and ethics on the other.[13] Our three theologians all presupposed the actual background horizon of sin in speaking of the need for purification and self-annihilation (Garrigou-Lagrange), forgiveness (Rahner), and mortification and ecclesial concorporation (de Lubac). Yet many discussions on the nature-and-grace relation, even on the part of those who reject the notion of "pure nature," seem to overlook the actually fallen condition of human nature and a person's native lack of soteriologically effective resources. The infusion of grace or the Holy Spirit as a new principle of action into the root of the human dynamism is incomprehensible apart from an accompanying divine intervention, made

11. E.g., see Maurice Nédoncelle, *Love and the Person*, trans. Ruth Adelaide (New York: Sheed & Ward, 1966); Karol Wojtyla, *Love and Responsibility*, trans. H. T. Willetts (London: Collins, 1981); Hans Urs von Balthasar, *Love Alone Is Credible*, trans. D. C. Schindler (San Francisco: Ignatius, 2004).

12. Ryan cites his dependence on Grisez at op. cit. 751, n. 104. For critical readings of the Neoclassicist project, see Fulvio di Blasi, *God and the Natural Law: A Rereading of Thomas Aquinas* (South Bend, IN: St. Augustine's, 2006); Russell Hittinger, *A Critique of the New Natural Law Theory* (Notre Dame: Notre Dame University Press, 1987).

13. On the relevance for deification of the doctrines of sin, merit, and friendship, see Melina, *The Epiphany of Love*, 146–62.

possible by universal atonement, in the form of merciful pardon and deliverance from slavery to sin. It is not incidental that the primary scriptural mention of our call to participation in the divine nature stresses the foundational mediation of the Savior's "great and precious promises" (2 Pet. 1:4), through which alone the passage to deiform assimilation begins.

Ryan is also unconvincing when he insists that deification brings about no fulfillment in human nature as such, as if that would imply an essential change in nature. On this point he over-interprets our authors and makes them say what in fact each denies. More importantly in the end, however, Ryan's comparative study, like so many other attempts to adjudicate discussion on these three figures, is hampered because it still remains locked within the polemically charged dialectical categories into which the nature-and-grace dispute so often falls. As long as one accepts as a point of departure, in the terms provided by postmedieval scholasticism, either the problem of believing that human nature's being ordered to beatitude obliges God in such a way that he "owes" it beatitude, or else the problem of believing that the gratuity of beatitude needs protecting from the threat of saying that human nature is innately inscribed with supernatural finality (as though this amounts to a "claim" on God), one is locked into a theological impasse. It was Rahner's and especially de Lubac's merit that they tackled the paradox of the natural desire for the supernatural by having recourse to a much broader range of concepts and metaphors than the debate as hitherto pursued had allowed for. Von Balthasar and others rightly referred to de Lubac's preferred mode of conceptualization as a "suspended middle" answering to neither philosophy nor (secondary) theology in precision of the other, but representing a paradoxical yet nondialectical zone in which each is concurrently affirmed and apophatically transcended. It will be recalled from earlier chapters that Garrigou-Lagrange, precisely in his attempts to communicate what is actualized in deification, occasionally broke free from the strictures of scholastic language and systematic categories, here and there approaching the mystical and "paradoxical" style so characteristic of de Lubac.

On the other hand, it is true that our three authors did not undertake their theological reflections in a vacuum, but within the cut-and-thrust context of their own theological polemics and in answer to pressing questions often arising not from detached reflection on the human condition and its beatified state but from politically charged embroilments over the accurate exposition of key texts in the Christian tradition and over the most coherent, theologically faithful appropriation of the divinely revealed and historically mediated givens of the faith. This is why the contemporary nature-and-grace controversy should not be treated as a mere academic contest, for it taps into concerns keenly felt by its earliest antagonists and of far-reaching relevance for current and future directions in theological education, ecclesial self-understanding, and world evangelization. Even so, it seems both plausible and worthwhile to have attempted in this book to consider aspects in the theological articulation of deification on the part of these authors in a way that focuses less on the specific problematics involved in the nature–and–grace debate and more upon their own particular use of sources, explanation of ideas, and employment of metaphors. Adopting this approach, I hope to have opened a way for the intelligent and interested reader to "get inside" their particular perspectives and rationales. For only in this way, it seems to me, can one conduct a properly critical and comprehensive appraisal of their relative value and make an informed judgment as to the coherence of their respective contributions to a genuinely christoform human culture.

Bibliography

Aherne, C. M. "Grace, Controversies On," in *The New Catholic Encyclopedia*, vol. 6. Detroit: Gale, 2003, 2nd ed.

Arintero, J. G. *The Mystical Evolution in the Development and Vitality of the Church*, vol. 1. Translated by J. Aumann. St. Louis: Herder, 1950.

Armstrong, A. H. "Image and Similitude in Augustine," *Revue des études augustiniennes* 10 (1964): 125–45.

Ashley, B. *Spiritual Direction in the Dominican Tradition.* New York: Paulist, 1995.

Augustine of Hippo. *Thirteen Homilies of St Augustine on St John XIV.* Translated by H. F. Stewart. Cambridge: Cambridge University Press, 1902.

———. *The Works of Saint Augustine: A Translation for the 21st Century* Part II – Letters, vol. 3 Letters, 156–210. Edited by B. Ramsey. Translated by R. Teske. New York: New City, 2004.

Badcock, F. J. "*Sanctorum Communio* as an Article in the Creed," *Journal of Theological Studies* 21, no. 1 (1920): 106–26.

Von Balthasar, H. U. *Love Alone Is Credible.* Translated by D. C. Schindler. San Francisco: Ignatius, 2004.

———. *The Moment of Christian Witness.* San Francisco: Ignatius, 1994.

———. *The Theology of Henri de Lubac: An Overview.* San Francisco: Ignatius 1991.

———. "On the Concept of Person," *Communio* 13, no. 1 (1986): 18–26.

Batlogg, A. R., and M. E. Michalski, eds. *Encounters with Karl Rahner: Remembrances of Rahner by Those Who Knew Him.* Milwaukee: Marquette University Press, 2009.

Benko, S. *The Meaning of "Sanctorum Communio."* London, 1964.

Di Blasi, F. *God and the Natural Law: A Rereading of Thomas Aquinas.* South Bend, IN: St. Augustine's, 2006.

Blondel, M. *Letter on Apologetics and History and Dogma.* Translated by A. Dru and I. Trethowan. Grand Rapids: Eerdmans, 1994.

Boersma, H. *Nouvelle Théologie and Sacramental Ontology: A Return to Mystery.* Oxford: Oxford University Press, 2009.

Bonino, S.-T., ed. *Surnaturel: A Controversy at the Heart of Twentieth-Century Thomistic Thought.* Translated by Robert Williams and Matthew Levering. Ave Maria, FL: Sapientia, 2009.

Bonner, G. "Augustine's Conception of Deification," *Journal of Theological Studies* 37 (1986): 369–86.

———. "Deification, Divinization." In A. D. Fitzgerald, ed., *Augustine Through the Ages: An Encyclopedia.* Grand Rapids: Eerdmans, 1999, 265–66.

———. "Deificare." In C. Mayer, ed., *Augustinus-Lexicon*, vol. 2. Basel: Schwabe, 1996, 265–67.

Borella, J. *The Sense of the Supernatural.* New York: Continuum, 2002.

Boyer, C. "Nature pure et surnaturel dans le 'Surnaturel' du Père de Lubac," *Gregorianum* 28 (1947): 379–96.

Braaten, C. E., and R. W. Jensen, eds. *Union with Christ: The New Finnish Interpretation of Luther.* Grand Rapids: Eerdmans, 1998.

Braine, D. "The Debate Between Henri de Lubac and His Critics," *Nova et Vetera* 6, no. 3 (2008): 543–90.

Brown, D. "'Necessary' and 'Fitting' Reasons in Christian Theology." In W. J. Abraham and S. W. Holzer, eds., *The Rationality of Religious Belief*. Oxford: Clarendon, 1987, 211–30.

Brooks, P., ed. *Christian Spirituality: Essays in Honour of Gordon Rupp*. London: SCM, 1975.

Bühler, P., ed. *Humain à l'image de Dieu*. Geneva: Labor et Fides, 1989.

Bulzacchelli, R. H. "Dives in Misericordia: The Pivotal Significance of a Forgotten Encyclical." In N. M. Billias et al., eds., *Karol Wojtyla's Philosophical Legacy*. Washington: DC: The Council for Research in Values and Philosophy, 2008, 125–62.

Burke, P. *Reinterpreting Rahner: A Critical Study of His Major Themes*. New York: Fordham University Press, 2002.

Caponi, F. J. "Karl Rahner and the Metaphysics of Participation," *The Thomist* 67 (2003): 375–408.

———. "Karl Rahner: Divinization in Roman Catholicism." In M. J. Christensen and J. A. Wittung, eds., *Partakers of the Divine Nature: The History and Development of Deification in the Christian Traditions*. Grand Rapids: Baker, 2007, 259–80.

Cessario, R. "Duplex Ordo Cognitionis." In Paul J. Griffiths and Reinhard Hütter, eds., *Reason and the Reasons of Faith*. New York: T. & T. Clark, 2005, 327–38.

Chadwick, H. "A Latin Epitome of Melito's Homily on the Pascha," *Journal of Theological Studies* 11, no. 1 (1960): 76–82.

Chenu, M.-D. *Faith and Theology*. Translated by D. Hickey. Dublin: Gill & Son, 1968.

Christensen, M. J., and J. A. Wittung, J. A., eds. *Partakers of the Divine Nature: The History and Development of Deification in the Christian Traditions*. Grand Rapids: Baker, 2007.

Cognet, L. *Post-Reformation Spirituality*. Translated by P. J. Hepburne-Scott. London: Burns & Oates, 1959.

Collins, P. M. *Partaking in Divine Nature: Deification and Communion*. New York: Continuum, 2008.

Colombo, J. A. "Rahner and His Critics: Lindbeck and Metz," *The Thomist* 56, no. 1 (1992): 71–96.

Congar, Y. "Peut-on definer l'Église? Destin et valeur de quatre notions qui s'offrent à la faire." In J. Leclercq, *L'homme, l'oeuvre et ses amis*. Paris and Tournai: Casterman, 1961, 233–54.

———. "'The Cross of Jesus' by Fr. Louis de Chardon, OP." In idem, *The Revelation of God*. Translated by A. Manson and L. C. Sheppard. London: Darton, Longman & Todd, 1968, 116–28.

———. *Jesus Christ*. Translated by Luke O'Neill. London: Geoffrey Chapman, 1966.

Cooper, A. G. *The Body in St Maximus the Confessor: Holy Flesh, Wholly Deified*. Oxford: Oxford University Press, 2005.

———. "Marriage and 'The Garments of Skin' in Irenaeus and the Greek Fathers," *Communio* 33, no. 2 (2006): 215–37.

———. "The Role of the Will in Conversion: Re-reading the Confessions with Thomas Aquinas," *Lutheran Theological Journal* 42, no. 1 (2008): 41–50.

———. "Criteria for Authentic Mystical Experience: Reginald Garrigou-Lagrange's Doctrine of Deification," *The Heythrop Journal* 55, no. 2 (2014): 230-43.

———. "Deification Between Vatican I and Vatican II." In David Meconi and Carl Olsen, eds., *Called to Be Children of God*. San Francisco: Ignatius, 2014.

Copleston, F. *A History of Philosophy: 19th and 20th Century French Philosophy*. London: Continuum, 1999.

Cunningham, C. "*Natura Pura*, the Invention of the Anti-Christ: A Week with No Sabbath," *Communio* 37 (2010): 243–54.

Cunningham, L. B. *The Indwelling of the Trinity: A Historico-Doctrinal Study of the Theory of St. Thomas Aquinas.* Dubuque, IA: Priory, 1955.

Cyril of Jerusalem. *St. Cyril of Jerusalem's Lectures on the Christian Sacraments: The Procatechesis and the Five Mystagogical Catecheses.* Edited by F. L. Cross. London: SPCK, 1951.

Daley, B. "The *Nouvelle Théologie* and the Patristic Revival: Sources, Symbols and the Science of Theology," *International Journal of Systematic Theology* 7, no. 4 (2005): 362–82.

Daniélou, J. *Platonisme et théologie mystique: Essai sur le doctrine spirituelle de Saint Grégoire de Nysse.* Paris: Aubier, 1944.

———. *Gospel Message and Hellenistic Culture: A History of Early Christian Doctrine Before the Council of Nicaea*, vol. 2. London: Darton, Longman & Todd, 1973.

Darlapp, A. "Nouvelle Théologie," *Lexikon für Theologie und Kirche*, vol. 7. Freiburg im Breisgau: Herder, 1963, 1060.

Dedek, J. F. "*Quasi Experimentalis Cognitio:* A Historical Approach to the Meaning of St. Thomas," *Theological Studies* 22 (1961): 357–90.

Deferrari, R. J. *A Lexicon of Saint Thomas Aquinas.* Fitzwilliam, NH: Loreto, 2004.

Del Colle, R. *Christ and the Spirit: Spirit-Christology in Trinitarian Perspective.* New York: Oxford University Press, 1994.

Deloffre, M.-H. *Thomas d'Aquin: Question disputée: L'union du Verbe incarne (De unione Verbi Incarnati).* Paris: Vrin, 2000.

————. "La Question disputée: L'union du Verbe incarné de saint Thomas d'Aquin," http://www.thomas-d-aquin.com/Pages/Articles/PresDeUnion.pdf.

————, and G. Delaporte. "Le 'esse secundarium' du Christ," http://www.thomas-d-aquin.com/Pages/Articles/EsseSecundarium.pdf.

Diepen, H. M. "L'existence humaine du Christ en métaphysique thomiste," *Revue Thomiste* 58 (1958): 197–213.

Dietrich, D. J., and M. J. Himes. *The Legacy of the Tübingen School: The Relevance of Nineteenth-Century Theology for the Twenty-First Century.* New York: Crossroad, 1997.

Donneaud, H. "*Surnaturel* through the Fine-Tooth Comb of Traditional Thomism." In S.-T. Bonino, ed., *Surnaturel: A Controversy at the Heart of Twentieth-Century Thomistic Thought.* Translated by R. Williams and M. Levering. Ave Maria, FL: Sapientia, 2009, 41–57.

Duffy, S. J. "Experience of Grace." In D. Marmion and M. E. Hines, eds., *The Cambridge Companion to Karl Rahner.* Cambridge: Cambridge University Press, 2005, 43–62.

Edwards, D. *How God Acts: Creation, Redemption and Special Divine Action.* Minneapolis: Fortress Press, 2010.

Egan, H. D. *The Spiritual Exercises and the Ignatian Mystical Horizon.* St. Louis, Institute of Jesuit Sources, 1976.

————. *Karl Rahner: The Mystic of Everyday Life.* New York: Crossroad, 1998.

————. "Theology and Spirituality." In D. Marmion and M. E. Hines, eds., *The Cambridge Companion to Karl Rahner.* Cambridge: Cambridge University Press, 2005, 13–28.

Eichrodt, W. *Theology of the Old Testament,* vol. 2. London: SCM, 1967.

Elert, W. *Eucharist and Fellowship in the First Four Centuries.* Translated by N. E. Nagel. St. Louis: Concordia, 1966.

Emery, G. "The Personal Mode of Trinitarian Action in St. Thomas Aquinas." In idem, *Trinity, Church, and the Human Person: Thomistic Essays*. Naples, FL: Sapientia, 2007.

Endean, P. "Rahner, Christology and Grace," *The Heythrop Journal* 37 (1996): 284–97.

———. *Karl Rahner and Ignatian Spirituality*. Oxford: Oxford University Press, 2001.

Fantino, J. *L'homme, image de Dieu chez S. Irénée de Lyon*. Paris: Cerf, 1986.

Feingold, L. *The Natural Desire to See God According to St. Thomas Aquinas and His Interpreters*. Naples, FL: Sapientia, 2010.

Ferguson, E. "God's Infinity and Man's Mutability: Perpetual Progress according to Gregory of Nyssa," *Greek Orthodox Theological Review* 18, no. 1–2 (1973): 59–78.

Fierro, A. *Sobre la Gloria en San Hilario: Una sintesis doctrinal sobre la noción biblica de «doxa»*, Analecta Gregoriana 144. Rome: Libreria editrice dell' Univ. Gregoriana, 1964.

Finland, S., and V. Kharlamov, eds. *Theosis: Deification in Christian Theology*. Eugene, OR: Pickwick, 2006.

Florovsky, G. "Cur Deus Homo? The Motive of the Incarnation." In H. S. Alivisatos, *Evharisterion*. Athens: 1957, 70–79, reprinted at http://www.holytrinitymission.org/books/english/ theology_redemption_florovsky_e.htm#_Toc104243114.

Gallagher, M. P. "Ignatian Dimensions of Rahner's Theology," *Louvain Studies* 29 (2004): 77–91.

Gallaher, B. "Graced Creatureliness: Ontological Tension in the Uncreated/ Created Distinction in the Sophiologies of Solov'ev, Bulgakov and Milbank," *Logos: A Journal of Eastern Christian Studies* 47 (2006): 163–90.

Garrigou-Lagrange, R. "Le désir naturel de bonheur: Prouve-t-il l'existence de Dieu?" *Angelicum* 8 (1931): 129–48.

————. "La nouvelle théologie: Où va-t-elle?" *Angelicum* 23 (1946): 126–45.

————. *The Love of God and the Cross of Jesus*, vol. 1. Translated by J. Marie. St. Louis: Herder, 1947 (= *L'Amour de Dieu et la Croix de Jésus*. Paris: Cerf, 1929).

————. *Grace: Commentary on the* Summa theologica *of St. Thomas, Ia IIae, q. 109-14.* Translated by the Dominican Nuns. St. Louis: Herder, 1952 (= *De Gratia: Commentarius in Summam Theologiae S. Thomae*. Torino: Berutti, 1946).

————. *Reality: A Synthesis of Thomistic Thought.* Translated by P. Cummins. London: Herder, 1950 (reprinted by Ex Fontibus, 2007) (= *La synthèse thomiste*. Paris: Desclée de Brouwer, 1946).

————. *Our Savior and His Love for Us.* Translated by A. Bouchard. St. Louis and London: Herder, 1951 (= *Le Sauveur et son amour pour nous*. Paris: Cerf, 1933).

————. *Beatitude: A Commentary on St. Thomas's Theological Summa, Ia IIae, qq.1-54.* Translated by P. Cummins. St. Louis: Herder, 1956 (= *De Beatitudine: De actibus humanis et habitibus. Commentarius in Summam theologicam S. Thomae.* Torino: Berruti, 1951).

————. *The Three Conversions in the Spiritual Life.* Rockford, IL: Tan Books 2002 (= *Les trois conversions et les trois voies*. Paris: Cerf, 1933).

Gavrilyuk, P. L. "The Retrieval of Deification: How a Once-Despised Archaism Became an Ecumenical Desideratum," *Modern Theology* 25, no. 4 (2009): 647–59.

Gertler, T. *Jesus Christus: Die Antwort der Kirche auf die Frage nach dem Menschsein*, Erfurt Theologischen Studien 52. Leipzig: St. Benno, 1986.

Gilbert, P., H. Kohlenberger, and E. Salmann, eds. *Cur Deus Homo*, Studia Anselmiana 128. Rome: S. Anselmo, 1999.

Gilson, E. *The Unity of Philosophical Experience.* San Francisco: Ignatius, 1964.

———. *Letters of Etienne Gilson to Henri de Lubac: Annotated by Father de Lubac.* Translated by M. E. Hamilton. San Francisco: Ignatius, 1988.

Giussani, L. *The Journey to Truth Is an Experience.* Translated by J. Zucchi. Montreal: McGill-Queen's University Press, 2006.

Gregory of Nyssa. *The Life of Moses.* Translated and edited by A. J. Malherbe and E. Ferguson. New York: Paulist, 1978.

Grillmeier, A. *Christ in Christian Tradition*, vol. 2, part 2: *The Church of Constantinople in the Sixth Century.* Translated by P. Allen and J. Cawte. London: Mowbray, 1995.

———. *Christ in Christian Tradition: From the Apostolic Age to Chalcedon (451).* Translated by J. S. Bowden. London: Mowbray, 1965.

Gross, J. *The Divinization of the Christian according to the Greek Fathers.* Translated by P. A. Onica. Anaheim, CA: A and C, 2002.

Grumett, D. *De Lubac: A Guide for the Perplexed.* London: T. & T. Clark, 2007.

De Halleux, A. "La Définition Christologique à Chalcédoine," *Revue théologique de Louvain* 7 (1976): 3–23, 155–70.

———. "Personalisme ou essentialisme trinitaire chez les Pères cappadociens?" *Revue théologique de Louvain* 17 (1986): 129–55, 265–92.

Hamann, A.-G. *L'homme, image de Dieu: Essai d'une anthropologie chrétienne dans l'Église des cinq premiers siècles.* Paris: Desclée de Brouwer, 1987.

Hankey, W. J. "One Hundred Years of Neoplatonism in France: A Brief Philosophical History." In J.-M. Narbonne and W. J. Hankey, *Levinas and the Greek Heritage Followed by One Hundred Years of Neoplatonism in France: A Brief Philosophical History.* Leuven: Peeters, 2006, 99–162.

Von Harnack, A. *History of Dogma*, vol. 2. Translated by Neil Buchanan. New York: Dover, 1961.

Healy, N. "Indirect Methods in Theology: Karl Rahner as an ad hoc Apologist," *The Thomist* 56 (1992): 613–34.

———. "Henri de Lubac on Nature and Grace: A Note on Some Recent Contributions to the Debate," *Communio* 35, no. 4 (2008): 535–64.

Hello, E. *Life, Science, Art: Being Leaves from Ernest Hello*. Translated by E. M. Walker. London: R. & T. Washbourne, 1912.

Himes, M. J. *Ongoing Incarnation: Johann Adam Möhler and the Beginning of Modern Ecclesiology*. New York: Crossroad 1997.

Hittinger, R. *A Critique of the New Natural Law Theory*. Notre Dame: Notre Dame University Press, 1987.

Höfer, J., and K. Rahner, eds. *Lexicon für Theologie und Kirche*, vol. 5. Freiburg im Breisgau: Herder, 1960.

Horan, D. P. "How Original Was Scotus on the Incarnation? Reconsidering the History of the Absolute Predestination of Christ in the Light of Robert Grosseteste," *The Heythrop Journal* 48 (2010): 1–18.

Hütter, R. "*Desiderium Naturale Visionis Dei-Est autem duplex hominis beatitude sive felicitas*: Some Observations about Lawrence Feingold's and John Milbank's Recent Interventions in the Debate over the Natural Desire for God," *Nova et Vetera* 5, no. 1 (2007): 81–131.

Kasper, W. *Jesus the Christ*. Translated by V. Green. London: Burns & Oates, 1976.

Kelly, B. "Divine Quasi-Formal Causality," *Irish Theological Quarterly* 28, no. 1 (1961): 16–28.

Kelly, J. N. D. *Early Christian Creeds*, 3rd ed. Harlow, UK: Longman, 1972.

Kerr, F. "Chenu's Little Book," *New Blackfriars* 66, no. 777 (1985): 108–12.

———. *Theology after Wittgenstein.* Oxford: Blackwell, 1986.

———. *After Aquinas: Versions of Thomism.* Oxford: Blackwell, 2002.

———. "A Different World: Neoscholasticism and Its Discontents," *International Journal of Systematic Theology* 8, no. 2 (2006): 128–48.

Kilby, K. *Karl Rahner: A Brief Introduction.* New York: Crossroad, 2007.

———. *Karl Rahner: Theology and Philosophy.* London: Routledge, 2004.

Komonchak, J. A. "Theology and Culture at Mid-Century: The Example of Henri de Lubac," *Theological Studies* 51 (1990): 579–602.

Kovacs, J. L. "'Servant of Christ' and 'Steward of the Mysteries of God': The Purpose of a Pauline Letter according to Origen's *Homilies on 1 Corinthians.*" In *In Dominico Eloquio / In Lordly Eloquence: Essays on Patristic Exegesis in Honor of Robert L. Wilken,* ed. Paul Blowers et al. Grand Rapids: Eerdmans, 2002, 147–71.

Lavaud, M.-B. "Le Père Garrigou-Lagrange: *In Memoriam,*" *Revue Thomiste* 64 (1964): 181–99.

Lehninger, P. D. "Luther and Theosis: Deification in the Theology of Martin Luther," Ph.D. Dissertation, Marquette University, 1999.

De Letter, P. "Created Actuation by the Uncreated Act: Difficulties and Answers," *Theological Studies* 18, no. 1 (1957): 60–92.

———. "Divine Quasi-Formal Causality," *Irish Theological Quarterly* 27, no. 3 (1960): 221–28.

———. "'Pure' of 'Quasi'-Formal Causality?" *Irish Theological Quarterly* 30, no. 1 (1963): 36–47.

———. "The Theology of God's Self-Gift," *Theological Studies* 24 (1963): 402–22.

Lewis, C. S. *The Four Loves*. London: Fontana, 1960.

Lonergan, B. *Grace and Freedom: Operative Grace in the Thought of St. Thomas Aquinas*. Edited by J. Patout Burns. London: Darton, Longman & Todd, 1971.

Long, S. A. "Obediential Potency, Human Knowledge, and the Natural Desire to See God," *International Philosophical Quarterly* 37 (1997): 47–63.

———. *Natura Pura: On the Recovery of Nature in the Doctrine of Grace*. New York: Fordham University Press, 2010.

Löser, W. "The Ignatian Exercises in the Work of Hans Urs von Balthasar." In D. L. Schindler, ed., *Hans Urs von Balthasar: His Life and Work*. San Francisco: Ignatius, 1991, 103–22.

———. "Hans Urs von Balthasar and Ignatius Loyola," *The Way* 44, no. 4 (2005): 115–30.

Lossky, V. *In the Image and Likeness of God*. London and Oxford: Mowbray, 1974.

Louth, A. *St John Damascene: Tradition and Originality in Byzantine Theology*. Oxford: Oxford University Press, 2002.

De Lubac, H. "Communauté et communion." In F. Perroux and J. Madaule, eds., *La Communauté Français: Cahiers d'études communautaires*, vol. 2. Paris: Presses Universitaires de France, 1942.

———. *Surnaturel: Études Historiques*. Paris: Aubier, 1946.

———. "Le Mystère du Surnaturel," *Recherches de Science Religieuse* 36 (1949): 80–121.

———. *Catholicism: Christ and the Common Destiny of Man*. Translated by L. C. Sheppard. London: Burns & Oates, 1950 (= *Catholicisme. Les Aspects sociaux du dogme*, 4th ed. Paris: Cerf, 1947).

——. *The Discovery of God*. Translated by A. Dru. Edinburgh, T. & T. Clark, 1996 (= *Sur le chemins de Dieu*. Paris: Aubier, 1956).

——. *Augustinianism and Modern Theology*. Translated by L. Sheppard. New York: Herder, 1969.

——. *The Church: Paradox and Mystery*. Translated by J. R. Dunne. Shannon, Ireland: Ecclesia, 1969 (= *Paradoxe et Mystère de L'Église*. Paris: Aubier-Montaigne, 1967).

——. *A Brief Catechesis on Nature and Grace*. Translated by R. Arnandez. San Francisco: Ignatius, 1984 (= *Petite catéchèse sur Nature et Grâce*. Paris: Librairie Arthème Fayard, 1980).

——. *Theological Fragments*. Translated by R. H. Balinski. San Francisco: Ignatius, 1989 (= *Théologies d'occasion*, Paris: Desclée de Brouwer, 1984).

——. *At the Service of the Church: Henri de Lubac Reflects on the Circumstances That Occasioned His Writings*. Translated by A. E. Englund. San Francisco: Ignatius, 1993 (= *Mémoire sur l'occasion de mes écrits*. Namur, Belgium, 1989).

——. *The Drama of Atheist Humanism*. Translated by E. M. Riley et al. San Francisco: Ignatius, 1995 (= *Le drame de l'humanisme athée*. Paris: Éditions Spes, 1945).

——. *Theology in History*. Translated by A. E. Nash. San Francisco: Ignatius, 1996 (= *Théologie dans l'Histoire*, 2 vols. Paris: Desclée de Brouwer, 1990).

——. *The Mystery of the Supernatural*. Translated by R. Sheed. New York: Crossroad, 1998 (= *Le Mystère du Surnaturel*. Paris: Aubier, 1965).

——. *Medieval Exegesis*, 3 vols. Translated by M. Sebanc, E. M. Macierowski, et al. Grand Rapids: Eerdmans, 1998–2009 (= *Exégèse médiévale: Les quatre sens de l'Écriture*. Paris: Aubier-Montaigne, 1959–64).

——. *Corpus Mysticum: The Eucharist and the Church in the Middle Ages*. Translated by G. Simmonds et al. Notre Dame: University of Notre Dame Press, 2006 (= *Corpus Mysticum: L'Eucharistie et l'Eglise au Moyen Age*. Paris: Aubier-Montaigne, 1944).

———. *History and Spirit: The Understanding of Scripture according to Origen.* Translated by A. E. Nash. San Francisco: Ignatius, 2007 (= *Histoire et esprit: L'Intelligence de l'Écriture d'après Origène.* Paris: Éditions Montaigne, 1950).

McCosker, P. "Middle Muddle?" *Reviews in Religion and Theology* 13, no. 3 (2006): 362–70.

McGrath, A. E. "Theology and Experience: Reflections on Cognitive and Experiential Approaches to Theology," *European Journal of Theology* 2 (1993): 65–74.

McInerny, R. M. *Praeambula fidei: Thomism and the God of the Philosophers.* Washington, DC: Catholic University of America Press, 2006.

McPartlan, P. *The Eucharist Makes the Church: Henri de Lubac and John Zizioulas in Dialogue.* Edinburgh: T. & T. Clark, 1993.

Madden, N. "Composite Hypostasis in Maximus the Confessor," *Studia Patristica* 27 (1993): 175–97.

Mannermaa, T. *Christ present in Faith: Luther's View of Justification.* Translated by Kirsi Irmeli Stjerna. Minneapolis: Fortress Press, 2005.

Mansini, G. "Quasi-Formal Causality and 'Change in the Other': A Note on Karl Rahner's Christology," *The Thomist* 52 (1988): 293–306.

———. *"What Is a Dogma?" The Meaning and Truth of Dogma in Eduoard le Roy and His Scholastic Opponents.* Rome: Editrice Pontificia Università Gregoriana, 1985.

———. "Henri de Lubac, the Natural Desire to See God, and Pure Nature," *Gregorianum* 83, no. 1 (2002): 89–109.

Marmion, D. "Rahner and His Critics: Revisiting the Dialogue," *Irish Theological Quarterly* 68 (2003): 195–212.

Marshall, B. D. *Christology in Conflict: The Identity of a Saviour in Rahner and Barth.* Oxford: Blackwell, 1987.

———. "Justification as Declaration and Deification," *International Journal of Systematic Theology* 4 (2002): 3–28.

———. "*Ex Occidente Lux?* Aquinas and Eastern Orthodox Theology," *Modern Theology* 20, no. 1 (2004): 23–50.

———. "*Beatus Vir:* Aquinas, Romans 4, and the Role of 'Reckoning' in Justification." In M. Levering and M. Dauphinais, eds., *Reading Romans with St. Thomas Aquinas: Ecumenical Explorations.* Washington, DC: Catholic University of America Press, 2012, 216–37.

Meconi, D. "Deification in the Thought of John Paul II," *Irish Theological Quarterly* 71 (2006): 127–41.

———. "The Consummation of the Christian Promise: Recent Studies in Deification," *New Blackfriars* 87, no. 1007 (2006): 3–12.

———. "Becoming Gods by Becoming God's: Augustine's Mystagogy of Identification," *Augustinian Studies* 39, no. 1 (2006): 61–74.

Melina, L. *The Epiphany of Love: Toward a Theological Understanding of Christian Action.* Grand Rapids: Eerdmans, 2010.

Mersch, E. *The Whole Christ: The Historical Development of the Doctrine of the Mystical Body in Scripture and Tradition.* Translated by J. R. Kelly. Milwaukee: Bruce, 1938.

———. "Filii in Filio," *Nouvelle Revue Théologique* 65 (1938): 551–82, 681–702, 809–30.

———. *The Theology of the Mystical Body.* Translated by C. Vollert. St. Louis: Herder, 1952.

Mettepenningen, J. *Nouvelle Théologie: Inheritor of Modernism, Precursor of Vatican II.* London: T. & T. Clark, 2010.

Milbank, J. *The Suspended Middle: Henri de Lubac and the Debate concerning the Supernatural.* Grand Rapids: Eerdmans, 2005.

De Moulins-Beaufort, E. "The Spiritual Man in the Thought of Henri de Lubac," *Communio* 25, no. 2 (1998): 287–302.

———. *Anthropologie et mystique selon Henri de Lubac.* Paris: Cerf, 2003.

Mouroux, J. *I Believe: The Personal Structure of Faith.* London: Geoffrey Chapman, 1959.

Muller, E. "Creation as Existential Contingency: A Response," *The Saint Anselm Journal* 1, no. 1 (2003): 65–78.

Narcisse, G. "The Supernatural in Contemporary Theology." In S.-T. Bonino, ed., *Surnaturel: A Controversy at the Heart of Twentieth-Century Thomistic Thought.* Translated by R. Williams and M. Levering. Ave Maria, FL: Sapientia, 2009, 295–310.

Nédoncelle, M. *Love and the Person.* Translated by Ruth Adelaide. New York: Sheed & Ward, 1966.

Nichols, A. "Thomism and the *Nouvelle Théologie*," *The Thomist* 64, no. 1 (2000): 1–19.

———. *Reason with Piety: Garrigou-Lagrange in the Service of Catholic Thought.* Ave Maria, FL: Sapientia, 2008.

Norris Clarke, W. *Person and Being.* Milwaukee: Marquette University Press, 1993.

O'Collins, G. *Jesus Our Redeemer: A Christian Approach to Salvation.* Oxford: Oxford University Press, 2007.

———. "Critical Issues." In S. T. Davis, D. Kendall, and G. O'Collins, eds., *The Incarnation: An Interdisciplinary Symposium on the Incarnation of the Son of God.* Oxford: Oxford University Press, 2002.

Olson, R. E. "Deification in Contemporary Theology," *Theology Today* 64, no. 2 (2007): 186–200.

Osborn, E. *Irenaeus of Lyons.* Cambridge: Cambridge University Press, 2001.

O'Shea, K. F. "Divinization: A Study in Theological Analogy," *The Thomist* 29, no. 1 (1965): 1–45.

———. "Pure Uncreated Unity," *Irish Theological Quarterly* 30, no. 4 (1963): 347–53.

———. "Pure Formal Actuation," *Irish Theological Quarterly* 28, no. 1 (1961): 1–15.

O'Sullivan, N. *Christ and Creation: Christology and the Key to Interpreting the Theology of Creation in the Works of Henri de Lubac.* Bern: Peter Lang, 2009.

Patfoort, A. "Missions divines et expérience des Personnes divines selon S. Thomas," *Angelicum* 63 (1986): 545–59.

Peddicord, R. *The Sacred Monster of Thomism: An Introduction to the Life and Legacy of Reginald Garrigou-Lagrange O.P.* South Bend, IN: St. Augustine's, 2005.

Peura, S., and A. Raunio, eds. *Luther und Theosis: Vergöttlichung als Thema der abendländischen Theologie.* Erlangen: Martin-Luther Verlag, 1990.

La Piana, G. "Recent Tendencies in Roman Catholic Theology," *Harvard Theological Review* 15, no. 3 (1922): 233–92.

Pieper, J. *Divine Madness: Plato's Case Against Secular Humanism.* Translated by L. Krauth. San Francisco: Ignatius, 1995.

Plass, P. "Transcendent Time and Eternity in Gregory of Nyssa," *Vigiliae Christianae* 34, no. 2 (1980): 180–92.

Quasten, J. *Patrology,* vol. 1. Allen, TX: Christian Classics (no date).

Von Rad, G. *Old Testament Theology*, vol. 1. Translated by D. G. Stalker. New York: Harper & Row, 1962.

Rahner, K. "E Latere Christi: Der Ursprung der Kirche als zweiter Eva aus der Seite Christi des zweiten Adam (1936)." In idem, *Sämtliche Werke*, vol. 3. *Spiritualität und Theologie der Kirchenväter*, ed. A. R. Batlogg et al. Einsiedeln: Benziger, 1999, 4–83.

——. Review of H. de Lubac's *Catholicisme* in *Zeitschrift für katholische Theologie* 63 (1939): 443–44.

——. "Ein Weg zur Bestimmung des Verhältnisses von Natur und Gnade," *Orientierung* 14 (1950): 138–41.

——. *Spirit in the World.* Translated by W. V. Dych. New York: Continuum, 1994 (= *Geist in Weld: Zur Metaphysik der endlichen Erkenntnis bei Thomas von Aquin*, 2nd ed. Munich: Kösel, 1957).

——. *Theological Investigations*, vols. 1–20. Translated by C. Ernst. London: Darton, Longman & Todd, 1961–81 (= *Schriften zur Theologie*, vols. 1–16. Einsiedeln: Benziger, 1954–84).

——, ed. *Encyclopedia of Theology: A Concise Sacramentum Mundi.* London: Burns & Oates, 1975.

——. *Foundations of Christian Faith: An Introduction to the Idea of Christianity.* Translated by W. V. Dych. New York: Crossroad, 1978.

——. "Ignatius of Loyola Speaks to a Modern Jesuit." In K. Rahner and P. Imhof, *Ignatius of Loyola*. London: Collins, 1979, 9–38.

——. *I Remember: An Autobiographical Interview with Meinold Krauss.* London: SCM, 1985.

——. *Faith in a Wintry Season: Conversations and Interviews with Karl Rahner in the Last Years of His Life.* Edited by P. Imhof and H. Biallowons. Translated by H. D. Egan. New York: Crossroad, 1991.

———. *The Content of Faith: The Best of Karl Rahner's Theological Writings.* Edited by K. Lehmann and A. Raffelt. Translated by H. D. Egan. New York: Crossroad, 1993.

———. *The Great Church Year: The Best of Karl Rahner's Homilies, Sermons, and Meditations.* Edited by A. Raffelt. Translated by H. D. Egan. New York: Crossroad, 1995.

———. *Spiritual Writings.* Edited by P. Endean. Maryknoll, NY: Orbis, 2004.

Ratzinger, J. *Church, Ecumenism, and Politics: New Essays in Ecclesiology.* New York: Crossroad, 1988.

———. "The Notion of Person in Theology," *Communio* 17, no. 3 (1990): 439–54.

———. *In the Beginning: A Catholic Understanding of the Story of Creation and the Fall.* Grand Rapids: Eerdmans, 1995.

———. *Introduction to Christianity.* Translated by J. R. Foster. San Francisco: Ignatius, 2004.

Reno, R. R. *The Ordinary Transformed: Karl Rahner and the Christian Vision of Transcendence.* Grand Rapids: Eerdmans, 1995.

Riches, A. "Church, Eucharist, and Predestination in Barth and de Lubac: Convergence and Divergence in *Communio*," *Communio* 35 (2008): 565–98.

———. "Christology and Anti-Humanism," *Modern Theology* 29, no. 3 (2013): 311–37.

Romanides, J. S. "Highlights in the Debate over Theodore of Mopsuestia's Christology and Some Suggestions for a Fresh Approach," *Greek Orthodox Theological Review* 5 (1959–60): 140–85.

Rowland, T. *Culture and the Thomist Tradition: After Vatican II.* London: Routledge, 2003.

Runia, D. T. *Philo of Alexandria and the Timaeus of Plato.* Leiden: Brill, 1986.

Russell, N. *The Doctrine of Deification in the Greek Patristic Tradition.* Oxford: Oxford University Press, 2004.

Ryan, P. F. "How Can the Beatific Vision both Fulfill Human Nature and Be Utterly Gratuitous?" *Gregorianum* 83, no. 4 (2002): 717–54.

Scheeben, M. *The Glories of Divine Grace, Part II: Union With God.* Translated by Patrick Shaughnessy. St. Meinrad, Ireland: Grail Publications, 1947.

———. *Mysteries of Christianity.* Translated by Cyril Vollert. St. Louis: Herder, 1964.

———. *Nature and Grace.* Translated by Cyril Vollert. St. Louis: Herder, 1954.

Schindler, D. L. "Norris Clarke on Person, Being, and St. Thomas," *Communio* 20, no. 3 (1993): 580–92.

———. "The Person: Philosophy, Theology, and Receptivity," *Communio* 21, no. 1 (1994): 172–90.

Schleiermacher, F. *The Christian Faith.* Translated by H. R. Mackintosh and J. S. Stewart. Edinburgh: T. & T. Clark, 1928.

Schneider, J. "ὁμοίωσις." In G. Friedrich and G. W. Bromiley, eds., *Theological Dictionary of the New Testament*, vol. 5. Grand Rapids: Eerdmans, 1967, 190–91.

Scola, A. "Christian Experience and Theology," *Communio* 23 (1996): 203–6.

Servais, J. *Théologie des Exercices spirituels: H. U. von Balthasar interprète saint Ignace.* Paris: Culture et vérité, 1996.

De La Soujeole, B.-D. *Le Sacrement de la communion: Essai d'ecclésiologie fondamentale.* Paris: Cerf, 1998.

Stump, E. *Aquinas.* London: Routledge, 2003.

De La Taille, M. *The Hypostatic Union and Created Actuation by Uncreated Act.* Translated by C. Vollert. West Baden Springs, IN: West Baden College, 1952.

Tanner, N. P., ed. *Decrees of the Ecumenical Councils*, 2 vols. London: Sheed & Ward, 1990.

Teilhard de Chardin, P. *Christianity and Evolution.* Translated by R. Hague. London: Collins, 1971.

Thompson, W. M., ed. *Bérulle and the French School: Selected Writings.* New York: Paulist, 1989.

Tillard, J.-M. R. *Chair de l'Église, chair du Christ: Aux sources de l'ecclésiologie de communion.* Paris: Cerf, 1992.

Törönen, M. *Union and Distinction in the Thought of St. Maximus the Confessor.* Oxford: Oxford University Press, 2007.

Torrell, J.-P. *Saint Thomas Aquinas*, vol. 2: *Spiritual Master.* Translated by R. Royal. Washington, DC: Catholic University of America Press, 2003.

———. "Le thomisme dans le débat christologique contemporain." In T. Bonino, ed., *Saint Thomas au XXe siècle. Colloque du centenaire de la "Revue Thomiste" (1893-1992)*, Toulouse, 25–28 mars 1993. Paris: Éditions Saint-Paul, 1994, 379–93.

———. "Nature and Grace in Thomas Aquinas." In S.-T. Bonino, ed., *Surnaturel: A Controversy at the Heart of Twentieth-Century Thomistic Thought.* Translated by Robert Williams and Matthew Levering. Ave Maria, FL: Sapientia, 2009, 155–88.

Turcescu, L. "'Person' versus 'Individual,' and Other Misreadings of Gregory of Nyssa." In S. Coakley, ed., *Re-Thinking Gregory of Nyssa.* Oxford: Blackwell, 2003, 97–109.

Tyrrell, G. "The 'Tabula Aurea' of Peter de Bergamo," *The Heythrop Journal* 10, no. 3 (1969): 275–79.

Voderholzer, R. *Meet Henri de Lubac: His Life and Work*. San Francisco: Ignatius, 2008.

Walsh, C. J. "Henri de Lubac in Connecticut: Unpublished Conferences on Renewal in the Postconciliar Period," *Communio* 23, no. 4 (1996): 786–805.

Weigel, G. *Witness to Hope: The Biography of Pope John Paul II 1920-2005*. London: HarperCollins, 2005.

Wicks, J. "Further Light on Vatican Council II," *Catholic Historical Review* 95 (2009): 546–69.

Wild, P. T. *The Divinization of Man According to Saint Hilary of Poitiers*. Mundelein, IL: Saint Mary of the Lake Seminary, 1950.

Wilhelm, J. and Scannell, T. B. *A Manual of Catholic Theology*, vol. 2. London: Kegan Paul, Trench, Kübner & Co., 1908.

Wilhelmsen, F. D. *The Paradoxical Structure of Existence*. Albany, NY: Preserving Christian Publications, 1991.

Williams, A. "Deification in the *Summa Theologiae*: A Structural Interpretation of the Prima Pars," *The Thomist* 61, no. 2 (1997): 219–55.

———. *The Ground of Union: Deification in Aquinas and Palamas*. New York: Oxford University Press, 1999.

Wilson, R. McL. "The Early History of the Exegesis of Gen 1:26," *Studia Patristica* 1, no. 1 (1957): 420–37.

Wingren, G. *Man and the Incarnation: A Study in the Biblical Theology of Irenaeus*. Translated by R. Mackenzie. Edinburgh: Oliver & Boyd, 1959.

Wojtyla, K. *Faith according to St. John of the Cross*. Translated by J. Aumann. San Francisco: Ignatius, 1981.

———. *Love and Responsibility*. Translated by H. T. Willetts. London: Collins, 1981.

Wolters, A. "Partners of the Deity: A Covenantal Reading of 2 Peter 1:4," *Calvin Theological Journal* 25 (1990): 28–40.

Wood, S. K. *Spiritual Exegesis and the Church in the Theology of Henri de Lubac.* Grand Rapids: Eerdmans, 1998.

Zahlauer, A. *Karl Rahner und sein "produktives Vorbild" Ignatius von Loyola.* Innsbruck: Tyrolia, 1996.

Index of Names

Index of Subjects